SPOTLIGHT on MUSIC

Authors

Judy Bond

René Boyer

Margaret Campbelle-Holman

Emily Crocker

Marilyn C. Davidson

Robert de Frece

Virginia Ebinger

Mary Goetze

Betsy M. Henderson

John Jacobson

Michael Jothen

Chris Judah-Lauder

Carol King

Vincent P. Lawrence

Ellen McCullough-Brabson

Janet McMillion

Nancy L. T. Miller

Ivy Rawlins

Susan Snyder

Gilberto D. Soto

Kodály Contributing Consultant

Sr. Lorna Zemke

McGraw Hill

HAL•LEONARD®

MACMILLAN McGRAW-HILL

i

ACKNOWLEDGMENTS

Creative Direction and Delivery: The Quarasan Group, Inc.

From the Top-On National Radio! selections are adapted from the nationally distributed public radio program, *From the Top.* CEOs/Executive Producers: Jennifer Hurley-Wales and Gerald Slavet. Authors: Ann Gregg and Joanne Robinson. © 2000, 2001, 2002, 2003 From the Top, Inc.

The Broadway Junior® logo and MTI® logo are trademarks of Music Theatre International. All rights reserved.

Grateful acknowledgment is given to the following authors, composers, and publishers. Every effort has been made to trace the ownership of all copyrighted material and to secure the necessary permissions to reprint these selections. In the case of some selections for which acknowledgment is not given, extensive research has failed to locate the copyright holders.

Songs and Speech Pieces

Angelina, Words and Music by Irving Burgie. Copyright © 1960. Renewed 1988. Cherry Lane Music Publishing Company, Inc. (ASCAP), Lord Burgess Music Publishing (ASCAP) and DreamWorks Songs (ASCAP). Worldwide Rights for Lord Burgess Music Publishing and DreamWorks Songs Administered by Cherry Lane Music Publishing Company, Inc. International Copyright Secured. All Rights Reserved.

Bashana Haba 'Ah (In the Year to Come), Lyrics by Ehud Manor. Music by Nurit Hirsh. Copyright © 1970. Renewed 1998. EMI SONGS (ISRAEL) LTD. All Rights Controlled and Administered by EMI BLACKWOOD MUSIC INC. All Rights Reserved. International Copyright Secured. Used by Permission.

Blue Suede Shoes, Words and Music by Carl Lee Perkins. Copyright © 1955, 1956. HI-LO MUSIC, INC. Renewed 1983, 1984. CARL PERKINS MUSIC, INC. (Administered by WREN MUSIC CO., A Division of MPL Music Publishing, Inc.) All Rights Reserved.

Body Talk, Words and Music by Nancy Telfer, Copyright © 1990 by Lenel Music Press. International Copyright Secured. All Rights Reserved.

Bop 'til You Drop, Words and Music by Douglas Colvin and John Cummings. Copyright © 1987. TACO TUNES. All Rights Administered by WB MUSIC CORP. All Rights Reserved. Used by Permission.

Camelot, from CAMELOT. Words by Alan Jay Lerner. Music by Frederick Loewe. Copyright © 1960, 1961 by Alan Jay Lerner and Frederick Loewe. Copyright Renewed. Chappell & Co. owner of publication and allied rights throughout the world. International Copyright Secured. All Rights Reserved.

Carol from an Irish Cabin. Words by Ruth Durand. Music by Dale Wood. Copyright © WARNER BROS. PUBLICATIONS U.S. INC. International Copyright Secured. All Rights Reserved.

Charleston, Words and Music by Cecil Mack and Jimmy Johnson. Copyright © 1923. Renewed. WARNER BROS. INC. All Rights Reserved.

Choo Choo Ch'Boogie, Words and Music by Vaughn Horton, Denver Darling and Milton Gabler. Copyright © 1945. Renewed. RYTVOC, INC. All Rights Reserved.

Comedy Tonight. from A FUNNY THING HAPPENED ON THE WAY TO THE FORUM. Words and Music by Stephen Sondheim. Copyright © 1962 by Stephen Sondheim. Copyright Renewed. Burthen Music Company, Inc. owner of publication and allied rights throughout the World. Chappell & Co. Sole Selling Agent. International Copyright Secured. All Rights Reserved.

Conga, Words and Music by Enrique Garcia. Copyright © 1985. FOREIGN IMPORTED PRODUCTIONS & PUBLISHING, INC. (BMI). International Copyright Secured. All Rights Reserved.

Cum-ma-la Be-stay, Words and Music by Donnie Burks, Jerry Vance and Terry Philips. Copyright © 1965. Renewed 1993 by Donny Burke, Jerry Vance and Terry Philips. International Copyright Secured. All Rights Reserved.

Dancing in the Street, Words and Music by Marvin Gaye, Ivy Hunter and William Stevenson. Copyright © 1964. Renewed 1992. FCG MUSIC, NMG MUSIC, MGIII MUSIC, JOBETE MUSIC CO., INC. and STONE AGATE MUSIC. All Rights Controlled and Administered by EMI APRIL MUSIC INC. and EMI BLACKWOOD MUSIC INC. on behalf of JOBETE MUSIC CO., INC. and STONE AGATE MUSIC (A Division of JOBETE MUSIC CO., INC.) All Rights Reserved. International Copyright Secured. Used by Permission.

Deep in the Heart of Texas, Words by June Hershey. Music by Don Swander. Copyright © 1941 by Melody Lane Publications, Inc. Copyright Renewed. International Copyright Secured. All Rights Reserved.

Doctor Jazz, Words and Music by John Jacobson and Steve Zegree. Copyright © 2001 by HAL LEONARD CORPORATION. International Copyright Secured. All Rights Reserved.

Doing the Latest Rag, from TITANIC. Music and Lyrics by Maury Yeston. Copyright © 1994. Yeston Music Ltd. (BMI). Worldwide Rights for Yeston Music Ltd. Administered by Cherry River Music Co. International Copyright Secured. All Rights Reserved.

Earth Child, Words and Music by Sharon Burch. Copyright © by Canyon Records. International Copyright Secured. All Rights Reserved.

El tambor (The Drum), Panamanian Folk Song. Spanish Words by Jose-Luis Orozco. Copyright © by Arcoiris Records, Inc. International Copyright Secured. All Rights Reserved.

continued on page 441

The McGraw-Hill Companies

Published by Macmillan/McGraw-Hill, of McGraw-Hill Education, a division of The McGraw-Hill Companies, Inc., Two Penn Plaza, New York, New York 10121.

Printed in the United States of America
ISBN 0-02-295912-2 / 6
5 6 7 8 9 027/043 10 09 08 07 06 05

CONTRIBUTORS

Consultants

Brian Burnett,
Movement

Stephen Gabriel,
Technology

Magali Iglesias,
English Language Learners

Roberta Newcomer,
Special Learners/Assessment

Frank Rodríguez,
English Language Learners

Jacque Schrader,
Movement

Kathy B. Sorensen,
International Phonetic
Alphabet

Patti Windes-Bridges,
Listening Maps

Linda Worsley,
Listening/Singable
English Translations

Sr. Lorna Zemke,
Kodály Contributing
Consultant

Contributing Writers

Allison Abucewicz
Sharon Berndt
Rhona Brink
Ann Burbridge
Debbie Helm Daniel
Katherine Domingo
Kari Gilbertson
Janet Graham
Hilree Hamilton
Linda Harley
Judy Henneberger
Carol Huffman
Bernie Hynson, Jr.
Sheila A. Kerley
Ellen Mendelsohn

Cristi Cary Miller
Leigh Ann Mock
Patricia O'Rourke
Barbara Resch
Isabel Romero
Carl B. Schmidt
Debra Shearer
Ellen Mundy Shuler
Rebecca Treadway
Carol Wheeler
Sheila Woodward

Recordings

Executive Producer
John Higgins

Senior Music Editor/Producer
Emily Crocker

Senior Recording Producer
Mark Brymer

Recording Producers
Steve Millikan
Andy Waterman

Associate Recording Producers
Alan Billingsley, Darrell
Bledsoe, Stacy Carson,
Emily Crocker, Rosanna

Eckert, John Egan, Chad
Evans, Darlene
Koldenhoven, Chris
Koszuta, Don Markese,
Matthew McGregor,
Steve Potts, Edwin
Schupman, Michael
Spresser, Frank Stegall,
David Vartanian, Mike
Wilson, Ted Wilson

Project/Mastering Engineer
Mark Aspinall

Post Production Engineer
Don Sternecker

Multicultural Consultants

William Anderson, Chet-Yeng Loong, Edwin Schupman, Kathy B.
Sorensen, Gilberto D. Soto, Judith Cook Tucker, Dennis Waringg

In the Spotlight Consultant

Willa Dunleavy

Multicultural Advisors

Brad Ahawanrathe Bonaparte (Mohawk), Emmanuel Akakpo (Ewe), Earlene Albano (Hawaiian), Luana Au (Maori), Ruby Beeston (Mandarin), Latif Bolat (Turkey), Estella Christensen (Spanish), Oussama Davis (Arabic), Mia Delguardo (Minahasa), Nolutho Ndengane Diko (Xhosa), Angela Fields (Hopi, Chemehuevi), Gary Fields (Lakota, Cree), Gilad Harel (Hebrew), Josephine Hetarihon (Bahasa Indonesian, Minahasa, and Maluko dialect), Judy Hirt-Manheimer (Hebrew), Rose Jakub (Navajo), Elizabeth Jarema (Fijian), Rita Jensen (Swedish), Malou Jewett (Visayan), Alejandro Jimenez (Hispanic), Chris Jones (Hungarian), Wendy Jyang Shamo (Mandarin), Amir Kalay (Hebrew), Michael Katsan (Greek), Silvi Madarajan (Tamil), Georgia Magpie (Comanche), Nona Mardi (Malay), Aida Mattingly (Tagalog), Mike Kanathohare McDonald (Mohawk), Vasana de Mel (Sinhala), Marion Miller (Czech), Etsuko Miskin (Japanese), Mogens Mogenson (Danish), Kenny Tahawisoren Perkins (Mohawk), Pradeep Nayyar (Punjabi, Hindi), Renu Nayyar (Punjabi), Mfanego Ngwenya (Zulu), Wil Numkena (Hopi), Samuel Owuru (Akan), Nina Padukone (Konkani), Hung Yong Park (Korean), James Parker (Finnish), Jose Pereira (Konkani), Berrit Price (Norwegian), John Rainer (Taos Pueblo, Creek), Lillian Rainer (Taos Pueblo, Creek, Apache), Arnold Richardson (Haliwa-Saponi), Ken Runnacles (German), Trudy Shenk (German), Ron Singer (Navajo), Ernest Siva (Cahuilla, Serrano [Maringa']), Bonnie Slade (Swedish), Cristina Sorrentino (Portuguese), Diane Thram (Xhosa), Elena Todorov (Bulgarian), Zlatina Todorov (Russian), Tom Toronto (Lao, Thai), Rebecca Wilberg (French, Italian), Sheila Woodward (Zulu), Keith Yackeyonny (Comanche)

Contents

Spotlight on Music Reading..........241

Texas

Focus the spotlight on Texas! Hear the music of the waves roll onto the shores of South Padre Island. Listen as your voice echoes across McKittrick Canyon in West Texas. Enjoy the quiet stillness of the East Texas pines. Experience the vast openness of the High Plains and the dramatic flow of the Rio Grande.

Focus the spotlight on Texas! Hear the blues as you stroll down the streets of Deep Ellum in Dallas. Feel the beat of rock and roll at Auditorium Shores in Austin. Experience a night of opera at the Houston Grand Opera. Hear the mariachis play charming serenades along the Riverwalk in San Antonio.

With an incredible history and rich diversity of cultures, Texas shines bright in the world.

Focus the spotlight on Texas and you'll discover that the possibilities are limitless.

◄ **Texan Dan Rather was honored by the Museum of Television & Radio for a commitment to fair and accurate news reporting.**

◄ **Tish Hinojosa**

Roger Clemens ►

A

in the Spotlight

Austin, the Rio Grande, and Houston—only a few of the special Texas places

Kirk Franklin

Norah Jones ▼

Texas in the Spotlight

Music is the language of Texas. Listen and you'll hear norteño, tejano, conjunto. Listen in Texas and you'll hear the blues. You'll hear boleros, ranchero, corridos. Hear country, cajun, zydeco, jazz, gospel, ragtime, and rock and roll.

Do you hear it? Music is the language of Texas.

step into the Spotlight

**Spotlight CD
Track 1**

Words and Music by John Jacobson,
Emily Crocker and John Higgins

1. Lis - ten to the world a - round you, There is
2. In a world of sound and col - or, in a

mu - sic ev - 'ry - where.___ Just step out - side___ your
rhy - thm all its own,___ It's the heart - beat of___ our

door - way, and you can hear mu - sic in the air!___
Tex - as, the land we proud - ly call our home!_

From the cit - y to the farm and field,___ to the
From the cit - y to the farm and field,___ there's a

Let's Talk Texas!

We are a part of something greater than ourselves. We walk in the footsteps of Sam Houston and Davy Crockett, of Barbara Jordan and Lady Bird Johnson. We breathe the air of ranger and rascal. We remember the Alamo and San Jacinto.

We are Anglo and Spanish, Mexican, mestizo, and African American. We are Native Americans: Comanche, Apache, Kiowa, Choctaw, Chickasaw, Cherokee, Creek, and Seminole.

We are mountain and valley, sand dune and chaparral, desert and mesa, hills and endless blue skies. We are the Rio Grande.

We are part of something greater than ourselves. We are Texas.

Stevie Ray Vaughan became ▲ world famous for his guitar playing. He won Grammys in both the rock and blues categories.

◄ Although Quanah Parker led Comanche fighters against the U.S. Army, he later led the Comanches in pursuing education and agriculture.

The Texas Flag

The Texas Seal

Map Legend

Green:
Forested/Vegetation
Areas

Brown:
Mountains
and Basins

Claudia "Lady Bird" Johnson, former First Lady, was best known for her interest in conserving the environment. She was also very involved in the Head Start program for preschool children.

The Texas Fruit:
Texas Red Grapefruit

The Texas Flying Mammal:
Mexican Free-tailed Bat

The Texas Stone:
Palmwood

The Texas Instrument:
Guitar

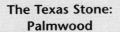

The Texas State Song

"Texas, Our Texas," the official state song of Texas, was adopted by the Legislature in 1929 after being selected in a statewide competition. It was composed by William J. Marsh of Fort Worth. The lyrics were written by Marsh and Gladys Yoakum Wright.

Texas, Our Texas

Spotlight CD Track 4

Words by Gladys Yoakum Wright and William J. Marsh
Music by William J. Marsh

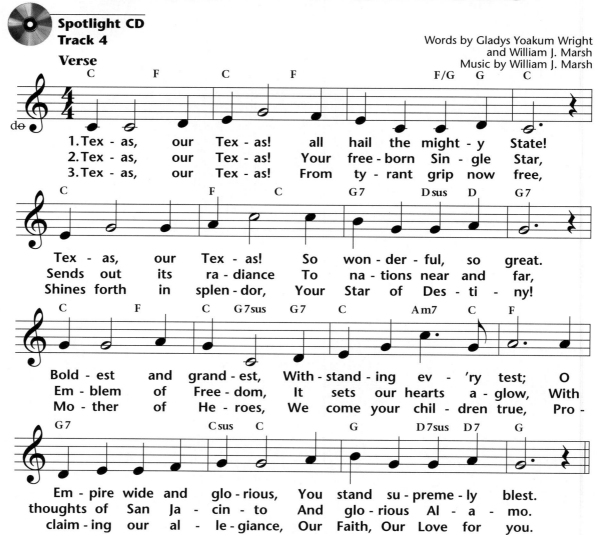

Verse

1. Tex - as, our Tex - as! all hail the might - y State!
2. Tex - as, our Tex - as! Your free - born Sin - gle Star,
3. Tex - as, our Tex - as! From ty - rant grip now free,

Tex - as, our Tex - as! So won - der - ful, so great.
Sends out its ra - diance To na - tions near and far,
Shines forth in splen - dor, Your Star of Des - ti - ny!

Bold - est and grand - est, With - stand - ing ev - 'ry test; O
Em - blem of Free - dom, It sets our hearts a - glow, With
Mo - ther of He - roes, We come your chil - dren true, Pro -

Em - pire wide and glo - rious, You stand su - preme - ly blest.
thoughts of San Ja - cin - to And glo - rious Al - a - mo.
claim - ing our al - le - giance, Our Faith, Our Love for you.

The Texas Pledge

Honor the Texas flag: I pledge allegiance
to thee, Texas, one and indivisible

Refrain

God bless you Tex - as! And keep you brave and strong, That
(repeat refrain)
you may grow in pow'r and worth, Through-out the ag - es long.

Texas Then and Now

Texas has been inhabited by many different people for the last 10,000 years. The largest growth in population started over three hundred years ago when the first European settlers arrived. Texas was once a province of Mexico but declared its independence in 1836. It was an independent republic for ten years, and in 1845 Texas joined the United States of America. Ever since then, Texas has enjoyed continuous population growth and economic success in many different industries. Today Texas is one of the most populous states and is still considered one of the fastest-growing states in the nation.

Scott Joplin ▲

The Alamo ▼

▲ Texas cowpunchers about 1885

Oil has been big business in Texas for more than a century. ▼

Boy in traditional dress and face paint at the National Championship Powwow in Grand Prairie ▶

◀ Miriam "Ma" Ferguson

Sam Houston was ▶ the first President of the Lone Star Republic.

Texas Presidents and First Ladies

Dwight and Mamie Eisenhower

Lyndon and Lady Bird Johnson

George and Barbara Bush

George and Laura Bush

A Texas Classic

Deep within each person's heart lies a melody. When we think of songs, we think of melody, rhythm, and harmony. But a song can also refer to the hopes, wishes, talents, and dreams that you hold in your heart. Can you recognize your song? From deep within your heart, can you sing it?

San Antonio Rose

**Spotlight CD
Track 7**

Words and Music by Bob Wills

1. Deep with - in my heart lies a mel - o -
(D.S.) Bro - ken song, emp - ty words I

dy, a song of old San An - tone,
know still live in my heart all a - lone.

where in dreams I live with a mem - o -
For that moon - lit pass by the Al - a -

ry, be - neath the stars all a - lone.___
mo, and Rose, my Rose of San An - tone.___

Fine

San Antonio Riverwalk

The Hispanic Influence

The uninterrupted Spanish occupation of Texas (1716–1821) ended more than 100 years ago, but the legacy of Spanish Texas is still significant today. We preserve and celebrate our Hispanic heritage.

MAP
UNITED STATES
TEXAS
MEXICO

▼ El Teatro La Paz, now the Xochil Art and Cultural Center in Mission, Texas

A Texas Star!

▲ Guitarrón player

▼ Former Hidalgo County Courthouse in Edinburg, Texas

Sandra Cisneros writes poems that tell stories. Or does she write stories that feel like poems? This author was born in Chicago, Illinois in 1954, the only daughter in a family with six sons. Her family seemed always to be moving back and forth between the United States and Mexico. As a result, she often felt disconnected and friendless, so she spent a lot of time reading and writing. Her parents did not have much money, but they made sure the children understood the importance of education. Since the middle 1980s, Cisneros has divided her time between Texas and California, but she lives primarily in San Antonio, Texas. Major themes in her writing are the strength and uniqueness of Mexican American women in difficult situations.

Mariachi music has been played and sung in Texas for nearly two hundred years. It can be sung at celebrations, for concerts, and even as a serenade.

Morena de mi corazón

Dark Haired Lady of My Heart

Words and Music by
Cesar Rosas

**Spotlight CD
Track 10
Verse**

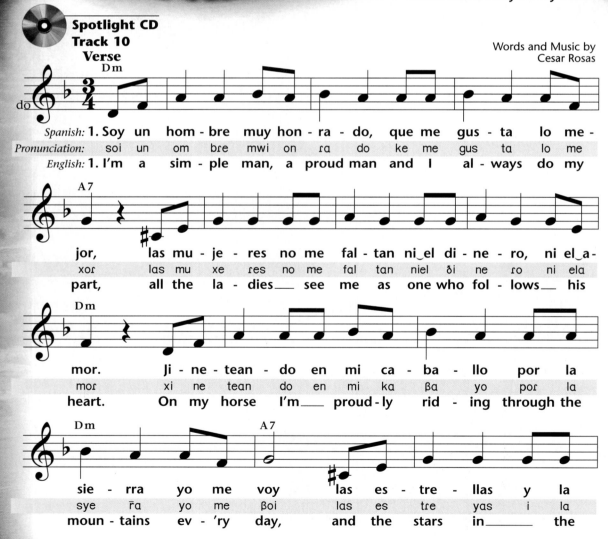

Spanish: 1. Soy un hom - bre muy hon - ra - do, que me gus - ta lo me -
Pronunciation: soi un om bɾe mwi on ɾa do ke me gus ta lo me
English: 1. I'm a sim - ple man, a proud man and I al - ways do my

jor, las mu - je - res no me fal - tan ni el di - ne - ro, ni el a -
xoɾ las mu xe ɾes no me fal tan niel ði ne ɾo ni ela
part, all the la - dies see me as one who fol - lows his

mor. Ji - ne - tean - do en mi ca - ba - llo por la
moɾ xi ne tean do en mi ka βa yo poɾ la
heart. On my horse I'm proud - ly rid - ing through the

sie - rra yo me voy las es - tre - llas y la
sye ɾa yo me βoi las es tɾe yas i la
moun - tains ev - 'ry day, and the stars in the

Refrain

lu - na e - llas me di - cen don - de voy.
lu na e yas me ði sen don de ßoi
night sky_____ they show me_____ the way.

Ay, ay, ay, ay,____ ay mi a - mor. Ay mi mo -
ai ai ai ai ai mi a moɾ ai mi mo

re - na de mi co - ra - zón. Ay, ay, ay, ay,____ ay mi a -
ɾe na ðe mi ko ɾa son ai ai ai ai ai mi a

mor. Ay mi mo - re - na de mi co - ra - zón.
moɾ ai mi mo ɾe na ðe mi ko ɾa son

2. Me gusta tocar guitarra, me gusta cantar el sol,
   el mariachi me acompaña cuando canto mi canción.
   Me gusta tocar guitarra me gusta cantar el sol,
   el mariachi me acompaña cuando canto mi canción.

   me gusta tokaɾ gitaɾa me gusta kantaɾ el sol
   el maɾiachi me akompanya kwando kanto mi kansyon
   me gusta tokaɾ gitaɾa me gusta kantaɾ el sol
   el maɾiachi me akompanya kwando kanto mi kansyon

2. In the sun I like to play my guitar and sing in the sun.
   All my friends are mariachis who join in with my song.
   In the sun I like to play my guitar and sing in the sun.
   All my friends are mariachis who join in with my song.

P

Big Cities, Small Towns

We are a part of something greater than ourselves.
We are a part of the community of Texas.
It takes large cities and very small towns,
rural and urban, metropolitan and provincial,
to make our community all that it can be.
We are a part of something greater than ourselves.
It's called Texas!

**Corpus Christi,
population 277,454**

Houston, population 1,953,631

Dallas, population 1,188,580

All population figures are from U.S. Census 2000.

Around the World in Texas Towns

Can you take a trip around the world and never leave Texas? London, Paris, Athens, Dublin, Denmark, Germany, Italy, Turkey, and China are all here in Texas.

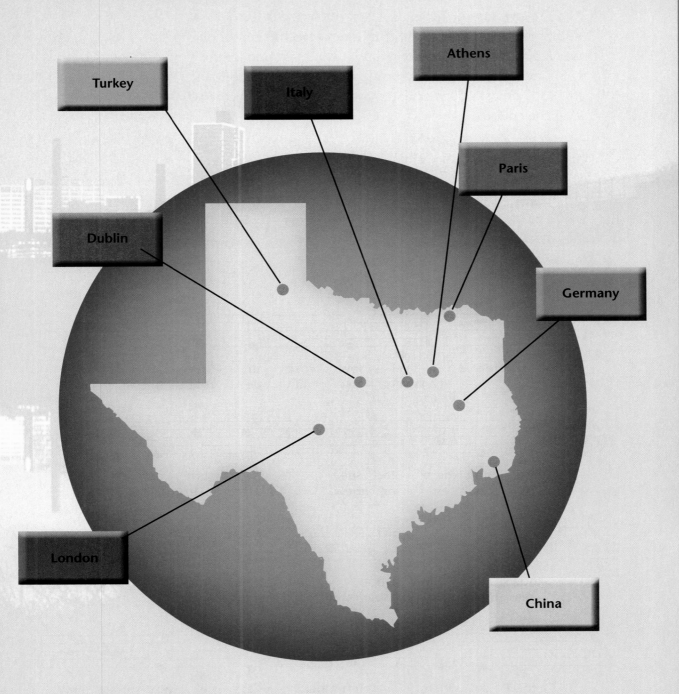

Athens

Turkey

Italy

Paris

Dublin

Germany

London

China

A Texas Medley

"**D**eep in the Heart of Texas" is a song that is especially important for Texans who have to leave their home state for a while. The words and melody take them back to the land that holds their heart.

"The Yellow Rose of Texas" was first published in 1853 by an author identified only as "J.K." In the nineteenth century it was a popular marching song, and it was also sung by the U.S. Cavalry on western outposts and along the cattle trails. In 1955, almost 100 years later, the tune was a hit record all over the country.

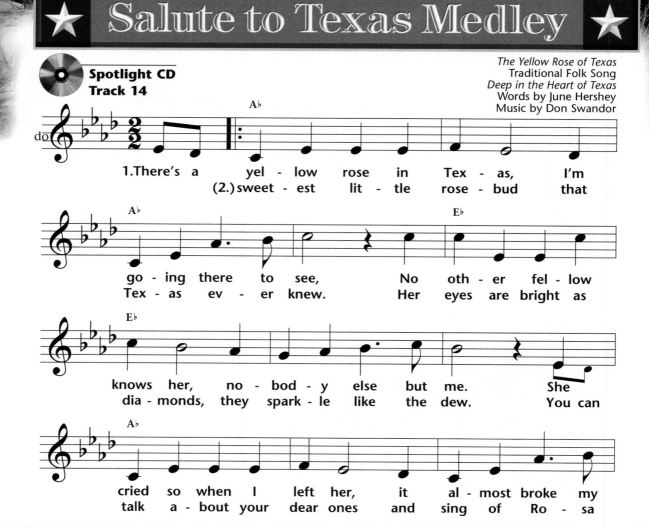

Salute to Texas Medley

**Spotlight CD
Track 14**

The Yellow Rose of Texas
Traditional Folk Song
Deep in the Heart of Texas
Words by June Hershey
Music by Don Swandor

1. There's a yel - low rose in Tex - as, I'm
(2.) sweet - est lit - tle rose - bud that

go - ing there to see, No oth - er fel - low
Tex - as ev - er knew. Her eyes are bright as

knows her, no - bod - y else but me. She
dia - monds, they spark - le like the dew. You can

cried so when I left her, it al - most broke my
talk a - bout your dear ones and sing of Ro - sa

Texas Art Gallery

Reservoir

Robert Rauschenberg (b. 1925), was born into poverty in Port Arthur, Texas. During his long career he has worked in a variety of styles, using highly personal techniques. Rauschenberg has created all-white pictures, all-black pictures, and all-red pictures, and he has painted with his fingers. This painting is in the style he calls "combine" paintings, which include actual objects, such as clocks, bottles, and clothing. He once said, "The world is a lot richer than we can comprehend."

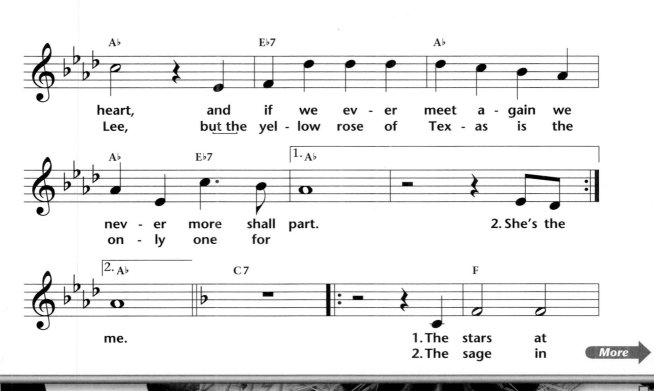

heart, and if we ev - er meet a - gain we
Lee, but the yel - low rose of Tex - as is the

nev - er more shall part. 2. She's the
on - ly one for

me.
1. The stars at
2. The sage in

More

night   are   big   and   bright,   deep   in   the
bloom   is   like   per - fume,   deep   in   the

heart   of   Tex - as.   The prai - rie   sky   is wide and
heart   of   Tex - as.   Re - minds me   of   the one   I

high,   deep in the heart   of   Tex - as.
love,   deep in the heart   of   Tex - as.

Deep   in   the   heart   of   Tex - as!

Kirk Franklin (b. 1970) is from Fort Worth. When he was young, he was very involved in church music, but in his teens, he got involved in activities that were not so positive. When one of his friends was killed in a shooting, he decided to change his life and spend all his time composing and performing gospel music. In 1991 he formed a 17-member choir called The Family, made up mostly of neighborhood friends. Their first album, in 1993, was called *Kirk Franklin & The Family,* and it became the first gospel album ever to go platinum, spending more than 100 weeks on the Billboard charts. In 1997 he began collaborating with an inner-city youth choir. Acting as producer and mentor, he worked with them to record the hit song "Stomp." Franklin likes to think that he has helped bring gospel music to the masses, and it all started in his home state of Texas!

Celebrate Texas!

Let's celebrate Texas! Celebrate its beautiful landscape, its colorful history, and its beautiful mix of people and cultures.

Let's celebrate Texas and all the unigue elements that make it a wonderful place to be. Let's play our guitars, beat our drums, dance our dances, and sing our songs with joy and pride.

Let's celebrate Texas, because Texas is truly something to celebrate!

Native American art displayed at National Championship Powwow ▶

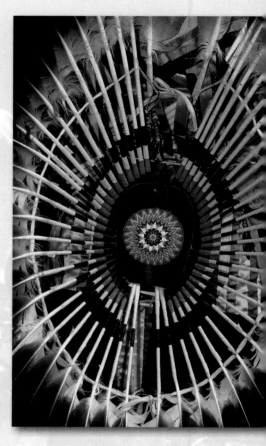

▲ **Texas Independence Day**

Fiesta Parade ▶

Cinco de Mayo ▶
celebration

Willie Nelson ▶

◀ San Antonio
Livestock Show
Parade

x

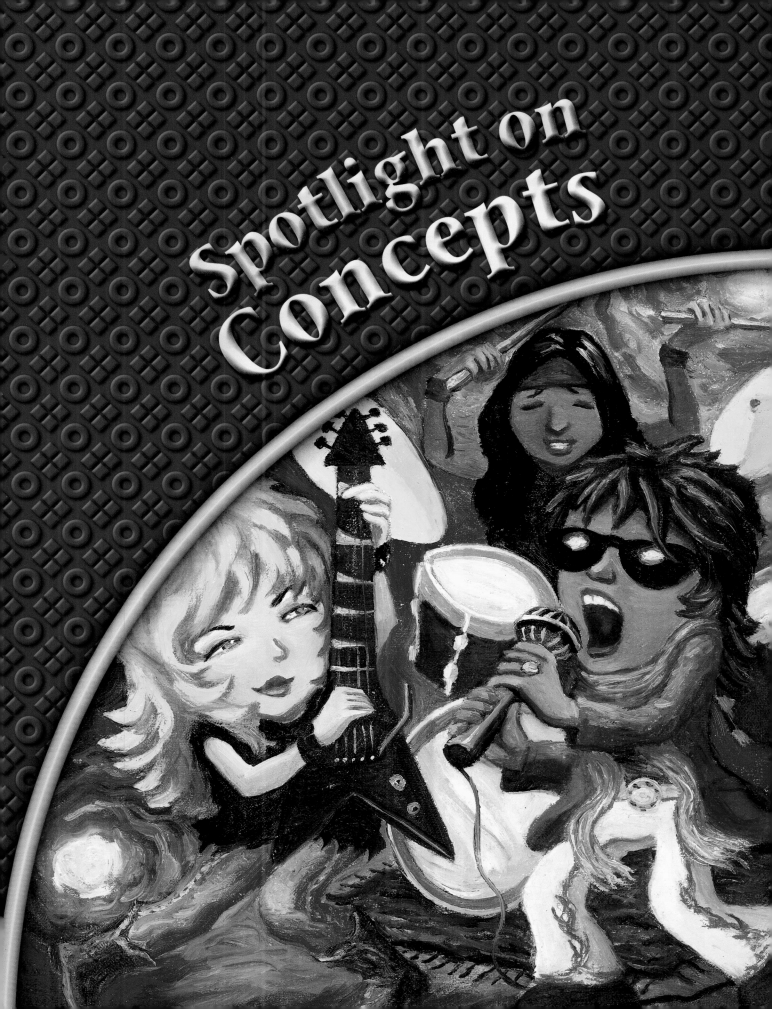

Spotlight on
Concepts

Spotlight on **Concepts**

Spotlight on Concepts

Rhythm Rocks the World

Rhythm has the power to move people and is basic to most music. You will create and perform rhythms in this unit. Rhythm is just one element of musical knowledge.

Building a mountain of musical knowledge takes time. The music mountain is built with rhythm, pitch, form, tempo, harmony, texture, and timbre. These musical elements occur in music of all times and places.

Coming Attractions

Perform Asian and African music.

Play syncopated rhythms.

Create drum conversations.

The song "Gonna Build a Mountain" has a powerful message about the importance of setting your goals and achieving your dreams. What are your musical goals? What can you do to try and achieve them?

CD 1:1

Words and Music by
Leslie Bricusse and Anthony Newley

1. Gon-na build a moun-tain   from a lit-tle hill.
2. Gon-na build a day-dream   from a lit-tle hope.

Gon-na build a moun-tain,   least I hope I will.
Gon-na push that day-dream   up the moun-tain slope.

Gon-na build a moun-tain,   gon-na build it high.
Gon-na build a day-dream,   gon-na see it through.

I   don't know   how I'm gon-na do it,
Gon-na build a   moun-tain and a day-dream,

on - ly know I'm gon-na   try.
gon-na make 'em both come   true.

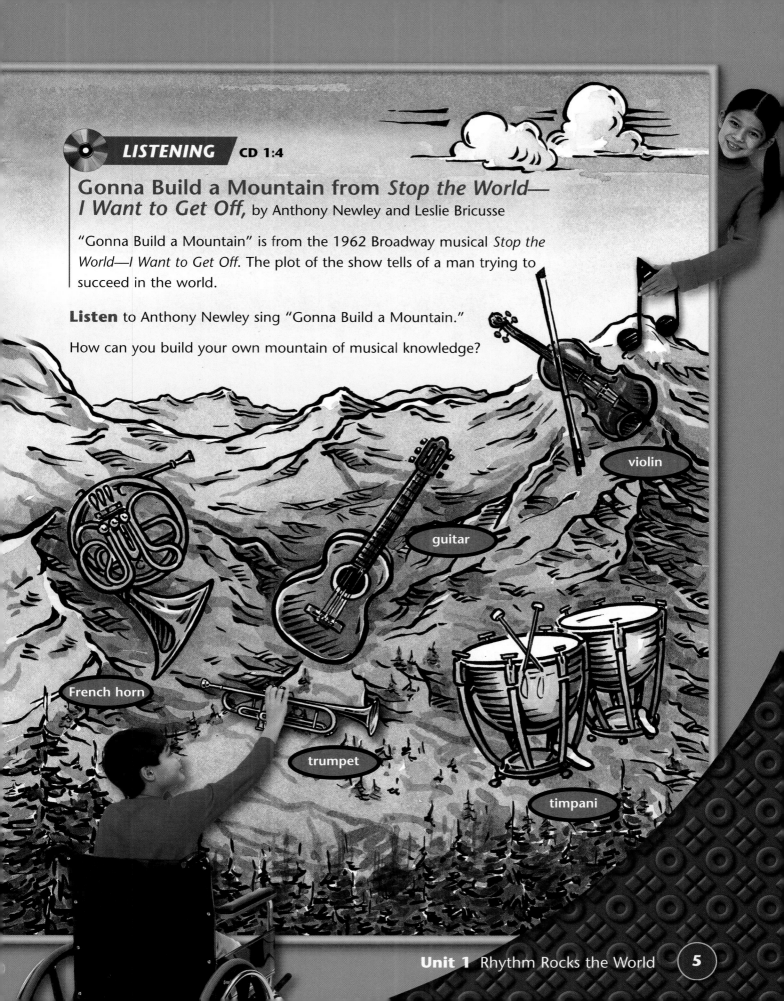

LISTENING · CD 1:4

Gonna Build a Mountain from *Stop the World—I Want to Get Off,* by Anthony Newley and Leslie Bricusse

"Gonna Build a Mountain" is from the 1962 Broadway musical *Stop the World—I Want to Get Off.* The plot of the show tells of a man trying to succeed in the world.

Listen to Anthony Newley sing "Gonna Build a Mountain."

How can you build your own mountain of musical knowledge?

violin

guitar

French horn

trumpet

timpani

Caribbean Connections

CONCEPT
RHYTHM
SKILLS
SING, IDENTIFY, PLAY
LINKS
HISTORY, CULTURES

Caribbean musical styles include interesting percussion tone colors and layered rhythms.

All music has one thing in common—**rhythm**. Rhythm is created by organizing sounds and silences of different lengths.

Identify the sounds of the instruments as you listen to the song.

O, LA LE!

CD 1:5

Words and Music by Hugh A. Davis

do O la le! O la la!

do O la le! O la la!

Al - le, al - le, al - le - lu - u - ia.

Al - le, al - le, al - le - lu - u - ia.

O_____ sing la la. O_____ sing la la.

O_____ la la O_____ la la

You can create percussion sounds by clapping, stamping, patting, and snapping. Almost anything that you can hit, scrape, shake, or rattle can become a percussion instrument. In Caribbean musical styles, you can hear unpitched percussion instruments such as conga drums, maracas, and güiros.

4 Beats of Sound—Note Values		4 Beats of Silence—Rest Values	
1 whole note	𝅝	1 whole rest	▬
2 half notes	𝅗𝅥　　𝅗𝅥	2 half rests	▬　　　▬
4 quarter notes	♩ ♩ ♩ ♩	4 quarter rests	𝄽 𝄽 𝄽 𝄽
8 eighth notes	♫ ♫ ♫ ♫	8 eighth rests	𝄾𝄾 𝄾𝄾 𝄾𝄾 𝄾𝄾
16 sixteenth notes	♬♬♬♬	16 sixteenth rests	𝄿𝄿𝄿𝄿 𝄿𝄿𝄿𝄿 𝄿𝄿𝄿𝄿 𝄿𝄿𝄿𝄿

Playalong

Play these ostinatos with body percussion. Then transfer the rhythms to instruments and perform them with the song.

O_____ sing la la.　　　O　　la la!

O_____　　　la la　O　　la la!

D.C. al Fine

Recycled Percussion

The joyful, bouncy sounds of the steel drum are unmistakably Caribbean! These drums were first made in Trinidad from the bottoms of large, discarded oil containers. The pitches are created by striking different-sized indentations on the upturned bottom, or "pan."

Sing "Angelina" and listen for the steel drums. Sing it again while playing the ostinatos from "O, La Le!"

MAP

TRINIDAD

VENEZUELA

Angelina

CD 1:10

Words and Music by Irving Burgie

Verse

C   F   C

1. It's so long since I've__ been home; seems like
said that you__ would wait, though I

C   F/A   G   C   F   C

there's no place_ to roam. I've sailed a-round_the Horn; been from
know I'm ra-ther late. But now I'm on__ my way with your

C   C/B♭   F/A   F6   C/G   G7   C

San Jo-se__ up to Baf-fin Bay,_ an' I've rode out man-y a storm.
mes-sage clear_ring-ing in my ear,__ An' I'll be home_ to stay.

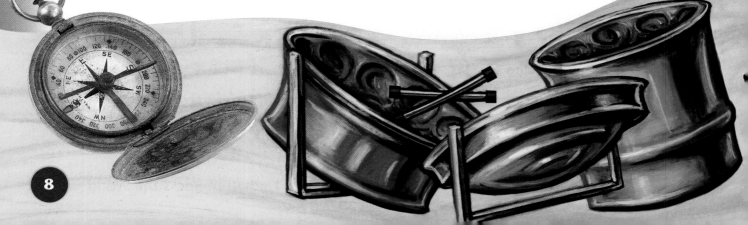

8

Refrain

An-ge-li-na, An-ge-li-na, bring down your con-cer-ti-na and

play a wel-come for me 'cause I'll be com-ing home from sea.

An-ge-li-na, An-ge-li-na, bring down your con-cer-ti-na and

2nd time to Coda

play a wel-come for me 'cause I'll be com-ing home from sea.

D.S. al Coda

2. Yes, you

Coda

com-ing home from sea.

concertina ▶

**THINK!** Why is it possible to play the same rhythmic patterns with both "O, La Le!" and "Angelina"?

A steel drum band

CONCEPT
MELODY
SKILLS
SING, PLAY,
DESCRIBE
LINKS
HISTORY, FINE ART

Moved by Melody

Have you ever noticed that some music can make hard jobs a little bit easier? Music can even help to get many people working together. The rhythm of a song can keep you moving through your work.

In the days when tall ships were powered by wind, sailors sang songs while they did their work. Singing together kept them working together as they did their chores—hauling on ropes, pulling up the sails, or mopping the deck—to the rhythm of the song.

Sing "Hullaballoo Balay."

▲ Defending a sailing ship

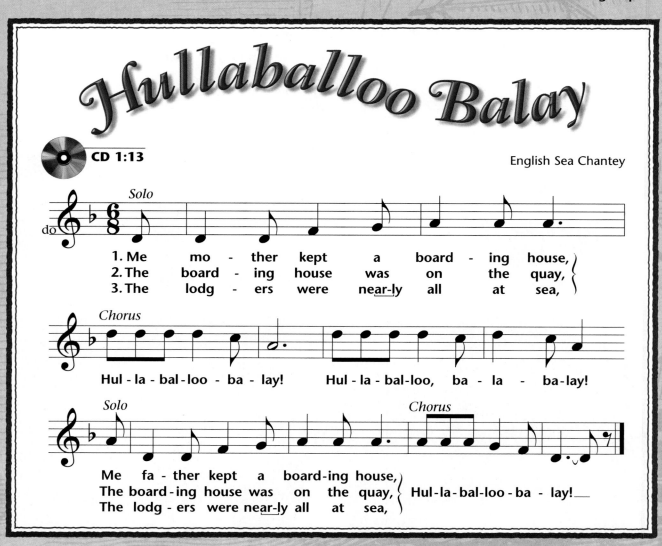

CD 1:13

English Sea Chantey

Solo

1. Me mo - ther kept a board - ing house,
2. The board - ing house was on the quay,
3. The lodg - ers were near-ly all at sea,

Chorus

Hul - la - bal - loo - ba - lay! Hul - la - bal - loo, ba - la - ba-lay!

Solo   *Chorus*

Me fa - ther kept a board-ing house,
The board - ing house was on the quay, } Hul - la - bal - loo - ba - lay!___
The lodg - ers were near-ly all at sea,

The song "Hullaballoo Balay" is a sailor song, or "chantey." Its repeating rhythm makes it a perfect song for work.

While doing their work, the sailors who originally sang "Hullabaloo Balay" probably had no accompaniment.

Play the following ostinatos to accompany the song.

See **music.mmhschool.com** to research sea chanteys.

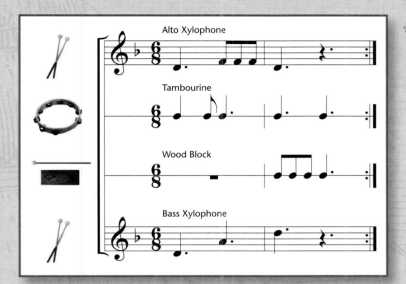

THINK! If you wanted to add instrumental sounds to the song, which instruments might you choose? To reflect the feeling of the song, would the accompaniment be rhythmic or melodic?

◀ Paul Bettany and Russell Crowe (right) in a scene from the film *Master and Commander*

Performing Ostinato Rhythms

"I Want to Be Ready" has optimistic lyrics that are supported by an upbeat rhythm. Also, the **pentatonic**, or five-pitch, melody is *do* centered. This gives it a bright sound.

Sing "I Want to Be Ready." What is the feeling of the words?

An **upbeat tempo** is quick and energetic. It often supports an optimistic musical mood. Does the rhythm of "I Want to Be Ready" contribute to that feeling?

The upbeat tempo of "I Want to Be Ready" is complemented by **syncopation** . Syncopation is a type of rhythm in which stressed sounds occur on weak beats or between beats. A rhythmic accompaniment can highlight a syncopated song.

Perform the two parts below with "I Want to Be Ready." Perform the first to accompany the whole song and the second for the verse only.

Spirituals such as "I Want to Be Ready" were created by enslaved African Americans in the 1800s. Some spirituals had a meaning related to gaining freedom as well as a religions meaning. Many freed slaves continued to farm after their emancipation. These workers are shown harvesting peanuts in Virginia in the 1890s. ▼

Japan: Two Musical Snapshots

CONCEPT
TONE COLOR
SKILLS
SING, PLAY, LISTEN
LINKS
HISTORY, CULTURES

The island country of Japan is full of contrasts—big cities and quiet countryside. Traditional ways and new technology contribute to its diverse culture. Japanese music is also full of contrasts. Japan's musical traditions go back many centuries, and much of this time-honored music is still performed. "Sakura" is a very old song. In Japan, it is known and sung by young and old.

Listen to "Sakura" and practice speaking the text in Japanese.

MAP
RUSSIA
CHINA
NORTH KOREA
JAPAN
SOUTH KOREA

Sakura

CD 1:19

Cherry Blossoms

Japanese Folk Song
English Version by MMH

Japanese: さ く ら　さ く ら　や よ い の　そ ら は
Pronunciation: sa ku ɾa　sa ku ɾa　ya yo i no　so ɾa wa
English: Cher-ry tree,　Cher-ry tree!　Cher-ry blossoms ev'-ry-where.

み わ た す か ぎ り　か す み か く も か
mi wa ta su ka gi ɾi　ka su mi ka ku mo ka
Far as an-y eye can see.　Mist and beau-ty fill the air,

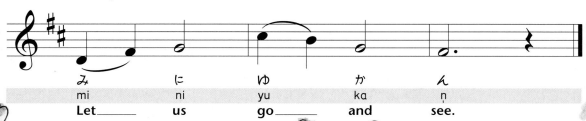

に お い ぞ い ず ろ　い ざ や い ざ や
ni o i zo i zu ɾu　i za ya i za ya
Love-ly blos-soms scent the breeze　Come with me,　come with me,

み に ゆ か ん
mi ni yu ka n
Let us go and see.

The koto is a string instrument that originated in China over two thousand years ago. It was then brought to Japan where it gained several more strings. The koto is a popular household instrument in Japan, much like the piano in the United States. For more than one hundred years, "Sakura" has been used to teach people to play the koto.

Sing "Sakura" as you listen to it being played on the koto.

CD-ROM

You can see how the koto is played on the *World Instruments* CD-ROM.

Play the following ostinato softly on resonator bells using the handles of the mallets. Notice that only five pitches are used.

koto

Playalong

For 12 measures

Last 3 measures

Playing the "Fat Drum"

Taiko drumming is a different kind of Japanese music. The word "taiko" in Japanese means "fat drum." If you look at the pictures of taiko drumming on these pages, you can see why this is such a good name for the drum.

Centuries ago these drums were played in religious festivals and ceremonies. In wartime, they were also used to frighten the enemy and give commands to the troops. In the last forty years, however, taiko drumming has become very popular all over the world. In the United States and Canada, there are over 150 taiko performing groups.

Listen to the rhythms of "Lion."

taiko drums

This six-man drumming team is playing a giant drum at a festival in Japan.

 LISTENING CD 1:23

Lion by Leonard Eto

"Lion" is a contemporary taiko composition for drums and voices. Kodo, an internationally recognized taiko ensemble, performs "Lion."

A Japanese taiko drummer in Los Angeles, CA

Listening Map for "Lion"

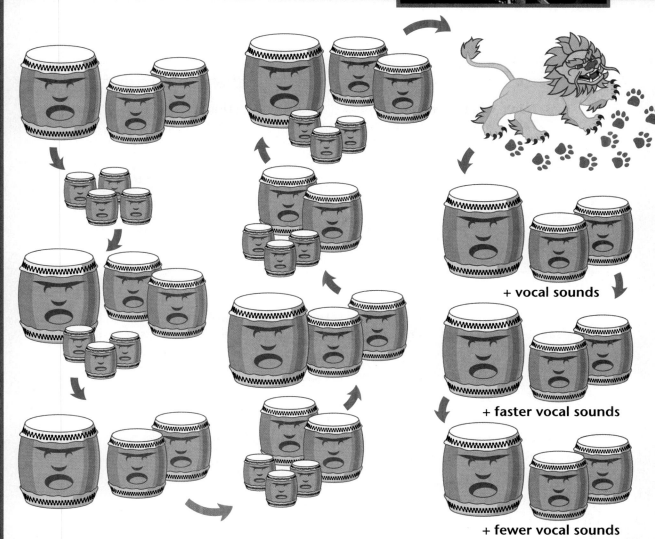

+ vocal sounds

+ faster vocal sounds

+ fewer vocal sounds

The Drummer in You!

CONCEPT
RHYTHM
SKILLS
LISTEN, PLAY
LINKS
MATHEMATICS, CULTURE

Listen to "Tain't What You Do" and tap with the beat. Then sing the song. Drums are the heart of the band. With a regular and steady beat, they help to keep the musicians together.

Bandleader Tommy Dorsey (trumpet) ▶ with Don Budge playing drums, 1938

Tain't What You Do

CD 1:24

Words and Music by
Sy Oliver and James Young

1., 3. Tain't what you do, it's the way that cha do it.
2. Tain't what you say, it's the way that cha say it.

Tain't what you do, it's the way that cha do it.
Tain't what you say, it's the way that cha say it.

Tain't what you do, it's the way that cha do it,
Tain't what you say, it's the way that cha say it,

1., 3. that's what gets___ re - sults.___ (3rd time) Fine
that's what gets___ re - sults.___

2. That's what gets__ re - sults.__ You can try hard,__

18

don't mean a thing.__

D.C. al Fine

Take it

ea - sy__   then your jive will swing.__

Playalong

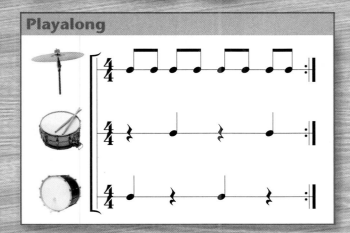

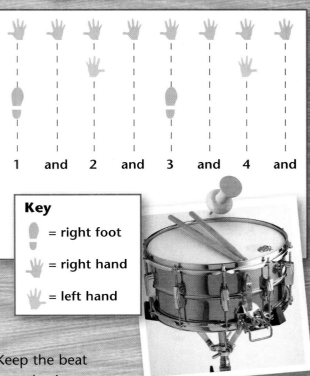

1 and 2 and 3 and 4 and

Key
= right foot
= right hand
= left hand

Discover the drummer in you! All you need are the basics!

The right foot plays the kick drum.
The left hand plays the snare drum.
The right hand plays the ride cymbal.
Work at a slow tempo until you get the hang of it. Keep the beat steady. Repeat this pattern over and over until you can play it comfortably and rapidly from memory.

You just played what is called the basic eighth $\frac{4}{4}$ beat.

Bandleader Tito Puente playing drums in concert

▲ snare drum

ride cymbal

kick drum

Unit 1 Rhythm Rocks the World **19**

The Alabama Beat

The down-home sound of country music makes it a favorite all over the world. Country music blends elements of folk music, gospel, and rock and roll to achieve its distinctive sound.

Meet the Musician

Randy Owen (born 1949) is a composer, singer, and guitarist. Randy Owen, Teddy Gentry, Jeff Cook, and Mark Herndon founded the country-western group Alabama in 1977 and named it after their home state. It is one of the most successful country-western groups in history.

Identify the parts of the song where you hear the basic eighth $\frac{4}{4}$ beat pattern in "Mountain Music."

MOUNTAIN MUSIC

CD 1:27

Words and Music by Randy Owen

Refrain F

Oh play me— some moun-tain mu - sic, Like grand-ma and grand-pa used to play.— Then I'll float_____ on down the ri - ver, to a Ca- - jun hide - a - way.

Verse
1. Drift a-way—
3. Play some

2. Climb
back - home

_____ like Tom Saw - yer Ride a raft_
ing tall hick' - ry bend - ing o -
come on mu - sic That

_____ like old_ Huck Finn, __ Take a nap_
- ver skin - nin' cats, __ Play - in' base-
comes_____ from the heart, __ Play

_____ like Rip_ Van Wink - le Daze
- ball_____ with chert_ rocks us-ing
some - thing_____ with lots_ of feel - ing 'cause that's where

dream - ing_____ a - gain.
saw - mill slabs_____ for bats.
mu - sic has__ to__ start.

THINK! **Compare** the drumming patterns in "Tain't What You Do" and "Mountain Music." How are they the same and how are they different?

Alabama performing at an open-air concert in Seymour, WI

21

A Partnership—Rhythm and Melody

CONCEPT
MELODY
SKILLS
READ, DESCRIBE
LINKS
HISTORY

MIDI

For another activity with "Down by the Riverside," see *Spotlight on MIDI*.

All music has two basic elements: rhythm and **melody** . Melody is the organization of pitches. The pitches are then arranged in rhythmic patterns.

Clap the rhythm of this song. Then play the first two lines of the melody on a keyboard.

Notice how the rhythm and melody combine in "Down by the Riverside" to create an upbeat feeling.

Down by the Riverside

CD 1:30

Traditional African American Spiritual
Arranged by Rollo Dilworth

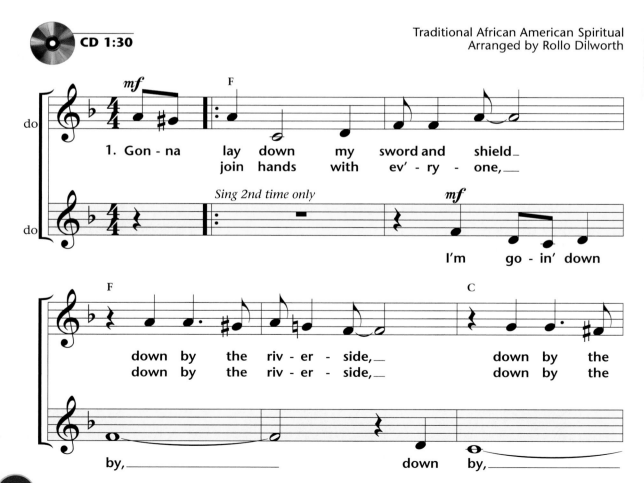

22

THINK! Describe how the song would sound if the melody had no syncopation.

The Shape of Melody

You probably know hundreds of songs without realizing it. You hear music every day—on radio, CDs, television, and in concerts. But of all the melodies you know, what makes each one sound different?

The way in which the notes of a melody are put together makes each song unique.

In melodies, pitches move up or down. They can:

. . . move by step up or down the scale.

. . . move in small hops, or skips.

. . . take big leaps up or down.

. . . stay the same as the previous pitch.

The shape and the direction of a melody's pitches are called **melodic contour**.

Chinese Music—Then and Now

CONCEPT
FORM
SKILLS
IMPROVISE,
PLAY
LINKS
CULTURES, HISTORY

Much of the music and art from China reflect ancient traditions and ceremonies. The music of the royal court and the folk songs of the people show a deep respect for the natural world and its beauty.

 **Art Gallery**

A Room in the House of Mr. Kong, a Peking Merchant

This watercolor was created in the 1800s. You can see Chinese instruments being played.

"Yüe líang wan wan" is an old and popular Chinese song. Notice the pentatonic melody as you sing the song.

MAP
RUSSIA
MONGOLIA
KOREA
CHINA
JAPAN
INDIA

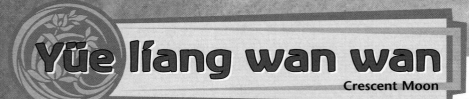 **Yüe líang wan wan**

Crescent Moon

CD 1:34

Folk Song from China

Mandarin:	跑	马	瘤	瘤	的	山	上	一	朵	溜 溜 的
Pronunciation:	pao	ma	lio	lio	di	shan	shang	i	dwɔ	lio lio di
English:	**Run - ning**	**horse,**	**to**	**the**	**moun-tain**	**top,**		**Lit - tle**	**clouds**	**in a**

云	哨	端	端	溜	溜	的	照	在
ün	yo	duan	duan	lio	lio	di	jao	tsai
clus - ter		**Face**	**to**	**face,**	**the__**		**moon and**	**cloud,**

The way sections of a piece of music are put together is called **form**. Blocks of music can be assembled in different patterns to create different forms.

Improvise an eight-measure phrase using the pitches D, E, F♯, A, and B on a keyboard or resonator bells.

While you are improvising, return to the notes B and F♯ as often as possible. This will help to establish the tonality.

Your improvisation can now function as a contrasting B section and the melody of "Yüe líang wan wan" will be the A section.

Perform the entire piece (with your improvisations) in an A B A form.

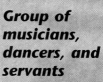 **THINK!** What other forms can you create using the song "Yüe líang wan wan" and your improvisations?

Chinese wood-block print
This print dates from about 1500. Look for the guzheng, a zitherlike instrument; the pipa, a four-stringed lute; and the dizi, a type of flute. ▼

Group of musicians, dancers, and servants
These Chinese terra cotta statuettes date from about the first century A.D. ▼

康 定 溜 溜 的 成 唷 月 亮 彎
kang dıng lio lio di chʌng yo üe liang wan
fly a - cross_ the_ vil - lage, Pale moon, Curv - ing,

彎 康 定 溜 溜 的 城 唷
wan kang dıng lio lio di chʌng yo
curv - ing,____ Cres - cent moon_ o - ver Cheng Yo.

Improvise a Drum Conversation

Listen for the different types of drumming and sticking techniques used in "Night Fight" from the film *Crouching Tiger, Hidden Dragon*. Can you describe them?

 LISTENING CD 2:1

Night Fight from *Crouching Tiger, Hidden Dragon* by Tan Dun

The music for the movie *Crouching Tiger, Hidden Dragon* uses many traditional Chinese and modern Western instruments. This blending of new and old sounds helps to express the mood of the film.

◀ Action scene from the film *Crouching Tiger, Hidden Dragon*

Learn About Chinese Instruments

Early Chinese musicians did not classify musical instruments the way Western musicians do (brass, woodwind, strings, and percussion). Instead, they were classified according to the materials from which they were made: earth, stone, metal, skin, wood, bamboo, and gourd.

Left to right: chanting drum, ceremonial drum, bronze drum and drumstick

Classify the instruments you hear in *Crouching Tiger, Hidden Dragon*. As you and your partner listen, use the seven Chinese categories to categorize the instruments.

In "Night Fight," you heard a conversation between several Chinese percussion instruments. You can have your own drum conversations.

Create a plan to improvise a drum conversation. Your plan might look like this:

1 Two or three drums begin softly (playing ostinatos) and continue throughout the piece.

2 A high-pitched drum and a low-pitched drum talk with each other.

3 Two other drums join the conversation.

4 A surprise ending!

When you are satisfied with your plan and the performance, record it.

Layers of sounds combine to create **texture**. Changes in texture are created by altering the number, type, range, and volume of voices or instruments used.

Listen to the recording of your improvisation. How does the texture change from the beginning to the end?

Left to right: waist drum (also called flower drum); hu-ch'in (violin) with bow, sheng (mouth organ), san-hsien (long-necked lute), pipa (lute); bronze cymbals

Making Music in Unusual Ways

CONCEPT
TONE COLOR
SKILLS
SING, MOVE, LISTEN
LINKS
CULTURES, SOCIAL STUDIES

In the early 1900s people throughout the southern United States formed jug bands, putting together instruments like the guitar, fiddle, or banjo with homemade instruments like kazoos, washboards, tubs, and jugs. The many folk songs of this region were often accompanied by local jug bands.

Listen to "The Wabash Cannonball."

The song "The Wabash Cannonball" is a about a mythical train that could take a person anywhere. Before airplanes, railroads were the most important form of long-distance transportation in the country. As the Industrial Revolution spread, these fast and powerful trains connected the nation and became more and more a part of the American scene. Railroad songs also became popular.

Sing "The Wabash Cannonball." Do you think a fictional train with amazing powers is an interesting subject for a song? Why?

The Wabash Cannonball

CD 2:2

Words and Music by William Kindt

1. From the great At - lan - tic O - cean to the
2. Now___ she came down from Bir-ming-ham on a
3. Now the East - ern states are dan - dy, so
4. So___ lis - ten to the jin - gle, the

wide Pa - cif - ic shore,
cold and frost - y day,
all the peo - ple say,
jum - ble and the roar,

To the green old flow - 'ring
As she rolled in - to the
From___ New York to Saint
As she glides a - long the

moun - tains   to   ice - bound   Lab - ra - dor,
sta - tion   you could   hear   the   peo - ple   say,
Lou - is   and Chi - ca - go   by   the   way,
wood - lands   through the hills   and   by   the   shore.

She's   long   and   tall   and   hand - some   and
"There's a   gal   out   there   from   Ten-nes - see,   she's
From the   lakes   of   Min - ne - so - ta   where the
Here the   might - y   rush   of   the   en - gine   and the

known quite well   to   all,   She's the   mod - ern   com - bin -
long,   and   she   is   tall,   She's the   mod - ern   com - bin -
rip - pling   wa - ters   fall,   No___ chan - ges   can   be
lone - some   ho - boes   squall,   While__ rid - ing through the

a - tion   called the   Wa - bash   Can - non - ball.
a - tion   called the   Wa - bash   Can - non - ball.
ta - ken   on   the   Wa - bash   Can - non - ball.
jun - gle   on   the   Wa - bash   Can - non - ball.

Move to "The Wabash Cannonball" and play the jug band sounds.

Found Objects? Sound Objects!

A jug band uses household or found objects to make music. The composer John Cage used household or found objects to alter the sounds of existing instruments.

Meet the Musician

John Cage (1912–1992) was an American composer. He loved to experiment with sounds. For example, he would place objects such as nuts, bolts, and pieces of rubber between the strings of the piano to change the sounds it made. He called this the "prepared piano."

A piano is "prepared" by inserting "foreign" objects between the strings, which changes the normal sound of the piano in surprising ways.

 LISTENING CD 2:5

Sonata X by John Cage

Listen to the sounds of this piece of music. What kinds of other instruments does the piano sound like?

Sounds of a Train

"The Wabash Cannonball" is about a fictional train. "Orange Blossom Special" is a song about a real train. Built in 1925, it ran the route from New York to Florida. This bluegrass song was written in 1938.

Listen for the fiddle in the opening of "Orange Blossom Special."

Orange Blossom Special train departing ▼

THINK! How does the music imitate the sound of the train?

32

Orange Blossom Special

CD 2:6

Words and Music by Ervin T. Rouse

1. Look a yon - der com - in', _____ com - in' down that rail - road _____ track!
2. Go - in' down to Flor - 'da _____ and ___ get some sand in _____ my _____ shoes,
3. Talk a - bout a - trav - 'lin', _____ she's the fast - est train on _____ the _____ line.

Hey, look a - yon - der com - in', _____ com-in' down that rail - road track!
or may - be Cal - i - for - nia _____ and ___ get some sand in _____ my track! shoes.
Talk a - bout a - trav - 'lin', _____ she's the fast - est train on ___ the line.

It's the Or - ange Blos - som Spe - cial _____ bring - in' my ba - by _____ back.
I'll ride that Or - ange Blos - som Spe - cial _____ and lose ___ these New ___ York ___ blues.
It's that Or - ange Blos - som Spe - cial _____ roll - in' down the Sea - board _ line.

United Through Music

CONCEPT
RHYTHM
SKILLS
SING, LISTEN
LINKS
SOCIAL STUDIES

Gloria Estefan has been entertaining the world since the 1980s. She has left a lasting mark on the music industry.

Sing "Conga." Tap, clap, or pat with the beat.

CD 2:9

Words and Music by Enrique Garcia

Refrain

Come___ on, move your bod-y, ba-by, do that con-ga, I know___
___ you can't con-trol your feet an-y lon-ger. Feel___
___ the rhy-thm of the mu-sic get-ting stron-ger. Don't___
___ you fight it till you've tried it; do that con-ga beat.

Fine

Verse

1. Ev'-ry-bod-y___ gath-er 'round now;___
2. Don't you wor-ry___ if you can't dance;___
3. It's the rhy-thm___ of the is-land___
4. If you want to___ do the con-ga,___

D.C. al Fine

let your bod-y feel___ the heat.___
let the mu-sic move___ your feet.___
from the sug-ar cane___ so sweet.___
you've got to lis-ten to___ the beat.___

Just as Gloria Estefan uses Hispanic music traditions in "Conga," Hossam Ramzy uses music styles of Egypt in his compositions.

◀ ceramic dumbeks

Meet the Musician

Hossam Ramzy was born in Cairo, Egypt. His musical career began at the age of three when he was given his first drum, an Egyptian tabla. His passion and talent for percussion have led him to explore the music of his native Egypt as a composer and performer.

 LISTENING CD 2:12

Belhadawa walla belshaawa
by Hossam Ramzy

Belhadawa walla belshaawa is a work for Egyptian percussion instruments. It means "Rough or Cool?" in Arabic, describing the playing style. Hossam Ramzy plays all the instruments, including tabla (goblet drum, also called dumbek), riqq (tambourine), and sagat and toura (small and large finger cymbals).

Listen and identify the sounds Ramzy uses.

Egyptian musicians playing the nai (flute), oud (lute), riqq (tamborine), and dumbek

◀ riqq

Join an African Drum Circle

Much of the excitement felt in African music is caused by syncopation and cross-rhythms. "Tina Singu" is a folk song from Lesotho, a country in southern Africa.

Cross-rhythms are created when different rhythm patterns occur at the same time. A common example in many African styles is groups of two beats against groups of three.

Listen for syncopation and cross rhythms in "Tina Singu." Where do you hear cross rhythms?

Drum circles are music-making events where people sit or stand in a circle while playing world percussion instruments. People improvise rhythms led by a facilitator in the center of the circle.

Create your own drum circle.

1. **Select** a leader.

2. **Begin** with the beat and layer on contrasting rhythms.

3. **Strive** to keep the beat and tempo steady.

4. **Listen** for variety in texture, dynamics, and tone color.

Spotlight Your Success!

REVIEW

1 Which of the notes/rests on the left are equal to the notes/rests on the right?

a.  b. c. d.

2 Which one of the following rhythms is syncopated?

a.

b.

c.

3 How many different pitches are in a pentatonic scale?

a. 4   b. 5   c. 6

4 What is a style of Japanese drumming?

a. upbeat tempo   b. syncopation   c. taiko

READ AND LISTEN

1 **Read** these rhythms. Then **listen**. Which rhythm do you hear?

 a. b. c.

2 **Read** these pitches. Then **listen**. Which pitches do you hear?

a.  b.

38

3 **Read** these pitches and rhythms. Then **listen**. Which one do you hear?

a.

b.

c.

THINK!

1 What is similar about the melody of "Sakura" and "Yüe líang wan wan"?

2 How do melody and rhythm combine to create a certain mood or feeling?

3 What kind of music sounds best with an upbeat tempo? Why?

4 **Write** about two pieces of music from the unit, one that uses syncopation and one that does not. Compare and contrast the sound and feel of both songs.

CREATE AND PERFORM

1 Use ♩, ♩, ♪, 𝄽, 𝄾, and ties.

2 Select one percussion instrument and create a four-measure rhythm using syncopation.

3 Select a contrasting percussion instrument and create a four-measure rhythm without syncopation to "answer" the first rhythm.

4 **Perform** your rhythms with a partner. Switch parts and perform again.

Meet the Musician
ON NATIONAL RADIO!

Name: Matthew Muckey
Age: 18
Instrument: Trumpet
Hometown: Sacramento, California

Not many musicians get to play *The Carnival of Venice* in the actual city of Venice, Italy, but trumpet player Matthew Muckey did just that. It was aboard a gondola while crowds gathered along the waterway to watch and listen. "I performed as a trio with two other trumpet players, and the bridges were packed with people," says Matthew. "It was so cool!"

Matthew has been able to travel extensively due to his involvement in music. He's a member of two youth orchestras that both tour around the world. Matthew has visited Italy, Switzerland, Austria, Germany, Russia, Lithuania, and Ireland.

Matthew is known not only for his musical talent but also for his very unusual pet, a shaggy donkey named Jasper. "My family has five acres of land, and we adopted Jasper," he explains. "He doesn't pull a plow or anything. I guess you could say he mows the lawn for us, but most of the time he just stands out there doing nothing."

 LISTENING   CD 2:19–21   **RECORDED INTERVIEW**

The Carnival of Venice
by J. B. Arban

Listen to Matthew's performance and interview on the national radio program **From the Top**.

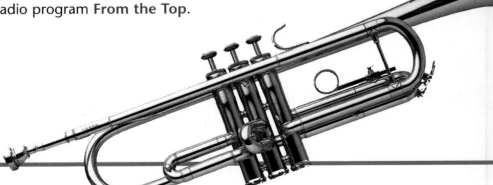

Spotlight on the Bassoon

Careers

John Hoey was the youngest child in a musical family. At home he listened to many records, his father singing, and a brother rehearsing his own band.

Mr. Hoey started playing the drums when he was three years old. As a skilled adult, he worked in many excellent bands. He enjoyed being part of those groups, but decided he wanted to do some musical things differently.

Ten years ago, Mr. Hoey formed The John Hoey Orchestra. His group includes drums, trumpets, saxophones, a keyboard, a guitar, a bass, and three singers. They're called an "orchestra" because they play many different musical styles. Mr. Hoey tells students to "Listen to as great a variety of music as possible" to become better musicians.

Did You Know?

The bassoon is a large woodwind instrument whose double-reed fits into a bent crook (the metal tube that holds the reed).

Almost eight feet long if it were straightened out, the bassoon's tubing is folded in half so it can be played more easily.

LISTENING   CD 2:22–24

Symphony No. 4, First Movement (excerpt), Second Movement (excerpt)
by Piotr Ilyich Tchaikovsky

Concerto for Orchestra, **Second Movement (Game of Pairs) (excerpt)**
by Béla Bartók

Listen to the wide range of sound the bassoon can create in these three excerpts. When played *staccato*, it can sound comic or playful. When played *legato,* in the higher register, it can sound sweet and lyrical. In the Bartók, two bassoons create a playful duet.

Singing
a Song

What would the world sound like if there were no singing? There would be no lullabies for babies, no rock or rap concerts, no singing around the campfire, no musical theater, and no "Happy Birthday" before blowing out the candles.

Singing is an important part of the human experience. People sing to express themselves. Singing brings us together.

What kinds of singing do you enjoy?

Coming Attractions

Sing in 2, 3, and 4 parts.

Move to a South African work song.

Listen to French Canadian "mouth music."

There are many different styles of singing—jazz, opera, blues, folk, and rap are just a few. You can practice and enjoy good singing in any style.

When I Sing

CD 3:1

Words and Music by Bill Henderson
Arranged by David J. Elliott

'Cause when I sing, I feel as light as spring.

It's a fun-ny___ thing, oo_____ I just

feel a lot bet-ter, feel a lot bet-ter, when I sing.___

I start to swing.__ It's a fun-ny thing__ oo___

I just feel a lot bet-ter, feel a lot bet-ter, feel a lot

bet-ter then. when I___ have to talk. A

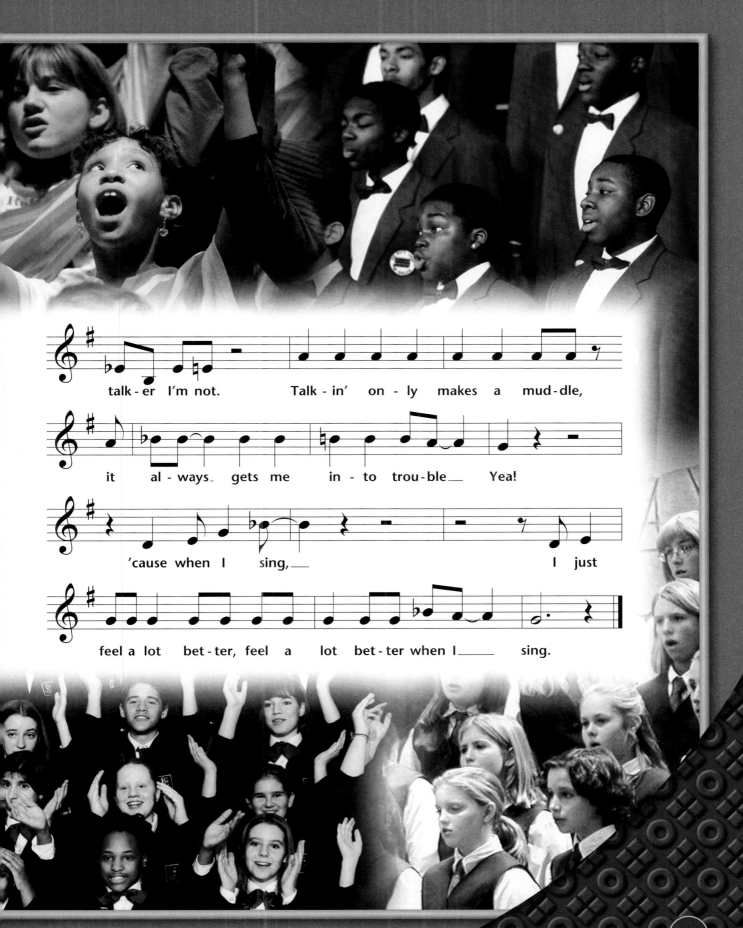

talk-er I'm not. Talk-in' on-ly makes a mud-dle,

it al-ways gets me in-to trou-ble__ Yea!

'cause when I sing,__ I just

feel a lot bet-ter, feel a lot bet-ter when I__ sing.

A Single Voice

Singing groups, or **choirs**, try to create the most beautiful sound possible. One way a choir does this is by striving for good **unison**. When everyone sings the exact same pitch at the same time, unison singing is achieved.

Singers can learn to blend their voices to create a good unison. One way is to work on singing the pitches perfectly in tune. Another is to practice singing vowels and consonants with exactly the same sounds and at the same time. These qualities all contribute to good unison singing.

Perform "The Water Is Wide" with good unison singing.

CONCEPT
MELODY
SKILLS
SING, LISTEN, ANALYZE
LINKS
FINE ART

MAP

SCOTLAND

IRELAND   ENGLAND
       WALES

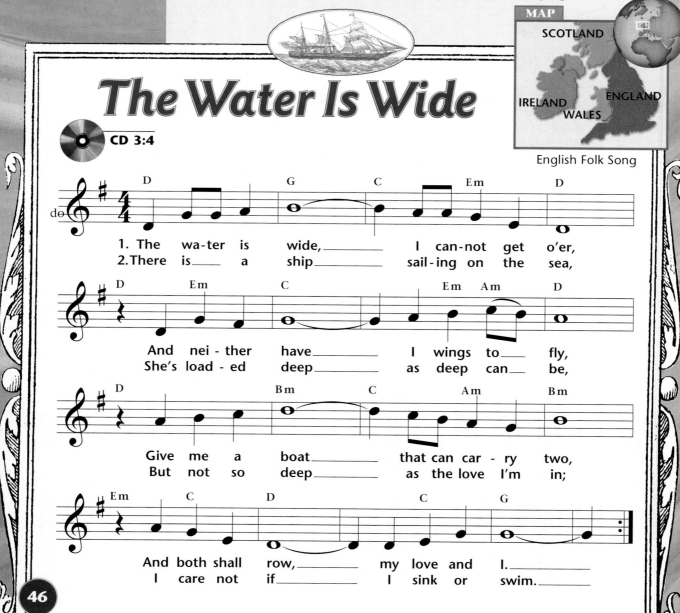

The Water Is Wide

CD 3:4

English Folk Song

1. The wa-ter is wide,_____ I can-not get o'er,
2. There is____ a ship_____ sail-ing on the sea,

And nei-ther have_____ I wings to___ fly,
She's load-ed deep_____ as deep can___ be,

Give me a boat_____ that can car - ry two,
But not so deep_____ as the love I'm in;

And both shall row,_____ my love and I._____
I care not if_____ I sink or swim._____

3. Oh, love is sweet._____ and love is fair,

Oh, love is sweet._____ and love is

Fresh as the dew_____ when it is___ new,

fair, Fresh as the dew_____ when it is___

But love grows old,_____ and_ it grows cold,

new, But love grows old,_____ and_ it grows

And fades a - way_____ like morn-ing dew.

cold, And fades a - way_____ like morn-ing dew.

Art Gallery

The Boating Party

Mary Cassatt (1845–1926) was an American painter. She created this oil-on-canvas painting in 1893–1894. What do you see?

Singing with Solfège

Rehearsing a song using pitch syllables, or **solfège**, is another technique singing groups use to develop a good unison sound. Solfège helps create better awareness for hearing and singing the pitches correctly.

Sing "Rage and Roar" in unison using solfège instead of the lyrics.

Repeat this exercise with the same pitch syllables but start on a lower or higher pitch. Listen carefully as you sing, and match your voice to the correct pitch. Singing or playing the correct pitch in tune is called **intonation** .

Rage and Roar

CD 3:7

Words and Music by Liz Gilpatrick

1

Though win-ter pounds its i-cy fist up-on the kitch-en___ door,

Solfège: so do' do' ti ti la la so so fa mi re so mi

2

We'll nev-er let it in, on nev-er let it in, though it may rage and roar!

re do re mi fa so mi fa so la ti do' mi' re' do' do' ti do'

3

Though it may rage and roar, we'll not let it in the door.

so mi mi so so do do do re mi fa so do

48

When a choir sings in unison, everyone is singing the same pitch at the same time, as you did when you sang "Rage and Roar" with solfège syllables.

Although you can sing "Rage and Roar" as a unison melody, it was written to be a **canon** . A canon, or round, occurs when the singers divide into smaller groups and sing the same melody, starting at different times. As the melody plays against itself, harmony is created.

Identify the moment in "Rage and Roar" when the unison becomes harmony.

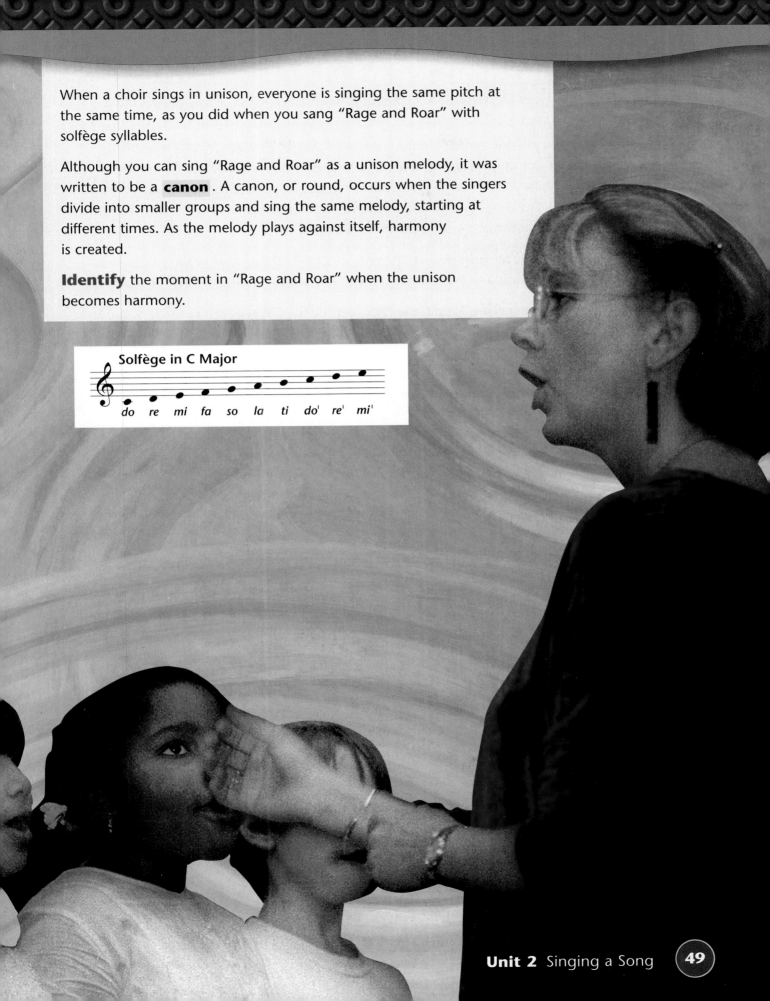

Solfège in C Major

do re mi fa so la ti do' re' mi'

We All Sing a Part

CONCEPT
MELODY

SKILLS
DESCRIBE,
SING, PLAY

LINKS
CULTURES

Music can be sung by soloists, groups, or a combination of both. A group may sing a melody in unison or a melody with harmony. Two separate melodies can even be sung together at the same time. Part-singing can add greater levels of expression and intensity to both the singing and listening experiences.

This **arrangement**, or version, of "O, Desayo" alternates between unison and part singing. There is a separate part for each group.

Describe the different sections of "O, Desayo." How many sections are there? How are they different?

MAP
DEMOCRATIC
REPUBLIC OF
CONGO

ANGOLA   ZAMBIA

NAMIBIA
BOTSWANA

O, DESAYO

CD 3:10

Angolan Folk Song
Arranged by Elliot Z. Levine
English Words by Elliot Z. Levine

Refrain

Portuguese: O, Des - ay - o!_____ O, Des - ay - o!
Pronunciation: o de sa yo   o de sa yo

O, Des - ay - o Me - ni - na, O, Des - ay - o!
o de sa yo me ni na o de sa yo

Verse 1
Part I

Rains are o - ver, it's fine and shin - y wea-ther O, Des - ay - o!

Part II

Fine and shin - y day for a get_ to - ge-ther, O, Des - ay - o!

Identify measures in which:

- Groups 1 and 2 sing in unison.
- Group 1 and Group 2 sing different melodies.

Sing "O, Desayo" in two parts.

Verse 2

Part I C   F

O, Des - ay - o,____ Me - ni - na. O, Des - ay - o,____ Me - ni - na,

Part II

Sing,   a   song__ and then   dance   a - long__ and then,

C   F

O, Des - ay - o,____ Me - ni - na O, Des - ay - o,____ Me - ni - na

drink   a   cup__ and then   stay   for sup - per then.

Verse 3

C   F

Off   they   go____ and good - bye,   we've

Off   we   go____ a - gain   down   the   stream_ a - gain

C   F

got   to   say____   good - bye!

off   we   go____ a - gain down   the   stream_ a - gain.

Singing the Accompaniment

In "Elijah Rock," you will hear two different vocal parts. One is the main melody of the song and the other is the accompanying part sung above the main melody.

 LISTENING CD 3:14

Elijah Rock African American spiritual

This exciting arrangement of "Elijah Rock" captures the mood of the original spiritual. It is performed by the Moses Hogan Chorale.

Listen to "Elijah Rock" and notice the higher vocal part that accompanies the melody. The higher part is called a **descant**.

THINK! Compare and contrast the similarities and differences in "Elijah Rock" and "O, Desayo."

Sing the melody or the descant of "Elijah Rock."

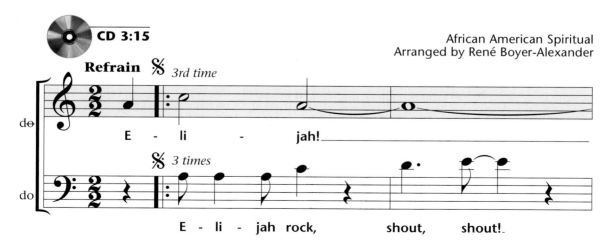

ELIJAH ROCK

CD 3:15

African American Spiritual
Arranged by René Boyer-Alexander

Refrain 𝄋 *3rd time*

E - li - jah!

𝄋 *3 times*

E - li - jah rock, shout, shout!

Play these parts with "Elijah Rock."

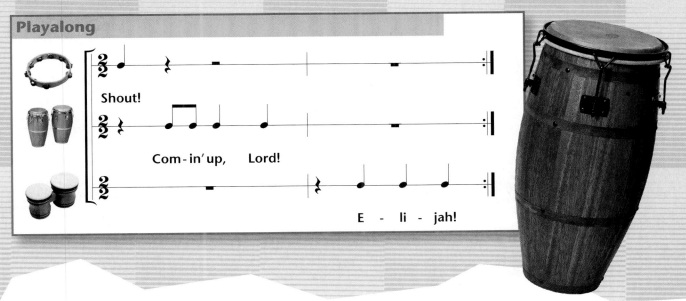

Playalong

Shout!

Com-in' up, Lord!

E - li - jah!

E - li - jah!____

E - li - jah rock, com - in' up Lord____ E - li - jah rock,

Fine

Fine

shout, shout! E - li - jah rock, com - in' up Lord

Verse

Who's that yon - der dressed in red?____ It

D.S. al Fine

must be the chil-dren that Mo - ses led.____

CONCEPT
MELODY
SKILLS
SING, EVALUATE, DESCRIBE
LINKS
CULTURES, THEATER

Some songs are favorites because of the melody, or the sound of the instruments, or the rhythm, or just the singer's voice. But in other favorites, the lyrics speak to you. In these songs the words are the most important feature.

Sing "One of Those Songs."

ONE OF THOSE SONGS

CD 3:19

English Words by Will Holt
Music by Gerald Calvi

1. Well this is one of those songs_ that you hear now and then,_ You
(2.) one of those songs_ that can make you re-call___ a
(3.) one of those songs_ that's so eas-y to hear,_ You

don't know just where,_____ you don't know just when,_ It's
ride in the spring-time, a walk in the fall,___ a
lis-ten just once,_ then you play it by ear,___ It's

one of those songs__ that are o-ver and then,___ It's
day in the coun-try, a night on the town,_ the
hummed on ver-ran-das and strummed on gui-tars,___ and

one of those songs__ that start play-ing a-gain,___ Yes it's just
sun com-ing up_____ or the rain com-ing down,_ Or else the
all your re-mem-ber is "lah-dee-dah-dah!"___ But la-ter

To fully communicate the meaning of a song, it is important to make the lyrics clear and understandable. You can do this if you **enunciate**, or clearly pronounce, the words in the song.

Sing "One of Those Songs" as though you are singing it to someone who has never heard it before. Try to enunciate clearly enough so that the first-time listener doesn't miss a word.

THINK!

In "One of Those Songs," which is more important—the melody or the lyrics? Why?

Let's Hear Those Words!

In the operetta *The Pirates of Penzance*, the character of the Major General sings about how much he knows but how little of it has to do with being a general.

LISTENING CD 3:22

A Modern Major General from *The Pirates of Penzance*

by W. S. Gilbert and A. Sullivan

In the operettas of Gilbert and Sullivan, there is always one song that requires a lot of words to be sung at high speed. These songs are called "patter songs." In the 1800s, "patter" was another word for quick talking.

Listen to "A Modern Major General" and hear the soloist and the chorus enunciate at a quick pace.

"Reel á Bouche" is French-Canadian "mouth music." There are no actual words. The syllables change often and go by quickly. Singers must enunciate clearly to make the music sound crisp and lively.

LISTENING CD 3:23

Reel á Bouche French Canadian song

The music of Canada is greatly influenced by the traditions and cultures of Native Americans, and of the French and English who settled there in the 1700s and 1800s.

Describe the clear enunciation of the choir in "Reel á Bouche." What would be a good way to learn a song like this?

On the next page is "Chiribim," an Eastern European song. The words are in Hebrew. The repetition of syllables and the quick rhythm make it challenging to enunciate clearly.

Sing "Chiribim." Practice the words in rhythm. Also, practice the melody on a neutral syllable, such as *la*. Then sing it with words.

▼ Scene from *The Pirates of Penzance*

◄ Rue Knapp as Major General Stanley from *The Pirates of Penzance*

Chiribim

MAP
POLAND
RUSSIA
GERMANY

Traditional Yiddish Song

Hebrew: מַר-אוֹשֶׁ-כּוּ ... בִּים רִי-בִּי רִי-צְ'י כֶּם-כּוּל רוּ-תֹּאמ דִי-דוֹ כַה-לְ
Pronunciation: uxɛ sheo maɾ   le xa do di tom ɾu kul xem chi ɾi bi ɾi bim

בּוֹם רִי-בִּי רִי-צְ'י   לָה-כַּ רַאת-לְק
lik ɾat ka la   chi ɾi bi ɾi bom

בּוֹם רִי-בִּי רִי-צְ'י לָה-כַּ רַאת-לְק בִּים רִי-בִּי רִי-צְ'י דִי-דוֹ כַה-לְ
le xa do di chi ɾi bi ɾi bim lik ɾat ka lah chi ɾi bi ɾi bom

רִי-צְ'י בּוֹם רִי-בִּי רִי-בִּי רִי-צְ'י לָה-כַּ רַאת-לְק דִי-דוֹ כַה-לְ
le xa do di lik ɾat ka la chi ɾi bi ɾi bi ɾi bi ɾi bom chi ɾi

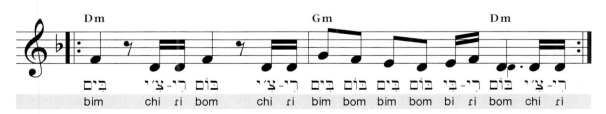

רִי-צְ'י בּוֹם רִי-בִּי בּוֹם בִּים בִּים בּוֹם בִּים רִי-צְ'י
bim chi ɾi bom chi ɾi bim bom bim bom bi ɾi bom chi ɾi

בּוֹם בּוֹם בִּים רִי-בִּי רִי-בִּי רִי-צְ'י אוֹי בּוֹם בּוֹם בִּים רִי-בִּי רִי-בִּי רִי-צְ'י אוֹי
oi chi ɾi bi ɾi bi ɾi bim bom bom oi chi ɾi bi ɾi bi ɾi bim bom bom

Thirds for Two Voices

CONCEPT
HARMONY
SKILLS
IDENTIFY, SING, PLAY
LINKS
SOCIAL STUDIES, HISTORY

Singers can perform simple melodies in several different ways; call and response, echo, and canon are just three possibilities.

Two voices can also sing together "in thirds." One voice sings at the interval of a third higher or lower from the melody, creating a harmony line that moves **parallel**, or in the same direction, with the first voice.

Listen to the accompanying melody in "Suliram," a lullaby from Indonesia. Is the accompanying melody a third lower or a third higher than the main melody?

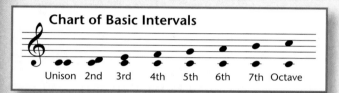

Chart of Basic Intervals

Unison 2nd 3rd 4th 5th 6th 7th Octave

Identify the intervals between the two voices in "Suliram." What other intervals are there besides thirds?

Sing "Suliram" in two parts. Just as you do when you sing in unison, be sure to match vowel and consonant sounds with the other singers.

Suliram

MAP
BRUNEI
SINGAPORE
INDONESIA
AUSTRALIA

 **CD 3:28**

Indonesian Folk Song
Arranged by Raymond J. Malone
English Words by Audrey Snyder

Indonesian: Su - li - ram,   su - li - ram, ram, ram, su - li -
Pronunciation: so   le   ɾam   so   le   ɾam ɾam   ɾam   so   le
English: Lit - tle child,   lit - tle tin - y   one,   lit - tle

ram   yang___   ma - nis,   a - du   hai   in -
ɾam   yang   ma   nis   a   du   hai   ɪn
child   you___   must know,   how we've longed, we've

Latin Thirds

When you hear "Mi caballo blanco," something about it might sound familiar to you. Can you identify the way in which the melody is harmonized?

Listen to "Mi caballo blanco" and follow along in your book.

Mi caballo blanco
My White Horse

CD 4:1

Words and Music by Francisco Flores del Campo
English Words by Linda Worsley

Spanish: Es mi ca-ba-llo blan-co___ Co-mo un a-ma-ne-cer
Pronunciation: es mi ka ba yo βlang ko ko mo un a ma ne seɾ
English: 1. This is my trus-ty white horse,___ I love him like a friend,
2. On wings of my good for-tune,___ he took me ev-'ry day,
3. When I am called to hea-ven,___ the an-gels have to know.

Siem-pre jun-ti-tos va-mos___ Es mi a-mi-go más fi-el.
syem pɾe xun ti tos βa mos es mi a mi go mas fi el
My horse is al-ways with me,___ True and loy-al to the end.
And on the wings of hard-ship,___ then he car-ried me a-way.
I'll ride my horse to hea-ven,___ For with-out him I'll not go!

Refrain

Mi ca-ba-llo mi ca-ba-llo ga-lo-pan-do va___
mi ka βa yo mi ca βa yo ga lo pan do βa
Mi ca-ba-llo, mi ca-ba-llo, As white as the dawn,___

Mi ca-ba-llo mi ca-ba-llo se va y se va.
mi ka βa yo mi ca βa yo sé βa i se βa
Mi ca-ba-llo, mi ca-ba-llo Run swift-ly on!

60

Harmonizing a melody in thirds is part of the musical tradition of many Spanish-speaking countries. "Mi caballo blanco," written by the Chilean composer Francisco Flores del Campo, is harmonized this way throughout the piece.

Practice the melody and the harmony separately. Then sing both parts together.

When a melody moves to a higher key it is called a **modulation**. It can create an interesting effect. As the music modulates up, its intensity increases.

Sing the song and perform these three melodic accompaniments for "Mi caballo blanco." Modulate from the key of D minor to E minor and then to F minor.

Playalong

D minor (3 times)

E minor (3 times)

F minor (3 times)

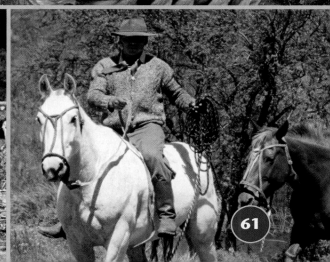

How Voices Come Together

CONCEPT
HARMONY
SKILLS
ANALYZE, SING, COMPARE
LINKS
CULTURE, LANGUAGE ARTS

Singing is so universal that it is often a subject for poets.

Read "Songs for the People" aloud. Think about the many ways that songs are a part of people's lives.

> from ★ **Songs for the People** ★
> Let me make the songs for the people
>   Songs for the old and young;
> Songs to stir like a battle-cry
>   Wherever they are sung.
> —*Frances Ellen Watkins Harper*

In "Listen to the Music" there are three separate melodies weaving in and out of each other all at the same time. The beginning of one melody overlaps with the ending of another, and so on.

Analyze the music. Look at the song and locate places where:

• a melody is repeated immediately after it is sung by another part.

• a part begins on the same note being sung of another part.

• a part begins an octave lower than the note of another part.

Singing in a good choir can be like playing on a championship baseball or football team. Everyone on the team has their role and everyone depends on one another to perform well. Everyone practices hard and works together to create a strong team. The more separate parts there are, the more dependent everyone is on everyone else—you must listen carefully and sing with precision.

Sing "Listen to the Music."

((((Listen to the Music))))

CD 4:6

Words and Music by Ed Robertson

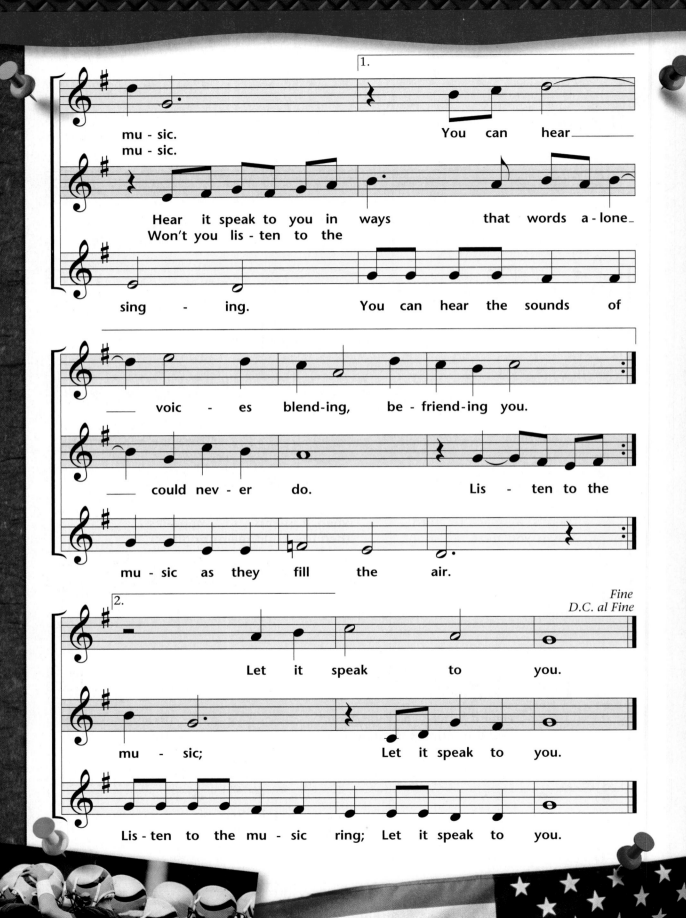

Choirs Around the World

Listen to the music of these three singing groups. They are each from different regions and different cultures. Notice the differences in tone quality, or **timbre**, of the voices.

LISTENING CD 4:11–13

Crazy Songs traditional Czech song
This song is sung by the Boni Puesi Choir, a Czech boys' choir.

Antiphonal Singing Song Chinese folk song
This song is sung by Red Leaf Girls Choir from China.

Mississippi Mud
by Harry Barris and James Cavanaugh
This song is performed by The Masters of Harmony, an American men's barbershop chorus.

Describe the timbre of the Chinese girls' choir.

Listen to the Czech boys' choir. Compare it with the Chinese girls' chorus. How is the timbre different?

Compare the singing and timbre of the American men's barbershop chorus with that of the other two singing groups.

▼ Boni Puesi Choir

▼ Barbershop performers

LESSON

6

CONCEPT
HARMONY

SKILLS
SING, LISTEN

LINKS
SCIENCE,
CULTURE

Tunes in Tune

There are special machines called tuners that can tell if you are singing or playing a note perfectly in tune. The machines can tell if a note is too high, too low, or just right.

A tuner measures the vibration of a sound. **Vibration** is rapid movement back and forth or up and down. Vibration at a frequency of 440 times per second or 440 hertz (Hz) produces the pitch A above middle C.

As a musician, you have special devices that tell you if a note is in or out of tune—your ears! By challenging yourself to listen and think carefully, you can sing or play any note perfectly in tune.

Singing in tune is not always easy, but it feels terrific when you sing so well in tune that your part harmonizes beautifully with the other parts.

Sing "Hava Nashira" in unison. Listen to make sure you sing with good intonation. What did you do to blend well with the other singers?

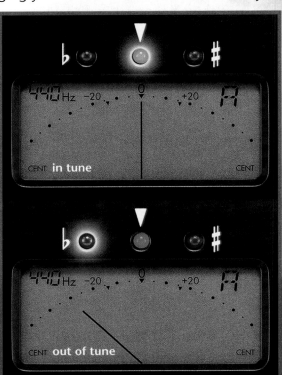

"Hava Nashira" was written more than 600 years ago. Now that you've sung it in unison, sing it as a canon, or round. How does the layering of voices change how it sounds?

Hava Nashira

Sing Alleluia

CD 4:14

Music by Johannes Ockeghem
Traditional Words

Music of Eastern Europe

The refrain of "Tum Balalaika" uses the musical device of harmonizing the melody in thirds. Find the measures in which this occurs.

Some pitch intervals, like thirds and sixths, are pleasing to the ear. On the other hand, seconds and sevenths sound jarring and harsh. The pleasant-sounding intervals are **consonances** and the harsh, jarring ones are **dissonances**. Dissonances create harmonic tension.

You can hear dissonance in the refrain. In measure 4, Voice 1 sustains an E as Voice 2 sings a D. And in measure 10, both voices start on a D, but Voice 2 moves down to a C.

▼ balalaika

Sing "Tum Balalaika," singing first the melody and then the harmony. Repeat, singing both parts together. Listen for consonances and dissonances.

MAP
ESTONIA
LATVIA
LITHUANIA
BELARUS
RUSSIA

Tum Balalaika

CD 4:18

Traditional Russian Yiddish Song
Arranged by Jay Broeker

1. Maid - en, maid - en, tell___ me true. What can grow with - out___ the dew? What___ can burn for years_ and years? What_ can cry and shed_ no tears?
2. Lis - ten, I've an an - swer for you, What stones can grow with - out___ the dew. Love___ can burn for years_ and years, Hearts_ can cry and shed_ no tears.

"Tum Balalaika" is arranged for three parts. Two of the parts are for voices and the third "voice" is a clarinet. Does the clarinet act and sound like a real voice or is it different? How?

Listen to or sing "Tum Balalaika." Notice the three different parts.

CD-ROM

Use *Orchestral Instruments* **CD-ROM** to learn more about the clarinet.

Refrain

Tum ba - la, tum ba - la - tum ba - la - lai - ka, Tum ba - la,

Tum ba - la, tum ba - la, tum ba - la - lai - ka, Tum ba - la,

tum ba - la, tum ba - la - lai - ka, Tum ba - la - lai - ka,

tum ba - la, tum ba - la - lai - ka, Tum ba - la - lai - ka,

tum ba - la - lai - ka, tum ba - la - lai - ka, tum ba - la - lai.

tum ba - la - lai - ka, tum ba - la - lai - ka, tum ba - la - lai.

African Voices

CONCEPT
CULTURAL
CONTEXT
SKILLS
MOVE, DESCRIBE,
PLAY
LINKS
CULTURES,
HISTORY

"Jikel' Emaweni" is a song of South African miners. Like many laborers all over the world, the miners sing to make the hard work go faster and easier. In the song, they are ready to "throw down their shovels" at the end of a hard day of digging.

Learn About Work Songs

Work songs have always been a part of the laborer's lot. They provide a regular beat to work to and help make the working day go faster. Sailors have used songs to row their oars together, and songs help fishermen pull in their nets. Farm workers sing to lift their spirits as they pick cotton, fruit, and vegetables.

MAP
NAMIBIA
BOTSWANA
SWAZILAND
LESOTHO
SOUTH AFRICA

Jikel' Emaweni
Throw It Down the Slope

CD 4:22

South African Work Song
Arranged by Cheryl Lavender

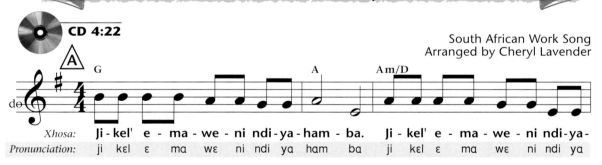

Xhosa: Ji - kel' e - ma - we - ni ndi - ya - ham - ba. Ji - kel' e - ma - we - ni ndi - ya-
Pronunciation: ji kεl ε ma we ni ndi ya ham ba ji kεl ε ma we ni ndi ya

ham-ba. ham-ba. A - jik' a - ma - do - da a - ji - ke lem - go - di - ni A
ham ba ham ba a jik a ma do da a ji kε lεm go di ni a

A - ji - kel' e - ma - we - ni. A-
a ji kεl ε ma we ni a

Move to "Jikel' Emaweni." What kinds of movement would go well with a work song like this? Would you move with the rhythm of the words or the beat of the music?

Moving to a Work Song

The rhythm of the melody of "Jikel' Emaweni" is made up of eighth, quarter, and half notes with no syncopation. The countermelody includes syncopation. In the main melody, all of the voices move in the same direction at the same time.

Explain how the syncopation accompanies the steady rhythm of the song.

Sing "Jikel' Emaweni" with all the vocal parts.

Perform the vocal and instrumental parts for "Jikel' Emaweni."

▲ Gold miners in Guateng, South Africa

(Bass part may be divided between two players)

▲ Sapphire miners in Ilakaka, Madagascar

More Guateng ▶ gold miners

Global Voices

LISTENING CD 5:1

Thula Sizwe, South African Freedom Song

"Thula Sizwe" was an important song to Black South Africans in the years before the fall of apartheid. They sang songs that sounded religious, but which were, in fact, carrying a message of hope for a day when they would be free.

MAP
NAMIBIA
BOTSWANA
SWAZILAND
LESOTHO
SOUTH AFRICA

Listen to the song and follow the lyrics.

Thula Sizwe

Thula Sizwe. Ungabokhala.
Ujehova wakho uzokunqobela.
Inkululeko. Uzoyithola.
Ujehova wakho uzokunqobela.

English Translation:
Be peaceful, Nation!

Be peaceful, Nation! Do not cry.
Your Jehovah will conquer for you.
Accept this freedom. You will find it.
Your Jehovah will conquer for you.

Say some phrases in IsiZulu:

Sawabonani	*Hello*
Ngiyabonga	*Thank you (to an individual)*
Ungabani?	*What's your name?*

Unjani?	*How are you?*
Ngiyaphila	*I'm fine.*

Digging for sapphires in Madagascar

Nelson Mandela, second from left, freedom fighter and former president of South Africa

Unit 2 Singing a Song

73

CONCEPT
HARMONY

SKILLS
SING, LISTEN,
ANALYZE

LINKS
HISTORY

"**W**alk by the River" is in four parts. One part is the main melody and there are three other accompanying vocal lines.

Sing the main melody of "Walk by The River."

Walk by the River

 CD 5:2

Words and Music by Holly Turnquist Fischer

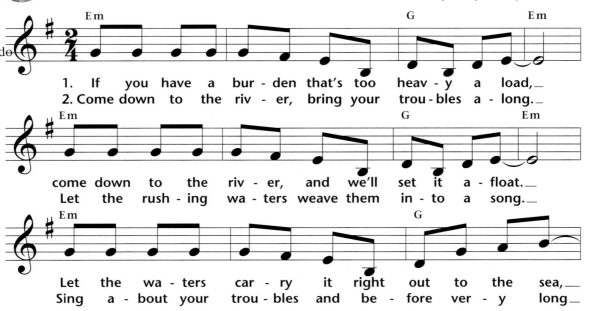

1. If you have a bur-den that's too heav-y a load,__
2. Come down to the riv-er, bring your trou-bles a-long.__

come down to the riv-er, and we'll set it a-float.__
Let the rush-ing wa-ters weave them in-to a song.__

Let the wa-ters car-ry it right out to the sea,__
Sing a-bout your trou-bles and be-fore ver-y long__

Four Parts to Sing

Practice the three-part accompaniment to "Walk by the River."

Now put it all together. As you sing the song in four parts, listen to the voices around you. Try and blend your voice with all the others using good enunciation and careful intonation.

Perform the entire song with melody and vocal accompaniment.

Harmony Parts

Words and Music by
Holly Turnquist Fischer

Walk_____ with your lov-in' hand_ in mine.
Stand_____ just to
Sing_____ with your

watch the wa - ter shine.   voi-ces mak-ing har-mo-ny in

notes so sweet and   fine._____
                     fine._____
                           fine._____

Ech-o,_____   ver-y   long   time._____

LISTENING CD 5:8

The Promise of Living
from *The Tender Land* by Aaron Copland

Copland wrote the opera *The Tender Land* for young
singers. Originally composed for television in 1952, it tells
about the lives of poor tenant farmers during the Great
Depression of the 1930s.

Listen to "The Promise of Living." How does the
composer blend the melody, vocal, and instrumental
accompaniment?

?THINK! Why are there so many different styles of
singing across the world? What are some possible reasons
for singing in one, two, three, or four parts? What is your
own favorite way to sing in parts?

Listening Map for The Promise of Living

Spotlight Your Success!

REVIEW

1 What is another name for using pitch syllables?

    a. parallel   **b.** solfège   **c.** choir

2 What is a higher accompanying melody?

    a. descant   **b.** canon   **c.** modulation

3 What is the word meaning to clearly pronounce the words of a song?

    a. intonation   **b.** arrangement   **c.** enunciate

4 When a song has modulations, what happens?

    a. changes keys   **b.** changes rhythms   **c.** changes dynamics

READ AND LISTEN

1 **Listen** to phrases from three songs. Which phrase is sung in unison?

    a. "O, Desayo"   **b.** "Mi caballo blanco"   **c.** "The Water Is Wide"

2 **Listen** to phrases from three songs. Which phrase is in $\frac{3}{4}$ meter?

    a. "O, Desayo"   **b.** "Mi caballo blanco"   **c.** "The Water Is Wide"

3 **Read** this phrase. Then **listen**. What is the interval between the first and last pitch?

    a. third   **b.** fourth   **c.** fifth

4 **Read** this phrase. Then **listen**. What is the interval between the last two pitches?

a. third   **b.** fourth   **c.** fifth

THINK!

1 What are different ways you can classify songs?

2 Choose two songs from the unit and identify the similarities and differences between each singing style .

3 List ways you can continue to improve your singing skills.

4 Choose your favorite song from this unit. Describe the song with as many details as possible. Then **write** about why this song has special appeal to you.

CREATE AND PERFORM

1 Form small groups and **create** a checklist to evaluate singing and vocal technique.

2 Choose and practice a part song. Videotape or audiotape your group's practice.

3 Evaluate the group's performance using the checklist.

4 Refine your performance.

5 **Perform** your song for the class or another audience.

Meet the Musician

ON NATIONAL RADIO!

Name: Deanna Talens
Age: 14
Instrument: Cello
Hometown: Appleton, Wisconsin

"I just get so impatient," says cellist Deanna Talens about the challenges of practicing. "It's so boring to drill passages over and over. I have a miserable time focusing!"

Deanna feels lucky, though, because she has a great cello teacher who's helped her improve her concentration. Whenever she has a distracting thought, he's taught her to stop playing, write it down, and assure herself she will devote time to it later. "It works!" says Deanna. "When I do that, I can clear my mind and start again."

Her teacher also has a knack for making lessons especially fun. When Deanna was learning "Requiebros," her teacher danced around the room like a bullfighter to demonstrate the exciting spirit of the music. "I loved it, and it actually made me play better!" says Deanna. "Now I try to bring that spirit into the piece whenever I perform it."

Deanna wants to be a professional cellist one day like her role models Yo-Yo Ma and Jacqueline du Pre. Deanna also has a fascination with film legend Audrey Hepburn. Says Deanna, "Audrey Hepburn was classic!"

 LISTENING CD 5:10–11 **RECORDED INTERVIEW**

Requiebros
by Gaspar Cassado

Listen to Deanna's performance and interview on the national radio program From the Top.

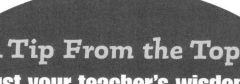

A Tip From the Top
"Trust your teacher's wisdom."
Deanna's teacher helped her solve problems and look at music in a fresh way. By following his advice, she's become a better musician.

Spotlight on the Harp

Did You Know?

The harp's beginnings go back to ancient times when strings were first stretched over wooden frames. These first harp strings may have come from an archer's bow.

A concert harp's 47 strings are plucked by the player's fingers. The right hand plays the shorter, higher strings, while the left hand plays the lower, longer strings.

A harp has seven foot pedals. These pedals activate a mechanism that raises or lowers the strings' pitches by shortening or lengthening the strings.

Harp strings are attached to a soundboard that amplifies the strings' vibrations.

 LISTENING CD 5:12–13

Concerto for Harp, Op. 4, No. 6, First Movement (excerpt)
by George Frideric Handel

Concerto for Harp, Third Movement (excerpt)
by Alberto Ginastera

Listen to Handel's concerto for harp. It was written in 1736. Over two hundred years later, Argentinian composer Ginastera wrote this colorful concerto for harp. The instrument has not changed much in 200 years, but musical styles are very different.

UNIT 3

Gotta Dance!

The urge to move to the music is universal. All over the world, people watch, listen, and dance as musicians perform. The music starts, you feel the beat, and the dancing begins. At parties or festivals, almost any kind of music can get people up and dancing.

Coming Attractions

Play a Polynesian stick game.

Create your own body percussion.

Move to dance music of the Renaissance.

"Dancing in the Street" invites people to come together and groove to the beat of the music. Wherever you're from, everyone is invited to get up and dance.

CD 5:14

Words and Music by Marvin Gaye,
Ivy Hunter and William Stevenson

Call - ing out___ a - round___ the world, "Are you

read - y for a brand new beat?" Sum-mer's here___ and the

time is right for danc - ing___ in the streets.

They're danc - ing in Chi - ca - go,___

down in New Or - leans,___ up in New York Cit -

Give Us a Hand

CONCEPT
RHYTHM

SKILLS
MOVE, CREATE

LINKS
DANCE

You don't have to dance to move to the music. Hand-jive, body percussion, and other combinations of movement let you keep the beat and create your own ways to move.

Perform the hand-jive below. When you are comfortable with the fast movement pattern, sing the refrain of "Bop 'til You Drop" while you do the hand-jive.

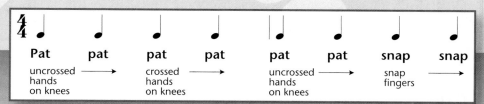

Pat	pat	pat	pat	pat	pat	snap	snap
uncrossed hands on knees →		crossed hands on knees →		uncrossed hands on knees →		snap fingers →	

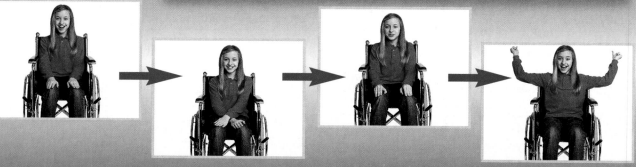

Doing the hand-jive in 1957

Bop 'til You Drop

CD 5:17

Words and Music by
Douglas Colvin and John Cummings

Refrain

Bop 'til you drop. Shake_ it 'til you break it. Move it 'til you lose it.

Dance, dance!_ Bop 'til you drop. Shake_ it 'til you break it.

Move it 'til you lose it. Dance, dance!_

Dance, dance!_ Dance, dance!_ D - d -dance!

The art of making up movement to music is called **choreography**. Can you choreograph your own hand-jive? Try making it longer and more complex.

Create your own hand-jive to the song. It can be one, two, or several measures long.

The Nylons made "Bop ▶ 'til You Drop" popular.

Body Choreography

Before you read the music for "Body Talk," study the key that tells you how to perform it. Experiment with all of the different types of body percussion and practice them separately.

Body Percussion

Pattern				
	H	F	Ch	T
Action	start with hands high above head and move hands slowly down in front as you clap	stamp feet: right left right	pat cheeks: right left	alternate hand slaps on thighs: start with right hand on right thigh; then left on left, etc.

Key
To make rhythmic sounds with the body for "Body Talk":

H – clap hands   F – stamp feet
T – pat hand(s) on thigh(s)
Ch – pat hands gently on cheeks

BODY TALK

Music by Nancy Telfer

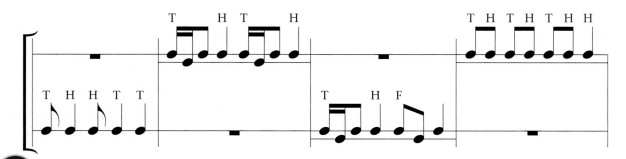

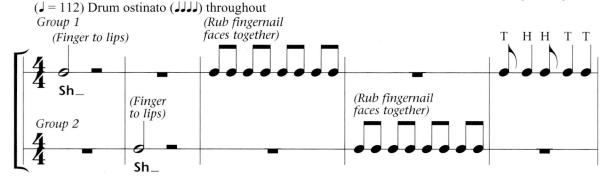

Perform "Body Talk." Be sure to perform the rhythms accurately and precisely—and don't be shy!

THINK!

How can you change the elements of body percussion in "Body Talk" to turn it into a dance?

On the Beat

CONCEPT
RHYTHM
SKILLS
MOVE, ANALYZE,
SING, READ
LINKS
SOCIAL STUDIES

Hand-jive is one of many types of movement that can be done to the beat of music. Another is a stick game, played on the Pacific Island of Tonga. Players sit on the floor in a circle and sing a song like "Ole La'u Papa e." While they are seated, they tap and pass sticks to the beat as they sing. One of the sticks is a different color, and whoever winds up with the "special" stick at the end of the song is the winner.

Keep a steady beat of quarter notes as you listen to "Ole La'u Papa e."

Analyze the instructions for the stick game. Do you move with the steady rhythm or in a syncopated rhythm?

Say:	Tap	Tap	Pass	Switch
	♩	♩	♩	♩
	Tap stick on floor in front with right hand	Tap stick on floor in front with right hand	Pass stick to right, take stick from left	Switch stick from your left hand to your right

"Ole La'u Papa e" is a rhythmic song from the Polynesian islands. The people there sing it on happy occasions. Its strong rhythm makes the song good for dancing or the stick game.

MAP

SOLOMON ISLANDS

CORAL SEA

FIJI ISLANDS

NEW CALEDONIA

TONGA

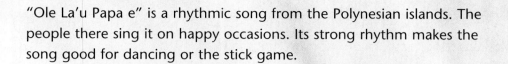
Ole La'u Papa e

CD 5:20

Tongan Stick Game Song
Collected and Transcribed by
Kathy B. Sorensen

Tongan: O - le la - 'u pa - pa e, O - le la - 'u pa - pa
Pronunciation: o le la 'u pa pa e o le la 'u pa

e, O - le la - 'u pa - pa, o - le la - 'u pa - pa,
e o le la 'u pa pa o le la 'u pa pa

O - le la - 'u pa - pa e. Ta la la la. e.
o le la 'u pa pa e ta la la la e

Perform the movements of the game. Then, as you learn to do them easily, sing "Ole La'u Papa e" as you do the stick movement patterns.

Young hula dancers playing ipu (gourds) ▶

Stick Games of Polynesia

There are many ways to play the stick game. In one version, the player holding the special stick at the end of the song gets to choose a percussion instrument to play during the next rounds of the game.

When you play the stick game, you can use one or more of these ostinatos to accompany "Ole La'u Papa e."

Read and practice the ostinatos. Decide which ostinatos you will play, and with which percussion instrument, when you win the stick game.

Now play the stick game. The game ends when there are no more instruments to be played or too few players to pass the sticks.

The ukulele is another ▶ popular Polynesian instrument.

Global Voices

Acitrón

Similar to the Polynesian stick game, "Acitrón" involves passing an object around a circle. Sitting in a circle, players focus on rhythm as they keep passing a stone to the beat. At the end of the song, the players move the stone back and forth without passing it. The trick is not to get confused.

MAP
UNITED STATES
MEXICO   BELIZE
GUATEMALA

 LISTENING CD 5:24

Acitrón Mexican Stone-Passing Game

Listen to "Acitrón." Compare it to the Polynesian stick game.

Acitrón de un fandango, zango, zango, sabaré.

Sabaré que va pasado con su triqui triqui tran.

Some of the song is nonsense. A few of the words are translated:

Acitrón — candied cactus

Fandango — dance, party

Que va pasado — passing by

There are many variations of the words to this favorite Mexican game.

Country Moves

CONCEPT
FORM
SKILLS
SING,
LISTEN, MOVE
LINKS
CULTURES

In the early years of the United States, dancing to fiddle music was a popular, and portable, form of entertainment. Dancers would be arranged in circles, squares, or lines and a leader would "call" the different steps. Many people still enjoy square, circle, and line dancing today.

Sing "The Old Barn Dance." Do you recognize the "called" steps?

The Old Barn Dance

CD 5:25

Words and Music by Jan Reese

(Sing 1st and 3rd times)

There's a sto - ry I love to hear my grand - pa tell 'bout the

(Sing 2nd and 3rd times)

Now we have our own tra - di - tion that we

things they did in his day. How they'd meet for a par - ty in the

keep right to this day. Once a year we meet at the

big red barn. He'd turn to the band and say,

big red barn. We turn to the band and say,

Refrain

"Fid-dle me a mel-o-dy and don't be slow. Get out on the floor and we'll do-si-do.

(3rd time to Coda)

Line up with your part-ner, now all shake hands. Get

read - y for some fun at the Old Barn Dance!"

Swing your part-ner 'round and 'round. Lift that gal up off the ground!

Greet your cor-ner, don't be slow, now back with your part-ner for a do-si-do.

3

(2nd time D.C. al Coda)

More

⊕ Coda

read - y for some fun at the Old Barn Dance! Get

read - y for some fun _____ at the Old Barn Dance!"

 Art Gallery

Dance of the Haymakers

In this lithograph by William Sidney Mount (1807–1868), dancers and musicians perform in a barn.

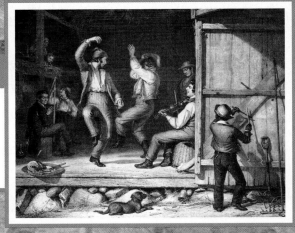

Calling All Dancers

In the refrain of "The Old Barn Dance," you sang "swing your partner" and "do-si-do." These are both calls for square dance **figures**, or steps.

 LISTENING CD 6:1

Red River Valley

Traditional American cowboy song

In "Red River Valley," you can hear the dance steps being called. This style of calling goes back over a hundred years and is still popular today.

Listen to "Red River Valley." Some of the figures sung in "The Old Barn Dance" are part of the "Red River Valley" dance.

Although traditional square dancing is still done today, the modern version of line dancing has been popular since the 1970s. Unlike square dances, the steps are not called, there are no partners and the number of dancers is limited only by space. Line dancing is similar to square dancing, however, in that there are basic figures that are used in all the dances. If you master these basic steps, you can learn any line dance.

 LISTENING CD 6:2

I Walk the Line
by Johnny Cash

"I Walk the Line" is a country-music song that is perfect for line dancing.

Perform the line dance steps to the song.

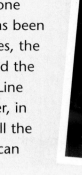

The Village and The Court

CONCEPT
FORM
SKILLS
LISTEN, SING, MOVE
LINKS
HISTORY,
FINE ART

Some of the steps used in modern square and line dances began in England as early as the 15th century. These dances were brought to America by the first settlers from Europe and later by other immigrants.

 LISTENING CD 6:3

Sellinger's Round English Renaissance Dance

"Sellinger's Round" isn't the kind of round you sing. It is called a **round** because it is danced in circle. The musical form is A B A B A B A B. In the dance, the second movement is repeated after each of the other movements. The dance has the following structure: A B C B D B E B.

Listen to "Sellinger's Round." Can you picture Renaissance-era English peasants dancing to it?

In the Renaissance, European noble families had private dance masters to teach them the dances performed at the royal court before the King and Queen. Some of these dances were the pavane (slow and somber), galliard (lively and vigorous), allemande (quick and leaping), and courante (a running dance).

Art Gallery

Festival in the Country

This 17th-century painting shows peasants dancing at a festival. It was created by David Teniers II (1610–1690), an artist who loved to paint village celebrations. How would you describe the dancing you see in this painting?

Belle Qui Tiens Ma Vie

My Love, You Hold My Life

CD 6:4

Words and Music by
Thoinot Arbeau

French: **Bel** - **le qui tiens ma vi** - **e cap** - **ti** - **ve dans tes yeux**
Pronunciation: bɛ lə ki tyɛ̃ ma vi ə kap ti və dã te zyö
English: **My love, you hold my life_____ a cap-tive in your eyes.**

Qui mas l'â - **me ra** - **vi** - **é d'un sou** - **ris gra** - **ci** - **eux**
kə ma la mə ra vi ə dœ̃ su ɾi gɾa si ö
As if a lit - tle mouse had been cap-tured in the house.

Viens tôt me se - **cou** - **rir ou me__ fau** - **dra mou** - **rir,**
vyɛ̃ to mə sə ku ɾir u mə fo dɾa mu ɾir
Come soon and res - cue me, Love, has-ten and set me free!

Viens tôt me se - **cou** - **rir ou me__ fau** - **dra mou** - **rir.**
vyɛ̃ to mə sə ku ɾir u mə fo dɾa mu ɾir
Come soon and res - cue me, Love, has-ten and set me free.

Dancing for the King and Queen

In the royal courts of Renaissance Europe, dancing was an important feature of social life. Members of the nobility and upper classes were all expected to be accomplished and graceful dancers.

 **LISTENING** CD 6:8

 LOG ON

See *music.mmhschool.com* to research Elizabethan folk songs.

Belle qui tiens ma vie by Thoinot Arbeau

The pavane was a stately dance which moved slowly across the ballroom giving the nobility an opportunity to show off their fine clothes and jewels to each other. The court dancing master would lead the procession around the dance floor. He would make sure that the dancers would pass all the most important people in the court, like the royal family and other high nobility.

Listen to the recording of "Belle qui tiens ma vie" played on Renaissance instruments. These string and wind instruments sound softer and more delicate than modern instruments.

THINK!

Do these instruments sound like they would be appropriate at a royal banquet and dance? Would they be a good choice for a boisterous country dance?

Art Gallery

1

1 ***The Wedding Ball of the Duc de Joyeuse***
This 16th-century anonymous French painting portrays a couple dancing at their wedding.

2 ***A Man and a Woman inside the Palace with Two Musicians***
This miniature is from an illuminated manuscript.

3 ***Scenes from the Life of the Prodigal Son***
This painting by Louis de Caullery (c.1580–1621) shows musicians and dancers at a banquet.

4 ***A Concert***
This enamel plaque by Limosin Leonard (1505–c.1577) shows musicians performing outdoors.

Perform this simple pavane. Here are the steps:

Formation: a column with couples standing side by side.
Do this 2-line sequence 3 times forward and 1 time backward

1. 2 measures: Step R, Touch L, Step L, Touch R

2. 2 measures: Step R, Step L, Step R, Touch L

Each time these movements repeat, they start on the opposite foot.

If you were the King's dancing master, you would line up the dancers and plan the route you and the dancers would follow. This is the first dance of the evening and you must decide when the procession will pass by the seated King and Queen.

Create a plan that will take the dancers all around the dance floor.

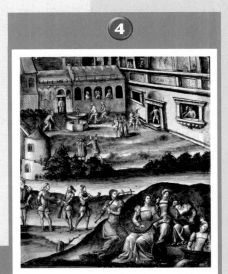

Round and Round We Go

CONCEPT
MELODY
SKILLS
SING, COMPARE, LISTEN, MOVE
LINKS
SOCIAL STUDIES, MATHEMATICS

"Mayim, Mayim" is an Israeli song that celebrates finding water in the desert. The song's joyful sentiments lend themselves to the simple and lively nature of the circle dance.

Sing "Mayim, Mayim." What kind of movements can you do in a circle dance?

MAP
ISRAEL
GAZA
WEST BANK
JORDAN
EGYPT
SAUDI ARABIA

MAYIM, MAYIM

CD 6:9

Words and Music by E. Amiran
Arranged by Valerie Shields

Perform the circle dance to "Mayim, Mayim."

THINK! Compare and contrast other songs of celebration to "Mayim, Mayim." How are they the same? How are they different?

חַי מַ-יִם בְּ-שָׂ-שׂוֹן חֵי חֵי מַ-יִם מַ-יִם מַ-יִם
hei ma yim be sa son hei hei ma yim ma yim ma yim
Hey! wa-ter, hap-pi-ness! Hey, hey, Wa-ter, wa-ter wa-ter,

מַ-יִם מַ-יִם מַ-יִם מַ-יִם בְּ-שָׂ-שׂוֹן מַ-יִם מַ-יִם
ma yim ma yim ma yim ma yim be sa son ma yim ma yim
wa-ter, wa-ter, wa-ter, wa-ter, hap-pi-ness, wa-ter wa-ter,

1.
2.
מַ-יִם מַ-יִם מַ-יִם מַ-יִם בְּ-שָׂ-שׂוֹן וּ-שְׂ-בְּ-שָׂ-שׂוֹן
ma yim ma yim ma yim ma yim be sa son ush be sa son
wa-ter wa-ter, wa-ter wa-ter, hap-pi-ness, You hap-pi-ness.

מַ-יִם חֵי מַ-יִם מַ-יִם חֵי מַ-יִם
ma yim hei ma yim ma yim hei ma yim

מַ-יִם חֵי מַ-יִם מַ-יִם מַ-יִם
ma yim hei ma yim ma yim ma yim

Breaking the Circle

The languages of music and dance have many words in common—beat, tempo, measure—but they may mean different things. For example, dances and music are both made up of steps, but they are not the same kind of steps. In dance, steps are made with your feet, but in music, steps identify the distance between pitches.

"Round and Round" is written in the **Dorian mode**, which is a type of musical scale. Its sound is different from that of a major or minor scale because of the way its whole steps and half steps are arranged.

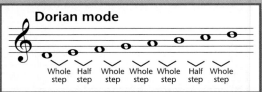

Dorian mode

Whole step / Half step / Whole step / Whole step / Whole step / Half step / Whole step

ROUND AND ROUND

CD 6:13

Anonymous

Round and round the Earth_ is turn-ing turn-ing al-ways round_ to morn-ing, and from morn-ing round_ to night.

Sing "Round and Round" in unison. When you know the melody, sing it in 3-part canon. Listen for the distinctive sound of the Dorian mode.

Now you can be your own dancing master using the steps you know. Create your own circle dance to "Round and Round." Can you make your own variations on a circle dance? How can you make the dance a canon?

Move as you sing "Round and Round."

Another form of the circle dance is the broken circle. When the circle "breaks," a leader is created who then directs the dancers into a line or back into a circle.

"Djurdjevka kolo" is a Yugoslavian dance which starts as a broken circle.

 **LISTENING** CD 6:16

Djurdjevka kolo Yugoslavian folk song

In "Djurdjevka kolo," traditional Yugoslavian instruments are used. For each section of the song, they are used differently. This helps to make the different sections of the song easier to identify.

Identify the number of sections in "Djurdjevka kolo."

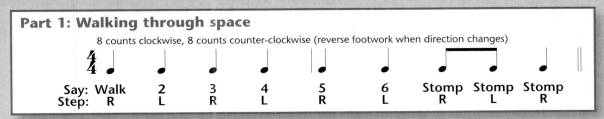

Part 1: Walking through space

8 counts clockwise, 8 counts counter-clockwise (reverse footwork when direction changes)

Say:	Walk	2	3	4	5	6	Stomp	Stomp	Stomp
Step:	R	L	R	L	R	L	R	L	R

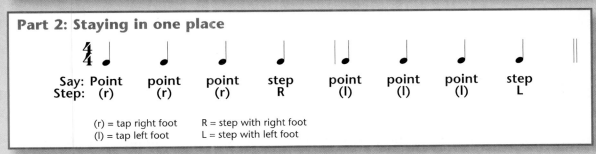

Part 2: Staying in one place

Say:	Point	point	point	step	point	point	point	step
Step:	(r)	(r)	(r)	R	(l)	(l)	(l)	L

(r) = tap right foot R = step with right foot
(l) = tap left foot L = step with left foot

Perform the steps as the leader takes the group on a new path.

American Dance Traditions

CD-ROM

Use **Orchestral Instruments** **CD-ROM** to learn more about violin and bass.

"**Y**ou Sing for Me" expresses the power singing and dancing has to bring people together. Two people are needed to sing in harmony or dance with a partner, so as the song says, "We need each other—yes, we do."

Sing "You Sing for Me." Join in with the harmony.

CD 6:17

Words and Music by Raymond K. McLain

I've come through storm - y weath - er, I'm sure you've seen it too.
I'll nev - er be more read - y to sing a - long with you.

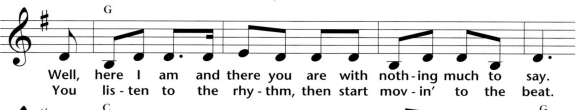

But now we're here to - geth - er and it's good to be with you.
To keep each oth - er stead - y,___ well, this is what to do.

Well, here I am and there you are with noth - ing much to say.
You lis - ten to the rhy - thm, then start mov - in' to the beat.

Sure - ly there's some bet - ter way to cel - e - brate to - day.
Come on, sweet mu - sic mak - er,___ let's give our - selves a treat.

The Del McCoury Band performing in Nashville, Tennessee

Refrain

Melody

You sing for me, _____ I'll sing for you. _____ We need each

You sing for me, I'll sing for you. We need each

oth - er, yes we do. _____ It takes sweet mu - sic

oth - er, yes we yes we do. It takes sweet mu - sic

ev - 'ry day to keep those lone - some blues_ a - way.

ev - 'rt day to keep those lone - some blues a - way.

Doot doot doo-dle-oo doot doot doot, doot doot doot doot doo-dle-oo doot.

Melody

Doot doot doo-dle-oo doot doot doot, doot doot doot doot doo-dle-oo doot.

Clogging Becomes Stomp Dancing

Clogging is a style of dancing that grew out of the Appalachian mountain folk dances of the 1800s. These mountain people were descended from English, German, Scottish, and Irish immigrants. Each of these separate cultures brought its own style of dance—jigs, reels, and step dances—to America. In rural areas, square dancing and clogging were the evening entertainment. Stomp dancing and African step dancing have evolved from clogging.

Perform "Bluegrass Stomp" while singing "You Sing for Me."

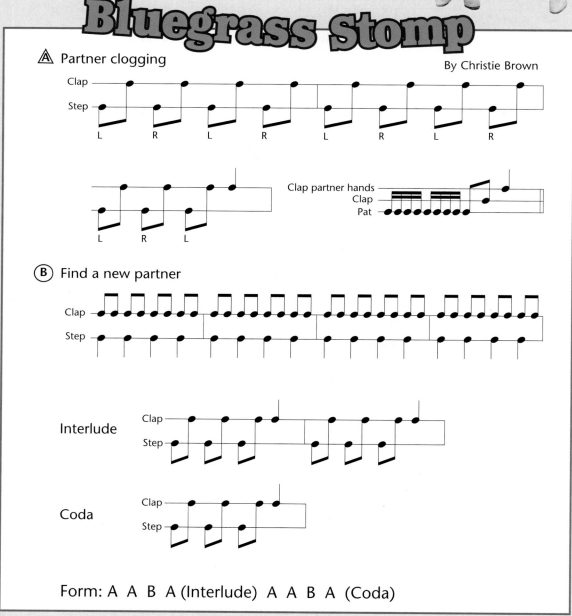

Form: A A B A (Interlude) A A B A (Coda)

Learn About "Tsiothwatasè:tha"

"Tsiothwatasè:tha" is an Iroquois round dance that originally came from Native American tribes of the Plains region. The Iroquois tribes in New York adapted it to fit their own style. In a circle, the dancers alternate movement to the right and left. Movement to the right stands for good and positive things and going to the left symbolizes negative things like sadness, grief, or anger. For the Iroquois, good always triumphs over bad and the dance always ends by moving to the right.

Tsiothwatasè:tha
Round Dance

CD 6:21

Iroquois Social Song and Dance
As Sung by Members of the Mohawk Nation

(a)
Mohawk: he   yo   he   yo   ha   hi   yo   ha   ya
Pronunciation: he   yo   he   yo   ha   hi   yo   ha   ya

(b)

(c)
he   yo   ha   hi   yo   ha   ya   he   yo   ha   hi   yo   ha   ya
he   yo   ha   hi   yo   ha   ya   he   yo   ha   hi   yo   ha   ya

(d)

(e)
he   yo   ha   hi   yo   ha   ya   he   yo   ha   hi   yo   ha   ya
he   yo   ha   hi   yo   ha   ya   he   yo   ha   hi   yo   ha   ya

(f)
ho   ya   he   ya   ha   ho   ya   he   ya   ha   yo - e   *(pitch fall off)*
ho   ya   he   ya   ha   ho   ya   he   ya   ha   yo   e

CONCEPT
STYLE

SKILLS
SING , ANALYZE, LISTEN

LINKS
HISTORY, DANCE

In the late 1890s a new form of popular music appeared. Marked by strong syncopated, or "ragged," rhythms, the music soon came to be known as "**ragtime**." For about twenty years, ragtime swept America and much of Europe, and became popular again in the 1970s with the release of the movie *The Sting*. The movie included several ragtime songs in the soundtrack.

A scene from the movie *Alexander's Ragtime Band* (1938) ▼

Meet the Musician

Scott Joplin (c.1867–1917), the "King of Ragtime Music," demonstrated extraordinary musical talent at an early age. With his parent's encouragement, he started studying piano and later focused on learning new kinds of harmony and style. He settled in St. Louis and became one of the first pianists to develop ragtime. His two most well-known pieces, "Maple Leaf Rag" and "The Entertainer," were written while he was living in St. Louis.

Sing "Mr. Scott Joplin's Ragtime Rag!"

Mr. Scott Joplin's Ragtime Rag!

CD 6:25

Music by Scott Joplin
Words by Mark Brymer

Lis-ten to Mis-ter Scott Jop-lin's rag - time, hear how his mel - o-dies shine.

On his pi - a - no he wrote his mu-sic, all A-

mer - i - can, by de - sign. He turned the cen - tur - y

on with his rag - time. Soon ev - 'ry pia - no had to have

Fine

one of his syn - co - pat - ed dit - ties, one of Jop - lin's rag - time rags!

Peo - ple___ danced_ the cake-walk when they_ heard_ that bass walk

and the_ jaun - ty rhy - thm of a rag-time band.

Folks in___ grand_ ho - tels, to folks in___ back - room swells

Da Capo al Fine

loved what that mu - sic had. It was rag-time razz-a - ma - tazz!

The two-step is a popular dance form that can be danced to many different kinds of music. It works well with ragtime music.

Perform the two-step. As you dance, listen to "Mr. Scott Joplin's Ragtime Rag!"

Charleston, Charleston

In the 1920s, as ragtime was starting to fade, the Charleston arrived to take its place. The strong syncopations in the dance, derived from ragtime, inspired a song of the same name.

Legend says the "Charleston" got its name because it started on a small island near Charleston, South Carolina. The term "flapper," for girls who flapped their arms and walked like birds as they danced, also came from the "Charleston" dance.

Sing "Charleston" and tap a steady beat with the syncopated melody.

CD 6:28

Music by James P. Johnson
Words by Cecil Mack

Charles - ton__ Charles - ton__ Made in__ Car-o-li - na__ Some dance,__ some prance,__ I'll say__ there's no-thing fin - er than the Charles - ton,__ Charles - ton,__ lord how__ you can shuf - fle__ ev-'ry step__you do leads to some-thing new, man I'mtell - ing you

Analyze the steps to the Charleston. Then dance while you listen to the recording.

🔘 **LISTENING** **CD 6:31**

La cumparsita by Gerardo Matos Rodríguez

The tango is another dance that was made popular in the mid-1900s. The famous Cuban-American band leader, Xavier Cugat, helped make this kind of music popular. This is his recording of "La cumparsita."

Listen to "La cumparsita." Describe the rhythm and melody.

▶ **Xavier Cugat in a scene from** *Holiday in Mexico* **(1946)**

It's a la - pa-zoo, buck dance,_ wing dance,_

We'll be_ a back num - ber_ but the Charles - ton_ the new

Charles - ton,_____ that dance_ is sure-ly a com - er

some - time_ you'll_ dance it one time_ the dance_ called the

Charles - ton_ made in South_ Car - o - line._

Cowboy Music

CONCEPT
TONE COLOR

SKILLS
SING, LISTEN, COMPARE

LINKS
HISTORY, CULTURE, FINE ART

Cowboys played an important role in the settling of the American West. Riding for many long days and nights, through all kinds of weather, and over treacherous trails, they would bring their herds to towns where the new railroads shipped them back East.

When their work was done, the cowboys would stay in town and maybe join in a Saturday-night hoedown, where there would be plenty of music and dancing.

Art Gallery

Untitled

This picture, by the artist Frederic Remington (1861–1909), shows cowboys leading a cattle drive.

"Doney Gal" is a term of affection for a cowboy's horse. Through all the long nights, bad weather and dangers of the cattle drive, a cowboy's horse was sometimes his best friend. Together, they took care of the herd, keeping them safe on the long drives to market.

Sing "Doney Gal."

Music on and off the Trail

LISTENING CD 7:1

Hoedown American folk song

"Hoedown" describes a Saturday night in a modern Western town.

Listen to "Hoedown." Does the song remind you of the old West? How?

Review the dance moves and skills you have learned in this unit. What steps and moves would fit "Hoedown?" Make up your own steps to "Hoedown."

Cowboys ride the ranges all over North and South America. In Argentina, in South America, cowboys are called gauchos, and the ranches they work on are called estancias.

LISTENING CD 7:2

Los trabajadores agricolas from *Estancia*
by Alberto Ginastera

The Argentine composer Alberto Ginastera composed a musical description of a day on the estancia. His ballet Estancia tells his story in four movements: Los trabajadores agricolas (The Farmers), Danza del trigo (Wheat Dance), Los peones de hacienda (The Ranch Workers), and Danza finale (Final Dance).

Follow the listening map as you picture the daily life on an Argentine ranch.

Listening Map for *Los trabajadores agricolas*

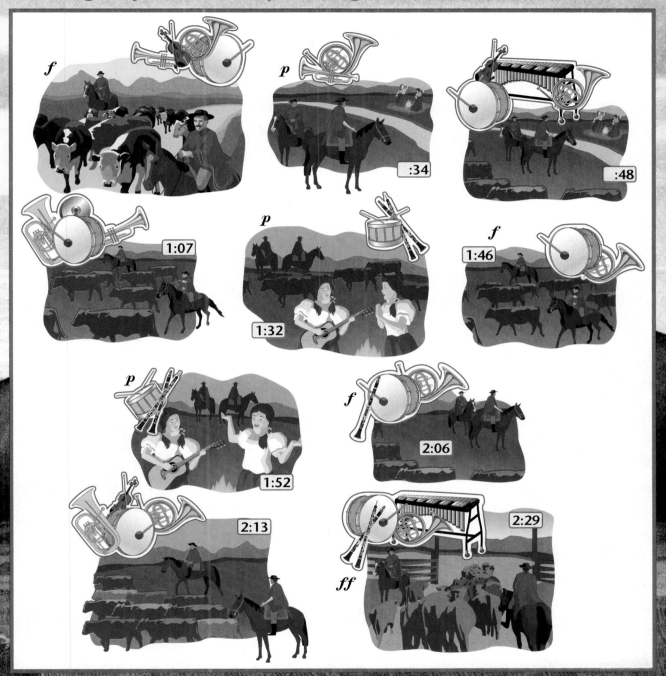

THINK! Compare and contrast "Los trabajadores agricolas," "Hoedown," and "Doney Gal." How are they different from each other?

Spotlight Your Success!

REVIEW

1 Which dance was popular with royalty during the Renaissance?

    a. Charleston   **b.** pavane   **c.** rhumba

2 Identify the whole steps and half steps in a major scale.

    a. w w h w w w h

    b. w w h w w h w

3 Which rhythm pattern shows syncopation?

  a.  **b.**  **c.**

4 Which is a description of a square dance?
    a. Dance that often tells a story
    b. Dance where a caller gives directions to the dancers
    c. 1920s American dance with syncopation

READ AND LISTEN

1 Read these melody patterns. Then listen. Which pattern is a major scale?

  a.

  b.

  c.

2 Read these melody patterns. Then listen. Which pattern includes a half step?

a.

b.

c.

3 Read these rhythm patterns. Then listen. Which rhythm pattern do you hear?

4 Read these rhythm patterns. Then listen. Which rhythm pattern do you hear?

THINK!

1 What are some common elements shared by the arts of music and dance?

2 Choose your favorite dance from this unit. Imagine teaching the dance to another person. **Write** about how you would do it.

3 Compare American country dances of the past with the popular country line dances of today. What things are similar? What things are different?

4 Name a dance you know in each category: **a.** ballroom dance, **b.** folk dance, **c.** historic court dance, **d.** ballet. Pick your personal favorite and tell why it is the most appealing to you.

CREATE AND PERFORM

Show what you know about rhythm by composing an eight-measure piece to perform on unpitched percussion instruments. Use syncopation, dotted quarter-eighth, and 16th-note patterns.

Meet the Musician

ON NATIONAL RADIO!

Name: Evan Premo
Age: 17
Instrument: String Bass
Hometown: Amasa, Michigan

Bassist Evan Premo lives in a beautiful rural area of Michigan. "There are only about 200 people in my town," says Evan. "The whole Upper Peninsula is very big in size, but has very few people." Evan loves living there and has found some advantages to being a musician in a very small town. "There's quite a few musical opportunities here, and not enough musicians to fill them," he states.

When he gets the opportunity to perform, Evan likes to share his thoughts with the audience before he plays. "I like to give an introduction to the music so the audience can understand more about it," he explains. "That way, they know what I'm thinking, and it gives them something to think about."

When Evan isn't playing music, he may be found exploring the great outdoors of his hometown. He does a lot of hiking, cross-country skiing, and kayaking, and also enjoys ice fishing with his dad.

LISTENING   CD 7:4–5   **RECORDED INTERVIEW**

Summertime from *Porgy and Bess*
by George and Ira Gershwin, arranged by Evan Premo

Listen to Evan's performance and interview on the national radio program **From the Top**.

Spotlight on the ☆Orchestra

Did You Know?

The first known orchestra was an ensemble of strings, trumpets, and trombones that played Giovanni Gabrieli's "Sacrae Symphonie" in 1597.

Orchestras can have from 30 to over 100 players from all four families of instruments: strings, brass, woodwinds, and percussion.

The role of conductor did not exist until the late 1800s. As orchestras grew, it became difficult for players to stay together just by listening to each other. It became necessary to have someone visually lead these larger ensembles.

 LISTENING CD 7:6–7

Rondeau from *Abdelazar*
by Henry Purcell

Benevenuto Cellini (Overture) (excerpt)
by Hector Berlioz

Since 1695, when Purcell wrote *Abdelazar*, the orchestra has evolved in many directions. **Compare** the sound of the modern symphony orchestra with the sound of an orchestra from Purcell's time.

UNIT 4

Play It Now

You see and hear musical instruments all the time—at school, on radio and television, in the movies, and at parties. Like people, musical instruments come in all sizes and shapes, and make all different kinds of sounds. Exploring musical instruments can be a lot of fun!

Coming Attractions

Play a melody on keyboard.

Read and play guitar chords.

Analyze tone color.

Musical instruments can be played alone or in large or small ensembles. Each instrument has a special function. It might play the melody, a harmony part, or perhaps a rhythm part. It might even do a combination of these.

Listen for the instruments as you hear "Let It Roll." As you listen, imagine the amount of time that might have been spent by the musicians to develop the skills for playing this piece.

CD 7:8

Words and Music by Paul Kennerley

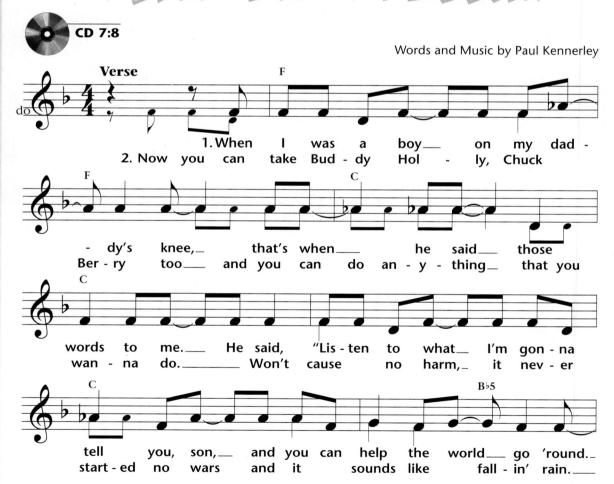

1. When I was a boy___ on my dad - dy's knee,___ that's when___ he said___ those words to me.___ He said, "Lis - ten to what___ I'm gon - na tell you, son,___ and you can help the world___ go 'round.

2. Now you can take Bud - dy Hol - ly, Chuck Ber - ry too___ and you can do an - y - thing___ that you wan - na do._____ Won't cause no harm,___ it nev - er start - ed no wars and it sounds like fall - in' rain.___

Think about what available percussion tone colors will sound the best with "Let It Roll." Create an eight-beat ostinato using that instrument or found sound.

Learning to Play

CONCEPT
TONE COLOR

SKILLS
SING, LISTEN, DECIDE

LINKS
HISTORY, DANCE

Playing a musical instrument is a lot of fun. But learning to play can sometimes be frustrating. The initial squeaks and squawks can also be painful to anyone close by.

"Mama Don't 'Low," is a humorous folk song about playing musical instruments in the house. As you learn to play an instrument, you'll probably be able to relate to the words of the song. Would your "Mama" tell you the same thing?

Sing "Mama Don't 'Low."

CD 7:11

American Folk Song

```
1. )
2. } Ma-ma don't 'low no  { gui - tar  play-in'  round   here._____
3. )                       { ban - jo  pick-in'  round   here,_____
                           { har - mo - niz - in' round  here,_____
```

```
Ma-ma don't   'low no  { gui - tar  play-in'  round   here,_____
                       { ban - jo   pick-in'  round   here,_____
                       { har - mo - niz - in' round   here,_____
```

```
I don't care what Ma-ma don't 'low, Gon-na { play   my gui-tar  an-y-how,
                                           { pick   my ban - jo  an-y-how,
                                           { har-mon-ize my songs an-y-how,
```

```
Ma-ma don't 'low no  { gui - tar  play-in'  round   here._____
                     { ban - jo   pick-in'  round   here._____
                     { har - mo - niz-in'  round   here._____
```

126

Explore the World of Musical Instruments

For thousands of years, people have been making instruments from materials they find around them. Early drums were made from tree trunks and early wind instruments from animal horns.

Even though they have diverse sounds and histories, all instruments fall into one of five families: strings, woodwinds, brass, percussion, and electronic instruments.

In the string family of instruments, sound is produced either by drawing a bow across the string or by plucking the string.

guitar △   harp △   violin △ and bow

Woodwinds and brass instruments can be made of wood or metal, but they have one thing in common: Their sound is produced by pushing air through the instrument.

Producing sound by hitting one material against another, as percussion instruments do, goes back to the Stone Age. This can be as simple as a stick hitting a log or piece of metal, or as complex as the keys of a piano striking the strings inside the case.

xylophone ▼

△ tuba

bassoon △

bass drum ▶

As technology progresses, the ability to synthesize, digitize, and computerize sound has become easier. Today a lot of popular music uses electronic instruments and electronically-created sounds. Electronic instruments are often used to substitute for other instruments when they are unavailable.

electronic ▼ keyboard

CD-ROM

Learn more about instruments with *Orchestral Instruments* CD-ROM.

Gigue

A popular dance of the 17th century was the gigue. The **gigue** was danced to fast music written with two beats to each measure. The composer Johann Sebastian Bach incorporated the gigue, and other dances, into much of his music.

MAP

DENMARK

NETHERLANDS

POLAND

GERMANY

CZECH REPUBLIC

FRANCE

AUSTRIA

Meet the Musician

Johann Sebastian Bach (1685–1750) is considered to be one of the greatest composers of all time. He spent most of his professional life as a church organist in Germany and wrote hundreds of pieces of music for chorus, orchestra, keyboard, and solo instruments. His music is still played today. Of his 20 children, four also became musicians.

 LISTENING CD 7:14

Brandenburg Concerto No. 5, Third Movement by Johann Sebastian Bach

J.S. Bach wrote his six "Brandenburg" concertos in 1721 for the Duke of Brandenburg. Each concerto spotlights different solo instruments. In the fifth concerto, the solo instruments are the flute, violin, and harpsichord.

Listen to the third movement of Bach's *Brandenburg Concerto No. 5*. Name the families of the solo instruments.

This movement from *Brandenburg Concerto No. 5* is written in $\frac{2}{4}$ time. You can hear that there are two strong beats in each measure. Often the beat is divided into three parts, which is called a triplet. Another important rhythm in this piece is the long-short dotted eighth and sixteenth pattern.

The main rhythm in the concerto is:

Playalong

THINK! If you were writing a piece for three instruments from different families, which would you choose? Why?

Playing on the Keyboard

CONCEPT
MELODY
SKILLS
LISTEN, PERFORM
LINKS
HISTORY

Keyboard instruments could be an instrumental family of their own. But because different keyboard instruments produce their sounds in different ways, keyboard instruments are members of all the different families of instruments.

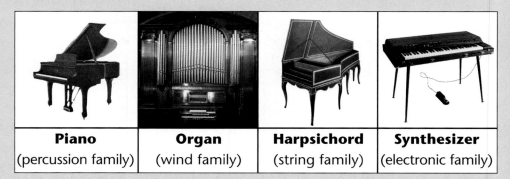

| Piano (percussion family) | Organ (wind family) | Harpsichord (string family) | Synthesizer (electronic family) |

Keyboard instruments have one important thing in common. No matter how their sounds are actually produced, pressing the keys sets the sound in motion. If you can play one keyboard instrument, you can basically play them all.

"I Love a Piano" is a song that talks about all the different styles of music you can play on just one versatile instrument—the piano.

Listen to "I Love a Piano." How does the accompaniment reflect the words of the song?

I Love a Piano

CD 7:15

Words and Music by Irving Berlin

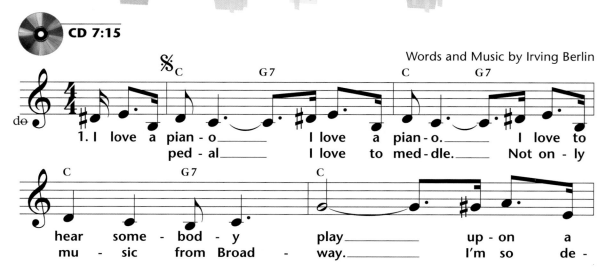

1. I love a pian-o.____ I love a pian-o.____ I love to
ped-al____ I love to med-dle.____ Not on-ly

hear some-bod-y play____ up-on a
mu-sic from Broad-way.____ I'm so de-

Easy Piano Melodies

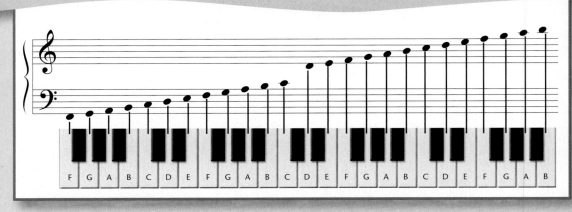

A full-size grand piano has 88 keys. Because of this large span, piano music is written across two staves with two different **clefs**. A clef is a symbol at the beginning of a staff of music that indicates the pitch of the notes. The treble clef, or G clef, indicates that the second line is G above middle C. The bass clef, or F clef, indicates that the fourth line is F below middle C.

"Winter ade" is written in the key of G major. Here are the notes for this key as they appear on the keyboard.

Play "Winter ade" with your right hand. Practice until it becomes easy.

Winter Ade

G Major

CD 7:18

German Folk Melody

German: Win - ter A - de schei - den - tut weh,
Pronunciation: vɪn tər ɑ de shaɪ dən tut ve
English: Win - ter, fare - well! part - ing is sad;

a - ber dein Schei - den macht, dass mir das Her - ze - lacht,
ɑ bər daɪn shaɪ dən mɑxt das mir das hɛrt sə laxt
But when at last you de - part, your leav - ing cheers my heart,

Win - ter a - de, Win - ter a - de.
vɪn tər ɑ de vɪn tər ɑ de
Win - ter, fare - well! Win - ter, fare - well!

Art Gallery

Return of the Hunters

This painting was created by Pieter Brueghel (c. 1520–1569) around 1565. Brueghel was the first in a family of Flemish painters.

By altering the key signature of this song, you change it from a major key to a minor key. In the key signature of G major, F is sharped, but in the key signature of G minor, the B and E are flatted.

Perform "Winter ade" in its minor-key version.

MAP

DENMARK
NETHERLANDS
POLAND
GERMANY
CZECH REPUBLIC
FRANCE
AUSTRIA

CD 7:22

Winter Ade
G Minor

German Folk Melody

German: Win - ter A - de schei - den - tut weh,
Pronunciation: vɪn tər a de shaɪ dən tut ve
English: Win - ter, fare - well! part - ing is sad;

a - ber dein Schei - den_ macht dass mir das Her - ze - lacht,
a bər daɪn shaɪ dən maxt das mir das hɛrt sə laxt
But when at last you de-part, your leav - ing cheers my_ heart,

Win - ter a - de, Win - ter a - de.
vɪn tər a de vɪn tər a de
Win - ter, fare - well! Win - ter, fare - well!

133

Playing in a Minor Key

CONCEPT
TONALITY

SKILLS
SING,
ANALYZE

LINKS
HISTORY,
GEOGRAPHY

As you have learned, music can be written in major or minor keys.

Sing "Red Iron Ore." Does it sound major or minor?

In the early part of the 20th century, there were keen rivalries between the ships that sailed between the ports of the Great Lakes. "Red Iron Ore" tells how one ship beat three others in a race to Cleveland.

RED IRON ORE

CD 7:25

Boat Song from the Great Lakes Region
Arranged by Michael Jothen

1. Come all ye bold sail-ors that fol-low the lake On an
2. In the month of Sep-tem-ber the sev-en-teenth day, Two
3. Next morn-ing we hove a-long-side the *Ex - ile.* And
4. The tug *Es - can - a - ba* she towed out the *Minch,* The
5. Through Louse Is-land it blew a fresh breeze; Made the
6. In Cleve-land's safe har-bour the *Rob - erts* now firm. Tis a

i - ron ore ves-sel your liv - ing to make. I
dol - lars and a quar-ter is all they would pay. And
soon was made fast to an i - ron ore pile, They
Rob - erts she thought she had left in a pinch And
Fox - es, the Bea-vers, the Skill - a - ge-les; We
big bit of boast-ing for which we all yearn! For

shipped in Chi-ca-go, Bid a-dieu to the shore, Bound a-
on Mon-day morn-ing the Bridge-port did take The
low - er'd their chutes and like thun-der did roar, They
as she passed by us, she bid us good-bye, Say-ing,
flew by the *Minch* for to show her the way, And she
ol' Cap-tain Shan-non had ought to stand treat, For

Ballads like "Red Iron Ore" were often sung as sailors worked or relaxed on board ship.

A small and portable keyboard instrument, the accordion was frequently carried aboard ships. It was a favorite accompaniment to the sailors' songs.

Listen to the sound of the accordion in "Red Iron Ore."

Verses 1-2 D.C.

way	to	Es - ca - na - ba	for	red	i - ron	ore.
ore	ship,	E. C. Rob - erts	far	out	in the	lake.
spout - ed	in - to	us	that	red	i - ron	ore.
"We'll meet	you in	Cleve - land	next	Fourth	of	Ju - ly!"
ne'er hove	in___	sight	till we were	off	Thun - der	Bay.
mak - ing	here___	safe - ly	a - head	of	the	fleet.

Refrain
Sing after verses 3-6 only

Part I

Down, down, down der - ry down.

Part II

Der - ry down, down, down der - ry down.

The Dorian Mode

"The Lumber Camp Song" is another song about hard work.
Lumberjacks' work is not easy. They have to be outside in all kinds
of weather, and cutting down towering trees can be dangerous.

The Lumber Camp Song

CD 7:28

Canadian Folk Song

1. Come all you jol - ly fel - lows and
2. At four o' - clock each morn - ing the
3. At six o' - clock it's break - fast, and
4. And then comes up the log - ger, all

lis - ten to my song; It's all a - bout the shan - ty boys and
boss be - gins to shout: "Heave out, my jol - ly team - sters; it's
ev - 'ry man is out, For ev - 'ry man who is not sick will
at the break of day: "Load up my slide, five hun - dred feet; to the

how they get a - long. We're the jol - liest bunch of
time to start the route." The team - sters they will
sure be on the route. There's saw - yers and there's
riv - er drive a - way." You can hear the a - xes

"The Lumber Camp Song" is written in the **Dorian** mode. Although slightly different from a true minor scale, the Dorian mode has a "minor" sound to it.

Sing "Red Iron Ore" and "The Lumber Camp Song." Can you hear any differences between the minor scale and the Dorian mode? What are they?

Analyze the Dorian mode. What is the order of whole steps and half steps that make up the Dorian mode?

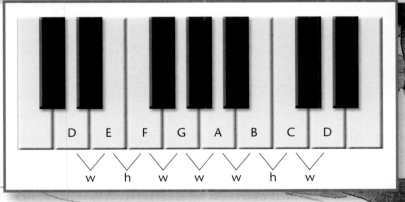

fel - lows that ev - er you could find; The way we spend our
all jump up in a most fret - ful way: "Where is me boots? Where
chop - pers to lay the tim - ber low; There's swam-pers and there's
ring - ing un - til the sun goes down. "Hur - rah, my boys! The

win - ter months is hurl - ing down the pine.
is me pants? Me socks is gone as - tray!"
log - gers to drag it to and fro.
day is spent. To the shan - ty we are bound."

◀ guitar pick

The guitar is one of the world's most popular instruments. In one form or another, it appears in the music of many cultures and countries. It has been a staple of popular music since the 1950s.

In "The Guitar Man," the performer expresses his feelings through his instrument. As he plays, he cheers the hearts of those who hear him.

Sing "The Guitar Man."

Carlos Santana ▶

◀ Bonnie Raitt

The Guitar Man

CD 8:1

Words and Music by Audrey Snyder

* 2nd time, 8-measure canon

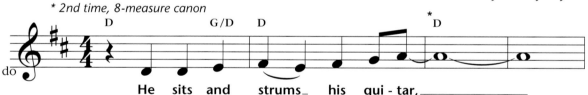

He sits and strums his gui - tar,
His mag - ic fin - gers touch the strings.

and weaves his thoughts in - to the mu - sic that he plays.
The in - stru - ment be - gins to sing

Peo - ple gath - er 'round, to hear the mag - ic sound.
a sim - ple mel - o - dy with six string har - mo - ny

Guitar Chords

Three or more pitches played together form a **chord**. Most often, these pitches are arranged in intervals of thirds, called **triads**. For example, a C major chord has the pitches C, E, and G. The E is a third higher than the C, and the G is a third higher than the E. What are the pitches for a G triad?

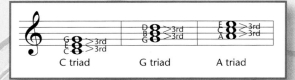

C triad   G triad   A triad

Analyze the chart below to see where to place your fingers on the guitar strings to play the chords. The fingers are numbered from "1" (index finger) to "4" (little finger). An "○" means the string should be played open, or without pressing it down. An "X" means that a string is not to be played.

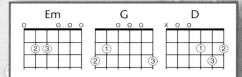

Hold the guitar as shown in the picture.

Strum the following rhythm with your right hand. Use your fingernails or a guitar pick to brush the strings.

José Feliciano ▲

$$\frac{4}{4}$$

↓ = strum down

 LISTENING CD 8:5

Jerry Douglas ▶
playing a Dobro

Foggy Mountain Breakdown by Earl Scruggs

"Foggy Mountain Breakdown" is a popular bluegrass song. In a "breakdown" song, each musician takes a solo turn playing the melody.

Listen to "Foggy Mountain Breakdown."
Use the rhythm you practiced to play the three chords in this order:
G G Em G Em G D G. Play one chord for each meaure.

thumb pick ▶
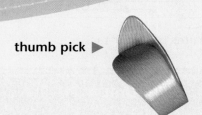

The guitar has a long tradition in Spanish folk music. In "Al lado de mi cabaña," the guitar provides a strong rhythmic accompaniment to the simple melody.

Sing "Al lado de mi cabaña." Listen for the guitar in the accompaniment.

MAP
FRANCE
PORTUGAL
SPAIN
MOROCCO   ALGERIA

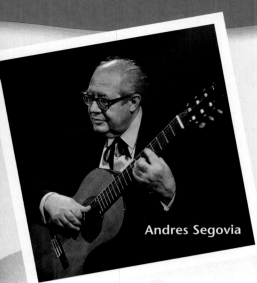

Andres Segovia

Al lado de mi cabaña

Beside My Cottage

CD 8:6

Spanish Folk Song

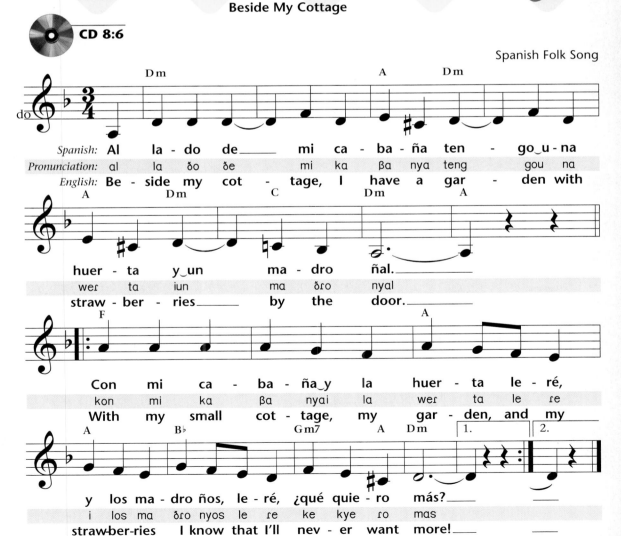

Spanish: Al la - do de____ mi ca - ba - ña ten - go u - na
Pronunciation: al la ðo ðe mi ka ßa nya teng gou na
English: Be - side my cot - tage, I have a gar - den with

huer - ta y un ma - dro ñal.
weɾ ta iun ma ðɾo nyal
straw - ber - ries____ by the door.

Con mi ca - ba - ña y la huer - ta le - ré,
kon mi ka ßa nyai la weɾ ta le ɾe
With my small cot - tage, my gar - den, and my

y los ma - dro ños, le - ré, ¿qué quie - ro más?____
i los ma ðɾo nyos le ɾe ke kye ɾo mas
straw - ber-ries I know that I'll nev - er want more!____

Unit 4 Play It Now

141

The Sounds of Japan

CONCEPT
TONALITY
SKILLS
SING,
IMPROVISE
LINKS
SOCIAL STUDIES,
CULTURES

A lot of the music of Japan uses five-pitch scales. This music can sound different to our ears because so much of Western music is written using major and minor scales.

"Joban Tanko Bushi" is about going to work in a mine. The workers carry their lanterns and sing about their feelings of friendship.

Sing "Joban Tanko Bushi." Practice clapping the rhythm of the melody as you sing and chant the song.

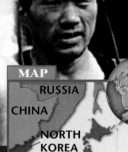

MAP
RUSSIA
CHINA
NORTH
KOREA
JAPAN
SOUTH KOREA

JOBAN TANKO BUSHI

CD 8:10

Joban Miners' Song

Japanese Folk Song
Arranged by Wendy B. Stuart

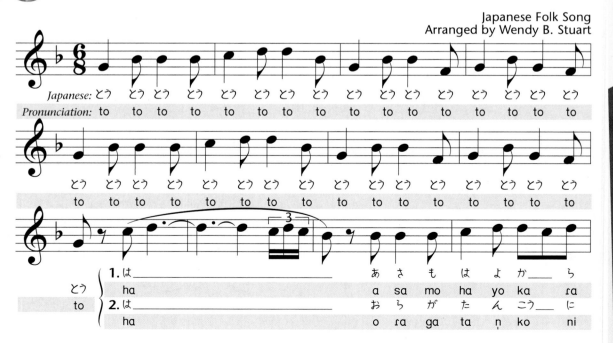

What are the notes of the scale used in "Joban Tanko Bushi?"

Improvise a descant part for "Joban Tanko Bushi" on the soprano recorder. Use only the following pitches and rhythms:

Always end your improvisation on the note G and with a ♩.

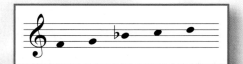

Global Voices

The Kokiriko

The **kokiriko** is an ancient Japanese percussion instrument. It is made up of short lengths of thin bamboo that have been used on the roofs of farmhouses for hundreds of years.

LISTENING CD 8:14

Kokiriko Traditional Japanese Folk Song

The words to "Kokiriko" tell about dancing and playing the kokiriko. "Kokiriko" comes from the village of Goka in the Toyama region of Japan. This area features unique ancient houses, built by farmers.

Listen for the sound of the bamboo slats in "Kokiriko."

THINK!

How might the sounds of bamboo slats have first been thought of as a musical instrument? Consider the fact that in this mountain region of Japan, there are often high winds and rain.

Mado no sansa mo dederekoden
Hare no sansa mo derderekoden

Kokiriko no take wa shichisun gobu ja
Nagai we ode no kanakai ja

The window (nonsense words)
The clear sky (nonsense words)
The height of the kokiriko
Is about ten inches tall.
The sleeve is so long
And there is a metal spoon.

The Bottom Line

In many musical ensembles, the instrument that plays the lowest notes, or **bass** notes, combines rhythm and harmony by providing both a strong beat and the main notes, or **root** notes, of chords. In early jazz, the string bass was the instrument most often used in this role.

The strings of the string bass can be bowed, plucked, or slapped, depending on the mood of the music. The bass plays music written in the bass clef.

"Slap That Bass" was written by brothers George and Ira Gershwin, and used in the 1937 movie, *Shall We Dance*. In the 1920s and 1930s the Gershwins wrote many songs for Broadway and Hollywood. George wrote the music and Ira the words. Together, they composed many classic songs of the American musical theater.

Sing "Slap That Bass." What do the words "zoom, zoom, zoom" mean in the context of the song?

Slap That Bass

CD 8:15

Lyrics by Ira Gershwin
Music by George Gershwin

Refrain

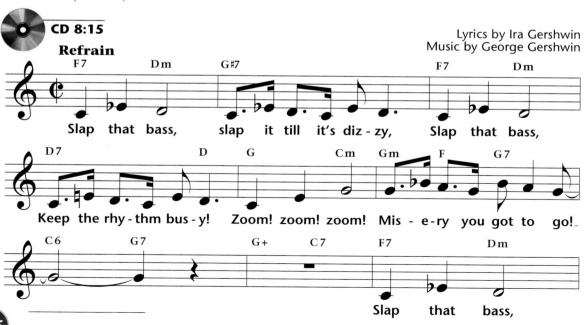

Slap that bass, slap it till it's diz-zy, Slap that bass,

Keep the rhy-thm bus-y! Zoom! zoom! zoom! Mis-e-ry you got to go!

Slap that bass,

G#7   **C#9**   **F7**   **Dm**   **D7**

Use it like a ton-ic! Slap that bass, Keep your Phil-har-mon-ic!

C   **Cm**   **Gm**   **F**   **G7**   **C7**

Zoom! zoom! zoom! And the milk and hon - ey - 'll flow! _____

Gm6   **C7**   **F**   **F**   **G7**

_____ Dic - ta - tors would be____ bet-ter off___ if they

C   **C9**   **F**

zoom zoomed now and then.___ To - day____ you can see_

F6   **G7**   **Cmaj7**   **G7**

_____ that the hap - pi - est men All got rhy-thm!

F7   **Dm**   **G#7**   **F7**   **Dm**

In which case If you want to bub-ble, Slap that bass,

D7   **D**   **C6**   **G7**   **C6**   **E♭**   **G7**

Slap a-way your trou-ble! Learn to zoom, zoom, zoom! Slap that

1. **C**   **Gm6**   **2.** **C**

bass!_____ bass!_____

**Fred Astaire and Ginger Rogers
in scenes from** *Shall We Dance* ▼

Notes from Underground

Other instruments that can provide an ensemble's bass notes are the tuba, bassoon, and bass clarinet. They all play music written in the bass clef. Often, the bass line can be a separate melody as well as a harmonic and rhythmic foundation.

Play the bass line for "Gee, Mom, I Want to Go Home" on an bass instrument.

Playalong

★Gee, Mom, I Want to Go Home★

 CD 8:18

Traditional Army Song
Adapted by Oscar Brand
Arranged by Douglas Townsend

1. They tell you in the Ar - my, The cof - fee's might - y
2. The bis - cuits that they give us, They say are might - y
3. The cloth - ing that they give us, They say is might - y
4. The sal - ar - y they pay us, They say is might - y

fine; It's good for cuts and bruis - es, It tastes like tur - pen - tine.
fine; Well, one fell off the ta - ble And crushed a pal of mine.
fine; Me and half my re - gi - ment Can all fit in - to mine.
fine; They pay you fif - ty dol - lars, And they take back six - ty - nine.

148

Sometimes, the bass line is the main melody. String bass player Edgar Meyer composes many works in which the bass is the main voice.

Meet the Musician

Edgar Meyer (b. 1960) has established himself as an innovative composer and one of today's best string bassists. In many styles, including classical and bluegrass, he performs his music all over the world.

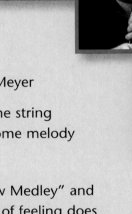

 LISTENING CD 8:21

Speed the Plow Medley by Edgar Meyer

In "Speed the Plow Medley" the low notes of the string bass provide the rhythm, harmony, and even some melody to the piece.

Listen to Edgar Meyer perform "Speed the Plow Medley" and describe the sound of the string bass. What kind of feeling does it give to the song?

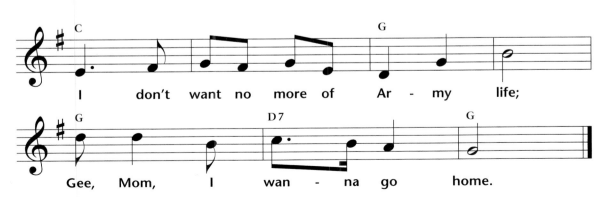

I don't want no more of Ar - my life;

Gee, Mom, I wan - na go home.

Songs for a Lifetime

CONCEPT
TONE COLOR
SKILLS
SING,
LISTEN
LINKS
HISTORY

Some songs make such an impression on you that you remember them for years. Many songs are remembered for their words, or **lyrics**. A song with powerful lyrics can leave a lasting impression.

Sing "Lean on Me." Why do you think the lyrics to "Lean on Me" are worth remembering?

CD 8:22

Words and Music by Bill Withers

1. Some - times in   our lives___   we all have pain___   we all have sor -
2. Please swal-low your pride___   if I have things_   you need to bor -

- row.___   But   if we are wise___   we know that there's_
- row___   for   no one can fill___   those of your needs_

_____ al - ways to - mor   -   row.___   } Lean on me   when you're not strong_
_____ that you won't let_____   show._ }

_____ and I'll be your friend___   I'll help you car   -   ry on___

Start the Overture!

An **overture** is an instrumental introduction, usually for either a musical or an opera. Often, melodies from the production are briefly quoted, or played, in the overture.

Meet the Musician

Gioacchino Rossini (1792–1868) was the most popular opera composer in Europe during his lifetime. He wrote over 40 operas, and his works were performed in England, Italy, France, Austria, and Russia. Although his operas are now somewhat forgotten, the overtures to his operas are still often performed in concert.

In the comic opera *The Barber of Seville*, a crafty barber uses trickery and deceit to help his friend win the hand of his beloved. Her miserly guardian is outwitted and the couple becomes free to marry.

LISTENING CD 8:25

The Barber of Seville (Overture)
Gioacchino Rossini

The overture sets the tone for the comedic action that follows. This first excerpt is from the original orchestral version that begins the opera.

The King's Singers, a vocal group, use their voices to imitate the instruments of the orchestra.

 **LISTENING** CD 8:26

The Barber of Seville (Overture) by Gioacchino Rossini, arr. by The King's Singers

The King's Singers have taken the overture to *The Barber of Seville* and arranged it for voices.

Listen to the two different versions of the overture to *The Barber of Seville*. How is the mood different in these two recordings?

Meet the Musicians

The King's Singers were formed in 1968 at King's College, Cambridge, England. The ensemble performs a diverse repertoire, ranging from folk songs to contemporary pop hits. The group's popularity stems from its ability to communicate the sheer enjoyment of singing.

Play It Again

CONCEPT
TEXTURE
SKILLS
SING, LISTEN
LINKS
LANGUAGE ARTS

Caribbean musicians use a variety of instruments—guitar, drums, steel drums, and other percussion. Caribbean music is passed down from one generation to the next.

"Yellow Bird" is a popular and fun Caribbean song about a talking bird.

Sing "Yellow Bird." What other instruments and accompaniments could you use to maintain the mood of the words?

MAP

CARIBBEAN
SEA

CD 8:27

Words and Music by Irving Burgie

My friend has a yel-low bird_ that goes with him_ for a walk,

but e-ven more than that,_ it al-so knows_ how to talk.

Yel-low bird, high up in co-co-nut tree.

See **music.mmhschool.com** to research Caribbean folk songs/music.

Jazzing It Up

The American poet Robert Frost wrote a poem about another kind of singing bird. What is his feeling about this "minor bird?"

A Minor Bird

I have wished a bird would fly away,
And not sing by my house all day;

Have clapped my hands at him from the door
When it seemed as if I could bear no more.

The fault must partly have been in me.
The bird was not to blame for his key.

And of course there must be something wrong
In wanting to silence any song.

—Robert Frost

Learn About Jazz

Jazz, an entirely American musical genre, has influenced music throughout the world. Begun in the early 20th century by African American musicians, jazz began by combining the rhythms and melodies of African music with the harmonic language of Western music. Jazz musicians create variations on popular songs through melodic improvisation and rhythmic syncopation.

At its beginning, jazz was more an approach to performance than a body of musical compositions. The marching bands of New Orleans, which often accompanied funeral processions, played traditional slow hymns on the way to the cemetery. On the way back to town, they broke into jazzed-up versions of the same hymns, ragtime tunes, or syncopated renditions of popular marches. The instruments in the marching band—trumpets, clarinets, trombones and drums—were the nucleus of the first jazz bands, usually adding only a piano, guitar, and string bass.

One of the greatest American musicians of the 20th century was John Coltrane. As a composer and jazz saxophonist, he influenced generations of musicians with his exciting style of playing. Musicians in all styles of music were influenced and inspired by him.

Meet the Musician

John Coltrane (1926–1967) grew up in North Carolina. Music was very important in his home and, like his father, he played several instruments. While still a teenager, he moved to Philadelphia to study music full-time. During World War II he played in the U.S. Navy Band in Hawaii.

After the war, he performed with all of the great jazz musicians of the 1940s and 1950s, including Dizzy Gillespie, Thelonious Monk and Miles Davis. Coltrane believed every person should work to create a better world, and music was his vehicle for inspiring happiness in others.

John Coltrane created a type of music that could sound playful, energetic, and technically complex, or simple, soulful and expressive.

 LISTENING CD 8:30

Locomotion by John Coltrane

In "Locomotion" an exciting drum introduction leads to a spontaneous sounding conversation between saxophone and trumpet.

Listen to "Locomotion." In addition to the drums, saxophone, and trumpet, what other instruments do you hear?

Spotlight Your Success!

REVIEW

1 Which instrument belongs to the brass family?

    a. piccolo   **b.** clarinet   **c.** tuba

2 What family of instruments includes the synthesizer?

    a. string   **b.** percussion   **c.** electronic

3 Which famous musician died in 1750?

    a. Johann Sebastian Bach   **b.** Edgar Meyer   **c.** Gioacchino Rossini

READ AND LISTEN

1 **Read** these rhythms. Then listen. Which rhythm do you hear?

2 **Read** these rhythms. Then listen. Which rhythm do you hear?

3 **Read** these melodies. Then listen. Which melody is in a minor key?

4 Read these melodies. Then listen. Which melody is in a major key?

a.

b.

c.

THINK!

1 Name the five instrument families. Then name at least two instruments in each family.

2 Choose your favorite song or listening selection from this unit. Describe your choice using musical terms and information you have learned. Then **write** about why this piece was your favorite.

3 Think about the musical instruments presented in this unit. If you were able to have lessons on one of the instruments, which one would you choose and why?

CREATE AND PERFORM

Show what you know about $\frac{6}{8}$ meter and minor tonality by composing a short piece to play on recorder or a barred or keyboard instrument:

1 Compose two different four measure rhythms in $\frac{6}{8}$ using ♩. ♪, ♪♪♪, and ♩ ♪

2 Decide on the form of your composition: ABA, AABA, ABAB, or AAAB.

3 Practice playing your composition as a rhythm piece. Start on D (pitch above middle C) and play a minor scale. Which pitch will be a flat? Write your scale.

4 Using pitches from the minor scale, compose a melody for your rhythm piece. Practice your piece until you can play it easily, and then take turns performing with your classmates.

Meet the Musician
ON NATIONAL RADIO!

Name: Lucy Tan
Age: 12
Instrument: Piano
Hometown: Lowell, Massachusetts

Lucy Tan remembers being drawn to the sound of the piano when she was a little girl. "We were living in an apartment, and the walls were really thin," recalls Lucy. "The neighbor had a piano, and I remember coming home from kindergarten every day and pressing my ear to the wall to listen to the music. I fell in love with the sound of the piano."

Lucy began taking piano lessons. She was committed to her music studies from the start, but when she was in fifth grade, an injury challenged her determination. One day when Lucy dropped her books in the school hallway, another student came charging down the hall. Lucy was accidentally kicked in the head as she was picking up her books. She suffered a serious concussion and for the next six months had terrible headaches. Still, she continued to play piano. "It's kind of like when an ice skater falls down," says Lucy of her determination to keep going. "No matter how many bruises they endure, they get up and keep on skating."

In addition to being a talented pianist, Lucy is also an award-winning writer. Her poem, "Visions in the Snow," won two rounds of a national poetry competition and is now published in a poetry collection.

LISTENING CD 9:1–2 **RECORDED INTERVIEW**

The Nightingale
by Franz Liszt

Listen to Lucy's performance and interview on the national radio program **From the Top**.

Spotlight on the Snare Drum

Did You Know?

Snare drums originated in Europe in the 1400s.

Snare drums were first played to signal soldiers on battlefields.

A snare drum's special sound comes from the tight wires, called snares, that are stretched across the drum's bottom. They vibrate when the drum is struck.

Snare drums are used in many types of ensembles: rock bands, military bands, and symphony orchestras.

 LISTENING CD 9:3–4

Ballerina's Dance from *Petrushka* (excerpt)
by Igor Stravinsky

Symphony No. 5, First Movement (excerpt)
by Dmitri Shostakovich

Listen to the varied uses of the snare drum in these two pieces. In *Petrushka*, the snare drum starts the dance of the ballerina with the villian. The puppet Petrushka interrupts them. In his Symphony No. 5, Shostakovich uses the snare drum in a powerful march.

Compose Yourself

Composers write the music you sing and play. All around the world, all kinds of people compose the music you listen to and enjoy.

When I get to be a composer
I'm gonna write me some
    music about
Daybreak in Alabama
And I'm gonna put the purtiest
    songs in it
Rising out of the ground like a
    swamp mist
And falling out of heaven like
    soft dew.
    from "Daybreak in Alabama"
    by Langston Hughes

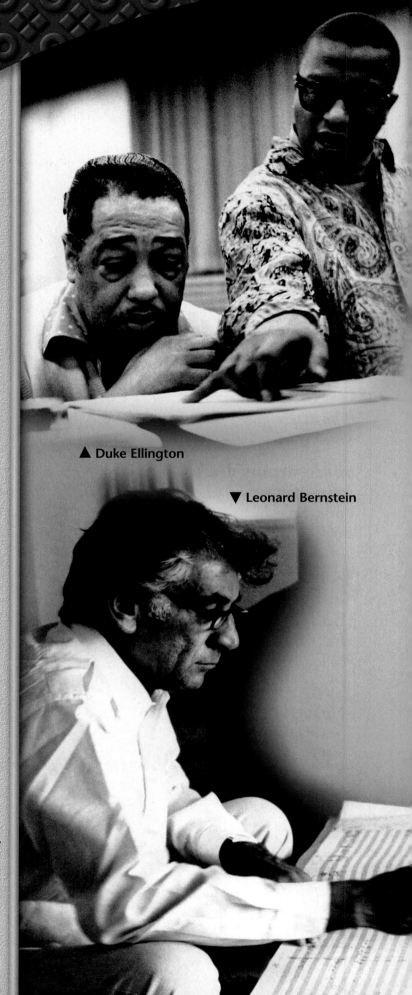

▲ Duke Ellington

▼ Leonard Bernstein

Coming Attractions

Discover how to improvise a rhythm or melody.

Listen to music of great composers, past and present.

Create and perform your own compositions.

Some musicians are performers—they sing, or play, or direct musical groups. Some compose and arrange music. Still others teach. But there are a few extraordinary musicians who can do it all. During his career, Edward Kennedy "Duke" Ellington excelled as a performer, educator, and composer.

Sing "It Don't Mean a Thing." Notice the repeated melodic phrases.

CD 9:5

Words and Music by
Duke Ellington and Irving Mills

From the words and phrases of "It Don't Mean a Thing," you can determine that the form is AABA.

 LISTENING CD 9:8

It Don't Mean a Thing by Duke Ellington

The swinging rhythm and witty lyrics of "It Don't Mean a Thing" have made this classic song popular to this day.

Listen to an arrangement of "It Don't Mean a Thing" sung by Ella Fitzgerald. Notice the AABA form. Notice the vocal and instrumental improvisations.

▲ Ella Fitzgerald

Meet the Musician

Duke Ellington (1899–1974) was an American jazz musician and composer. His famous orchestra played his own compositions and arrangements and made many innovations in the jazz idiom. Ellington traveled around the world bringing his music to distant lands and cultures. In 1969 he received the Presidential Medal of Freedom.

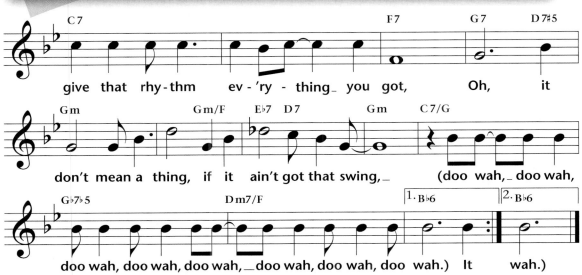

give that rhy-thm ev-'ry-thing_ you got, Oh, it

don't mean a thing, if it ain't got that swing,_ (doo wah,_ doo wah,

doo wah, doo wah, doo wah,_doo wah, doo wah, doo wah.) It wah.)

You've Heard This Form Before

CONCEPT
FORM
SKILLS
SING, PLAY
LINKS
THEATER

Composers can get ideas for music from many different sources. The composing team of Richard Adler and Jerry Ross based their musical *Damn Yankees* on a baseball novel, *The Year the Yankees Lost the Pennant.*

Sing "Heart." What is the message the composers give about what it takes to be a winner?

Heart

CD 9:9

Words and Music by
Richard Adler and Jerry Ross

You've got-ta have heart; All you real-ly need is heart. When the odds are say-in' you'll nev-er win,__ That's when the grin__ should start. You've got-ta have hope, Must-n't sit a-round and mope. Noth-in's half as bad as

THINK!

What are the similarities in form between "Heart" and "It Don't Mean a Thing?"

Music with a Heart

Because the form of "Heart" is **AABA** , you can play an accompaniment for it with just two phrases of music—one for each of the A sections and one for the B section.

Play the bass line accompaniment below with the song. The accompaniment is transposed to the key of F major, so your instrument will need a B♭. After you are comfortable playing these patterns, try improvising new rhythms for the B section as you play.

The message in "Heart," of hope and overcoming life's obstacles, is one that has appeared in many songs in a variety of styles. In "Va Pensiero," from the opera *Nabucco*, the composer Giuseppe Verdi deals with the same theme.

 LISTENING CD 9:12

Va Pensiero from *Nabucco*
by Giuseppe Verdi

The opera *Nabucco* is a biblical story about the struggle for freedom. In this chorus, the enslaved Hebrews sing about one day being free from their Babylonian oppressors.

Analyze "Va Pensiero." Does it have the same form as "Heart?"

Sing Another Verse

CONCEPT
HARMONY
SKILLS
SING, PLAY
LINKS
SOCIAL STUDIES

Folk songs were originally passed down from one person to another without being written down. It is as though each performer is one in a series of composers, each passing their version to the next performer.

Observing where and how the lyrics repeat can help you determine the form of a song.

Sing "Jack Was Ev'ry Bit a Sailor." What is the form of this Newfoundland folk song?

MAP

CANADA

NEWFOUNDLAND

Jack Was Ev'ry Bit a Sailor

CD 9:13

Newfoundland Sea Chantey

1. 'Twas twen-ty-five or thir-ty years since Jack first saw the light. He
2. When Jack grew up to be a man, he went to La-bra-dor; He
3. The whale went straight for Baf-fin's Bay 'bout nine-ty knots an hour. And

came in-to this world of woe one dark and storm-y night. He was
fished in In-dian Har-bor where his fa-ther fished be-fore; On____
ev-'ry time he'd blow a spray, he'd send it in a shower. "Oh,____

born on board his fa-ther's ship as she was ly-ing to, 'bout
his re-turn-ing in the fog he met a heav-y gale, And
now," says Jack un-to him-self, I must see what he's a-bout." He

Play this bass part with "Jack Was Ev'ry Bit a Sailor." Because I and V chords are the only ones used in this C major song, the pitches C (I) and G (V) are the only ones in the accompaniment patterns.

▲ These men cod fishing were shown in a magazine in 1885.

Art Gallery

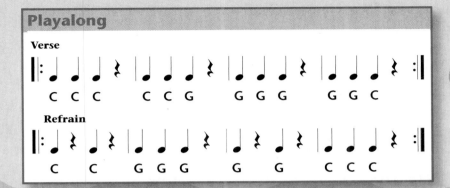

Playalong

Verse

C   C   C   C   C   G   G   G   G   G   G   C

Refrain

C   C   G   G   G   G   G   C   C   C

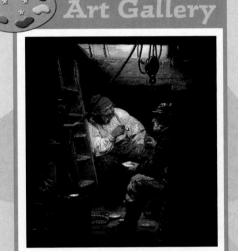

THINK! The lives of common people become the subjects of many folk songs. What are some events that might become subjects of folk songs?

▲ This nineteenth-century painting shows two fishermen and a boy gossiping in the hold of a boat.

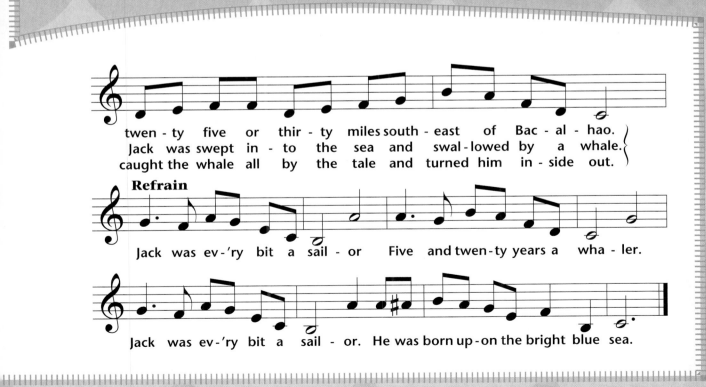

twen - ty five or thir - ty miles south - east of Bac - al - hao.
Jack was swept in - to the sea and swal - lowed by a whale.
caught the whale all by the tale and turned him in - side out.

Refrain

Jack was ev - 'ry bit a sail - or Five and twen - ty years a wha - ler.

Jack was ev - 'ry bit a sail - or. He was born up - on the bright blue sea.

Making Chords

In every major and minor scale, the notes of the scale can be numbered from 1 to 7 (1 and 8 are the same pitch) with Roman numerals—I to VII. A chord built on any one of these notes is called by that number of the scale. For example, in B♭ major the I chord is built on B♭, the IV chord is built on E♭, and the V chord is built on F:

See
music.mmhschool.com
to research
South American
folk songs/music.

MAP
CHILE
URUGUAY
ARGENTINA

Some of the same forms that we find in our own music can be found in music from all over the world.

Sing "Chiu, Chiu, Chiu." Look closely at this folk song from Uruguay. Does it have the same form as "Jack Was Ev'ry Bit a Sailor?"

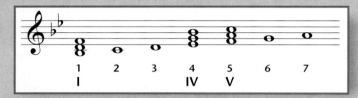

CD 9:16

Uruguayan Folk Song
English Version by MMH

Spanish: Can - ta, can - ta, pa - ja - ri - to.___ Can - ta, can - ta tu can -
Pronunciation: kan ta kan ta pa xa ɾi to kan ta kan ta tu kan
English: Can - ta, can - ta pa - ja - ri - to.___ Sing the songs that cheer me

ción, Mi - ra que la vi - da_es tris - te y tu can -
syon mi ɾa ke la βi da es tris te i tu kan
so. See, my life is full of sor - row, your mer - ry

tar me_a - le - gra_el co - ra - zon. Chí - u, chí - u, chí - u,
taɾ mea le gɾael ko ɾa son chi u chi u chi u
sing - ing sets my heart a - glow. Chí - u, chí - u, chí - u,

172

In "Chiu, Chiu, Chiu," the harmony serves to set the verse and refrain apart from each other. The verse includes I and V chords, and the refrain uses I, IV and V chords.

chí - u,_____ chí - u, chí-u, chí-u, chí-u._____ Can-ta, can-ta pa-ja-
chi u   chi   u chi u chi u   chi u   kan ta kan ta pa xa
chí - u,_____ chí - u, chí-u, chí-u, chí-u._____ Can-ta, can-ta pa-ja-

ri - to.   Que tu can - tar   me_a-le-gra_el co - ra - zon.
ri to   ke tu kan tar   mea le gra el ko ra   son
ri - to.   Your mer-ry sing - ing sets my heart a - glow.

Refrain

Con tus gor - je - os,_____ con tu tri - nar,   Des - pier-ta_el
kon tus gor   xe os   kon tu tri nar   ðes pyer tael
Your mer - ry   chirp-ing;_____ your roun-de - lay,   You bring the

al - ba, la no-che ya se va.   Con tus gor-je-os,_____con tu tri-
al ßa la no che ya se ßa   kon tus gor xe os   kon tu tri
dawn-ing, the shad-ows fade a-way,   Your mer-ry chirp-ing;_____your roun-de-

nar,_____ Des - pier-ta_el al - ba, la no-che ya se va.
nar   ðes pyer tael al ßa la no che ya se ßa
lay._____ You bring the dawn-ing, the shad-ows fade a - way.

Chords Can Help You Compose

CONCEPT
TONALITY

SKILLS
SING,
ANALYZE

LINKS
HISTORY

Folk songs are passed down from generation to generation and form an important part of any culture's identity. Folk songs have a unique way of connecting with the listener's emotions, and some modern composers even try to make their songs sound like folk melodies.

Folk Song Characteristics
- Lyrics about common experiences
- Uncomplicated melodies
- Repetition of words and phrases

"If I Had a Hammer" may sound like a traditional folk melody, but it was actually written by composers Pete Seeger and Lee Hays in 1958.

◀ **Pete Seeger and Lee Hays**

If I Had a Hammer

CD 9:20

Words and Music by
Lee Hays and Pete Seeger

1. If I had a ham-mer,— I'd ham-mer in the
(2.) bell,_____ I'd ring it in the
(3.) song,_____ I'd sing it in the
(4.) ham - mer,— And I've— got a

morn - ing,— I'd ham-mer in the ev - 'ning,—
morn - ing,— I'd ring it in the ev - 'ning,—
morn - ing,— I'd sing it in the ev - 'ning,—
bell,_____ And I've got— a song to sing,

All o - ver this land. I'd ham-mer out
All o - ver this land. I'd ring— out
All o - ver this land. I'd sing— out
All o - ver this land. It's the ham-mer of

dan - ger,___   I'd ham-mer out a warn - ing,___
dan - ger,___   I'd ring___ out a warn - ing,___
dan - ger,___   I'd sing___ out a warn - ing,___
jus - tice,___   It's the bell___ of___ free - dom,_

I'd ham-mer out love be-tween my broth-ers and my sis - ters,
I'd ring___ out love be-tween my broth-ers and my sis - ters,
I'd sing___ out love be-tween my broth-ers and my sis - ters,
It's a song a-bout love be-tween my broth-ers and my sis - ters,

1., 2., 3.
All_____ o - ver this land.   2. If I had a
                                                          3. If I had a
                                                           4. Well, I got a

4.
All_____ o - ver this land._____

Analyze the key signature of this music. This is the key of E-flat major. What are the letter names of the flats?

Compare the key signatures of "Jack Was Ev'ry Bit a Sailor," "Chiu, Chiu, Chiu," and "If I Had a Hammer." Name the key signature for each song.

The Weavers with Pete Seeger and Lee Hays ▶

Unit 5 Compose Yourself   175

The Folk Song Revival

Pete Seeger has composed many songs and performed for generations of music lovers. In "River of My People," he gives us an important message in just a few measures with only three simple chords.

Meet the Musician

Pete Seeger (b. 1919) was one of the pioneers of the American folk music revival of the late 1950s and early 1960s. He helped to transform folk music from an orally transmitted body of traditional songs found mainly among rural dwellers to a popular form of mass entertainment. His songs often contain messages of peace, tolerance, and universal brotherhood.

Sing "River of My People" What is the song's message? What is the name of its key signature?

River of My People

 CD 9:23

Words and Music by Peter Seeger
Music based on Traditional Russian Folk Song

1. There's a riv-er of my peo-ple And its flow is swift and
2. Man-y rocks and reefs and moun-tains, See to bar its storm-y
3. You will find me in the main-stream, Steer-ing sure-ly through the
4. For_____ I have mapped this riv-er, And I know its liv-ing
5. Oh,_____ riv-er of my peo-ple, To-geth-er we must

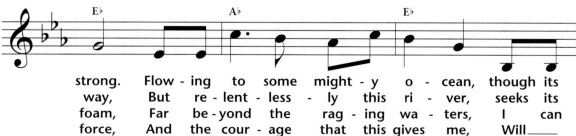

strong. Flow-ing to some might-y o-cean, though its
way, But re-lent-less-ly this ri-ver, seeks its
foam, Far be-yond the rag-ing wa-ters, I can
force, And the cour-age that this gives me, Will_____
go, Has-ten on-ward to that meet-ing, Where my

The three chords in "River of My People" are I, IV, and V7. These are the same three chords in the refrain of "Chiu, Chiu, Chiu." Are the roots of the chords the same pitches in both songs? Why?

What does the "7" in a V7 chord mean? (Hint: Think about the number of notes from the chord root.)

Play a bass accompaniment in the key of C using the root pitches of the I, IV, and V7 chords. The letters above the staff tell you to change from one pitch to the next on the right beat. Transpose the letters: E♭ = C; B♭ = G; A♭ = F.

In the key of C major, these are the I, IV, V7 chords shown on a piano keyboard. What pitches are the roots of each chord?

Compose a **countermelody** to be played during the last phrase of "River of My People" (the last four measures with the pick-up). Use notes from the chords indicated on the keyboard as well as passing tones.

A countermelody is a melody written as a contrast to the main melody of a song. It is also played at the same time as the main melody and can be higher or lower than the main melody.

The countermelody:
- can have either the same or different rhythm as the melody.
- can use the same words as the melody or a neutral syllable.
- will always be on a different pitch than the melody.
- will flow best if there are no big interval leaps.

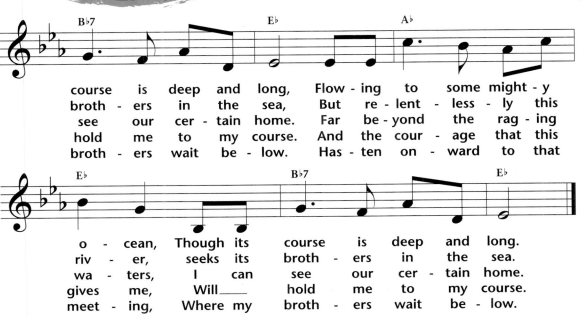

	B♭7				E♭		A♭		
course	is	deep	and	long,	Flow - ing	to	some	might -	y
broth - ers	in	the	sea,		But	re - lent -	less -	ly	this
see	our	cer - tain	home.		Far	be - yond	the	rag -	ing
hold	me	to	my	course.	And	the	cour -	age	that this
broth - ers	wait	be - low.			Has - ten	on - ward	to		that

E♭				B♭7			E♭
o - cean,	Though its	course	is	deep	and	long.
riv - er,	seeks its	broth - ers	in	the	sea.
wa - ters,	I can	see	our	cer - tain	home.
gives me,	Will___	hold	me	to	my	course.
meet - ing,	Where my	broth - ers	wait	be - low.

The Birth of the Blues

CONCEPT ◄
FORM
SKILLS
SING, MOVE
LINKS
HISTORY

The **blues** is a style of music born of suffering. The singer/songwriter shares his or her pain in a way that we can understand and identify with. "Blind" Lemon Jefferson was one of the most popular blues recording artists of the 1920s.

Sing "One Dime Blues." Think about the meaning of the lyrics. How do they make you feel?

One Dime Blues

CD 10:1

Words and Music by Blind Lemon Jefferson

1. I'm broke an' I ain't got a dime. I'm
2. I was stand-in' on East Cair-o street one day, I was
3. One dime was all that I had. One

broke an' I ain't got a dime. I'm
stand-in' on East Cair-o street one day, I was
dime was all that I had. One

broke an' I ain't got a dime. Ev-'ry-
stand-in' on East Cair-o street one day, One
dime was all that I had. Got a

bod-y gets in hard luck some-time.
dime was all that I had.
meal be-fore the last.

Learn About the Blues

The blues is a musical style that grew out of African American spirituals and work songs. Originating in the rural Mississippi Delta region at the beginning of the 20th century, the blues descended from earlier work shouts or calls called "arhoolies." The blues is primarily a vocal narrative for solo voice with instrumental accompaniment and a fixed harmonic progression.

The sufferings endured by generations of African American people found expression in these early blues. As people migrated to cities in search of work, the blues gradually became an urban phenomenon. Blues music has contributed significantly to the development of jazz, rock and roll, and country and western music.

"Blind" Lemon Jefferson ▼

"One Dime Blues" is a **16-bar blues**. There are two major characteristics to a 16-bar blues. The first concerns the lyrics:

- A statement is made (*I'm broke an' I ain't got a dime*).
- This statement is sung two more times.
- A closing statement is made, commenting on the first statement (*Ev'rybody gets in hard luck sometime*).

The second characteristic in this blues is its chord progression.

Josh White singing and playing the blues ▼

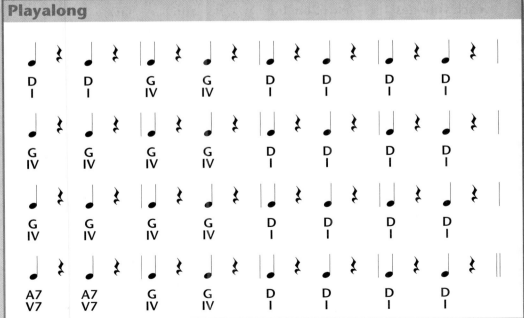

Playalong

D	D	G	G	D	D	D	D
I	I	IV	IV	I	I	I	I

G	G	G	G	D	D	D	D
IV	IV	IV	IV	I	I	I	I

G	G	G	G	D	D	D	D
IV	IV	IV	IV	I	I	I	I

A7	A7	G	G	D	D	D	D
V7	V7	IV	IV	I	I	I	I

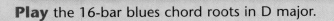
Play the 16-bar blues chord roots in D major.

179

Boogie on Down

"Choo, Choo, Ch'Boogie" has basically the same three chords—I, IV, and V7—as "One Dime Blues," in a similar progression. A boogie-woogie is a style of playing the blues on the piano with a steady repeated pattern in the bass and improvised melodic work. What is the difference in mood between "One Dime Blues" and "Choo, Choo, Ch'Boogie"?

Move to "Choo, Choo Ch'Boogie" with a partner. One leads the other, improvising fancy footwork. Notice the chord progression.

John Lee Hooker, one of the world's greatest blues singers

Choo, Choo, Ch'Boogie

CD 10:4

Words and Music by Vaughn Horton, Denver Darling and Milton Gabler

1. I'm head-in' for the sta-tion with my pack on my back,_ I'm
reach your des-ti-na-tion but a-las and a-lack,_ You

tired of trans-port-a-tion in the back of a hack,_ I
need some com-pen-sa-tion to get back in the black,_ You

love to hear the rhy-thm of the click-a-ty clack,_ And
take a morn-in' pa-per from the top of the stack,_ And

hear the lone-some whis-tle, See the smoke from the stack,_ And
read the sit-u-a-tions from the front to the back,_ The

Analyze the chord progression in "Choo, Choo, Ch'Boogie." What are the chord roots in this F major song?

Play along with the recording as you follow the chord changes indicated in the music.

Howlin' Wolf, a Chicago bluesman, known for his powerful "howling" voice and loud electric blues ▶

C7

pal   a - round with dem - o - crat - ic   fel - lows named "Mac"_   So,
on - ly   job that's o - pen needs a   man with   a   knack,_   You

F   3   Bb   3   F   Bb7

take me right back to the track,   Jack!_ }
put   it right back in the rack,   Jack!_ }   Choo-Choo_   Choo-

Bb7   F

- Choo-Ch-Boogie, Woo   -   Woo_   Woo - woo ch' boo-gie Choo-

Bb7   1.
                            C7   3   C dim 3

- Choo_   Choo - Choo-Ch-Boo-gie_ Take me right back to the

C7   2.
                            C7   3   3   F

track,   Jack!_   2. You   Take me right back to the track,   Jack!_

LESSON 5

CONCEPT
RHYTHM
SKILLS
SING, MOVE
LINKS
THEATER

Meter Makes a Difference

Besides the lyrics, a song's meaning can often be found in other musical elements. The key, tempo, rhythm, instrumentation, and meter can either reinforce or contradict the meaning of a song's words. The organization of beats within a measure is **meter**.

Sing "Lullaby of Broadway." Step-clap during the verse and do smooth arm movement in the refrain.

LULLABY OF BROADWAY

CD 10:7

Words and Music by Al Dubin and Harry Warren

1. Come on a-long and lis-ten to ___ The lull-a-by of Broad - way. ___
2. Come on a-long and lis-ten to ___ The lull-a-by of Broad - way. ___

The hip hoo-ray and bal - ly - hoo, _ The lull-a - by of Broad - way. ___
The hi-dee-hi and boop-a - doo, _ The lull-a - by of Broad - way. ___

The rum-ble of a subway train, _ The rat-tle of the tax - is, ___
The band be-gins to go to town, _ And ev-'ry-one goes cra - zy. ___

The daf-fy-dils who en - ter - tain ___ At An-ge - lo's and Max-ie's. When a
You rock-a-bye your ba - by round _ Till ev-'ry-thing gets ha - zy. "Hush-a-

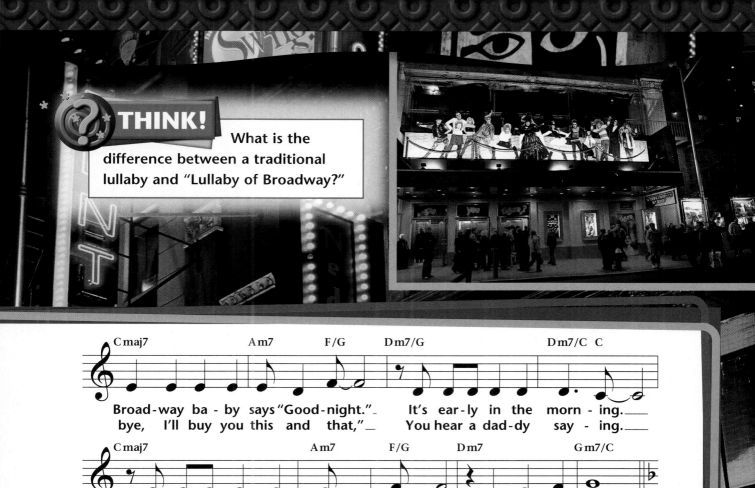

Broad-way ba - by says "Good-night."_ It's ear-ly in the morn - ing.___
bye, I'll buy you this and that,"_ You hear a dad-dy say - ing.___

Man-hat-tan ba - bies don't sleep tight___ Un - til the dawn.
And Ba - by goes home to her flat___ to sleep all day.

Good - night, Ba - by, Good - night,

Milk-man's on his way.___ Sleep tight, Ba - by,

Sleep tight, Let's call it a day. Hey!_ Let's call it a day!

Lis-ten to___ the lull-a-by___ of old Broad - way.___

Lullabies Are Not Just for Sleeping

"Sweet and Low" is a more traditional lullaby. A mother sings to her baby about her hopes that the "wind of the Western sea" will carry her sailor husband back to her.

Move to "Sweet and Low" by swaying from side to side with the $\frac{6}{8}$ meter. How are the unspoken messages in this song different from those in "Lullaby of Broadway?"

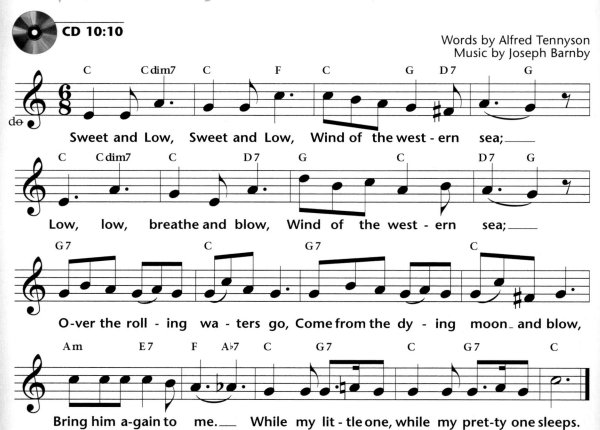

CD 10:10

Words by Alfred Tennyson
Music by Joseph Barnby

Sweet and Low, Sweet and Low, Wind of the west - ern sea;

Low, low, breathe and blow, Wind of the west - ern sea;

O - ver the roll - ing wa - ters go, Come from the dy - ing moon and blow,

Bring him a-gain to me. While my lit - tle one, while my pret-ty one sleeps.

These two lullabies ("Lullaby of Broadway" and "Sweet and Low") sound and feel very different from each other. One of the reasons for the different feeling between these two songs is their different meter.

Improvise by singing "Lullaby of Broadway" in a slow $\frac{6}{8}$ meter.

Describe how the change of meter changes the "unspoken" message of the song.

Come on a-long and list-en to a lull-a-by of Broad-way.

Young Composers

CONCEPT
HARMONY
SKILLS
SING, LISTEN
LINKS
HISTORY

The majority of professional musicians train all their lives to achieve, and maintain, a high level of excellence and musicality. In some very rare cases, however, people show great musical talent and ability at a very early age. The rest of the world often sits up and takes notice of these young geniuses.

This was certainly the case with young Wolfgang Amadeus Mozart. He was already composing and performing music when he was only five years old.

Sing Mozart's "Alleluia." The canon is taken from a larger work composed in 1773, when Mozart was 17 years old. Practice it in unison first, and then sing it as a three part canon.

MAP

GERMANY
AUSTRIA
POLAND
SLOVENIA
ITALY
CROATIA BOSNIA
YUGOSLAVIA

ALLELUIA

CD 10:13

Words and Music by Wolfgang Amadeus Mozart

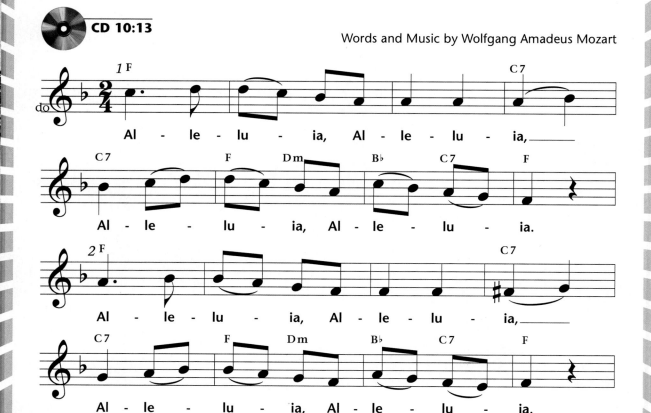

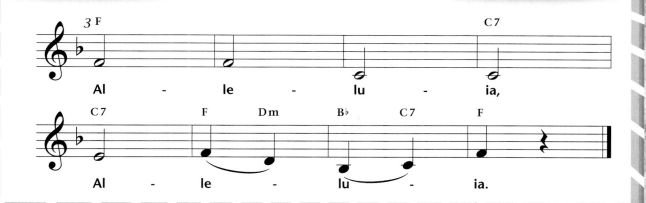

3 F   C 7

Al - le - lu - ia,

C 7   F   Dm   B♭   C 7   F

Al - le - lu - ia.

LISTENING CD 10:16

Exsultate, jubilate, Third Movement

by Wolfgang Amadeus Mozart

The "Alleluia" canon is taken from the third movement of Mozart's *Exsultate, jubilate,* a piece for soprano and orchestra.

Listen to *Exsultate, jubilate* sung by Kathleen Battle. Do you hear the repetitions of the first melodic theme? What is the form of this music?

MIDI

For another activity with "Alleluia," see *Spotlight on MIDI.*

Meet the Musician

Wolfgang Amadeus Mozart (1756–1791) was perhaps the most famous child prodigy the world has ever known. It is reported that he could read music even before he learned to talk. Mozart played the piano, violin, and viola. Although he died at the early age of 35, he wrote over five hundred pieces of music, including operas, symphonies, concertos, and songs.

When Mozart was still very young, his father took him and his sister (also a gifted young musician) on a tour of Europe. They traveled from their native Austria and performed for large audiences and many of the royal courts across Europe.

Sing Hallelujah!

"Heleluyan" is another type of "Alleluia," but written by a Native American in the Muscogee language.

Sing "Heleluyan."

CD 10:17

Heleluyan
Alleluia

Muscogee Song
Transcribed by Charles Webb

Muscogee: He - le - lu - yan, he - le - lu - yan;_ he - le, he - le - lu - yan;
Pronunciation: hɛ lɛ lu yan hɛ lɛ lu yan hɛ lɛ hɛ lɛ lu yan

he - le - lu - yan, he - le - lu - yan;_ he - le, he - le - lu - yan.
hɛ lɛ lu yan hɛ lɛ lu yan hɛ lɛ hɛ lɛ lu yan

Creek Grass Dancers

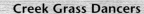

THINK! How do you think the Native American composer intended this song to be sung? Why?

188

Today, there are many young composers writing many different styles of music. In 2003, while still a college student, Aaron Marx wrote this piece for clarinet and piano.

Use **Orchestral Instruments CD-ROM** to learn more about clarinet.

LISTENING CD 10:19

Dance for Clarinet and Piano by Aaron Marx

Dance for Clarinet and Piano is written in a musical style called "klezmer." Klezmer music originated in Eastern Europe and is based on the music and chants of Hebrew prayers.

Listen to *Dance for Clarinet and Piano*. Follow the listening map.

Listening Map for *Dance for Clarinet and Piano*

A

B

C slow lyrical section in ¾ meter

A

A melodic ornamentation in clarinet

Instruments Set the Scene

There are many elements that make up a finished piece of music. Composers and arrangers have many tools to use and choices to make. Fast or slow? Loud or soft? High or low? Every choice is important. One of the biggest is which instruments and voices to use. Instrumentation can have a dramatic effect on music, and can give clues to the culture or region from which a song originates.

Sing "Samba de Orfeu." Do the instruments used give you any clue about where the song comes from? Which instruments and where?

MAP

BRAZIL

SOUTH AMERICA

Samba de Orfeu

Dance of Orpheus

CD 10:20

Words by Antonio Maria
Music by Luiz Bonfa

B♭maj7

Portuguese: Que - ro vi - ver,_____ que - ro___ sam - bar
Pronunciation: ke ɾu vi veɾ ke ɾu sã baɾ

B♭maj7   C m7

A - té sen-tir___ a_es-sen-cia da vi - da, Me fal - tar_____
a te sẽ tiɾ aes sen sya da vi da me fal taɾ

C m7

Que - ro sam - bar,___ que - ro___ vi - ver,
ke ɾu sã baɾ ke ɾu vi veɾ

C m7   F 7   1.   B♭maj7

De-pois do sam - ba, ta bem, Meu a - mor pos - so mor - rer.___
de pois du sã ba ta bẽ meu a moɾ pos so mo heɾ

190

The Brazilian Beat

Brazil is a country in South America that was colonized by the Portuguese. It has a strong local culture as well as strong ties to the culture of Portugal. The lyrics for "Samba de Orfeu" are written in Portuguese, still the national language of Brazil.

The diverse traditions of Africa, Portugal, and Native South America have all influenced the culture of Brazil.

The samba originated in Brazil between the late 1800s and early 1900s and is danced during festivals and celebrations. In the 1920s, the samba was introduced to the United States in a Broadway play called *Street Carnival.* The festive style and mood of the dance has kept it alive and popular to this day. Samba is a fun dance that fits much of today's popular music.

Allegretto by Xavier Montsalvatge

"Allegretto" is a lively piece for solo piano. Spanish composer Xavier Montsavatge wrote it as a birthday present for his 10-year old daughter, Yvette. He included a piece of a famous song in this selection—a musical "quote."

Listen to "Allegretto." Do you recognize the musical "quotation?" What is it?

Heavenly Music

CONCEPT
STYLE

SKILLS
SING, LISTEN

LINKS
SCIENCE

What if you were able to fly into space? What would you see as you looked back at your home planet? Mountains and oceans? Continents, with their coastlines and rivers? How would you feel as you sped away from Earth past the moon and the Sun?

Sing "This Pretty Planet." How does the rhythm remind you of something spinning?

This Pretty Planet

CD 10:25

Words and Music by
John Forster and Tom Chapin
Adapted by MMH

This pret - ty plan - et spin - ning through space. You're a
gar - den. You're a har - bor. You're a ho - ly place.
Gold - en sun go-ing down. Gen-tle blue gi - ant, spin us a-round.
All through the night. Safe 'til the morn - ing light.

Perform this 4-part vocal accompaniment to "This Pretty Planet." Practice each part separately, then all 4 parts together. Finally, sing them with the song.

"This Pretty Planet" is in G major. Use Roman numerals and root notes to name the chords in the vocal accompaniment.

Spin, spin-ning in space, round and a-round, a ho - ly place.

Music of the Spheres

In addition to the stars, the ancient Greeks were able to see seven celestial bodies in the sky—the Sun, the Moon, Mercury, Venus, Mars, Jupiter, and Saturn. It was their belief that when these bodies moved through space, their vibrations, with mathematical precision, created the purest of sounds—the "Music of the Spheres." Throughout the centuries, composers have tried to re-create these celestial sounds here on Earth.

Meet the Musician

British composer **Gustav Holst** (1874–1934) was well known during his lifetime as a composer of operas, chamber music, vocal pieces, and orchestral music of many different styles. His compositions were based on subjects as varied as Renaissance music, folk songs, Sanskrit literature, modern poetry, and astrology. His most famous piece, *The Planets*, is still popular today.

In ancient Rome, the god of war—Mars—was so important that a month (March) was named in his honor. At one time March was the first month of the year in the Roman calendar.

LISTENING CD 10:28

Mars from *The Planets*
by Gustav Holst

Holst composed an orchestral suite called *The Planets*. In it, he wrote musical portraits of Mars, Venus, Mercury, Jupiter, Saturn, Uranus, and Neptune. Since astronomers did not discover Pluto until 1930 (ten years after the suite was written), there is no piece representing that planet.

▶ Roman mosaic of the
Greek god Oceanus
(son of Uranus),
circa 2nd century

Listen to Holst's "Mars" and follow the listening map. What is the meter? Does the meter stay the same throughout?

Tap and clap a $\frac{5}{4}$ pattern of quarter notes as you listen.

Tap   clap   clap   tap   clap

Clap the ostinato rhythm from "Mars" when you hear it.

Can you devise a word pattern to fit this ostinato?

Listening Map for Mars

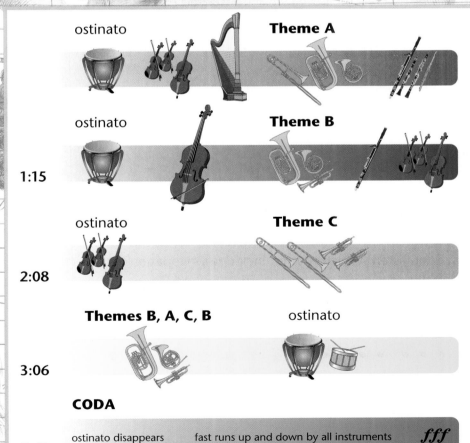

Spotlight Your Success!

REVIEW

1 A major song with a key signature of two flats is in what key?

  a. C   **b.** E♭   **c.** B♭

2 What chords are most used in a blues progression?

  a. I ii vii   **b.** I IV V   **c.** iii IV V

3 Which pattern shows syncopation?

  a.    **b.**    **c.**

4 What would these chords (D G A) be if they were transposed from the key of D to the key of F?

  a. F B♭ C   **b.** F C D   **c.** F G A

READ AND LISTEN

1 Read these bass lines using chord roots. Then listen. Which bass line do you hear?

2 Read these rhythms. Then listen. Which rhythm includes syncopation?

a.

b.

c.

3 Read these chord progressions. Then listen. Which chord progression do you hear?

4 Read these chord progressions. Then listen. Which chord progression do you hear?

a.

b.

c.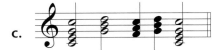

THINK!

1 Compare two contrasting styles of composition by describing how musical elements are used in each: How does an opera chorus, such as "Va pensiero," differ from a song composed in folk style, like "If I Had a Hammer"?

2 Choose your favorite music from this unit. Describe it using musical terms and information you have learned, including something about the choices made by the composer. **Write** about why this piece was your favorite.

3 What kind of knowledge and skill is needed to transfer ideas about sound and emotion from one person to another? What do you already know that would help you get started?

CREATE AND PERFORM

1 Compose a song! Start by writing or finding a short poem that expresses something you find interesting. It can be sad or funny, or have any feeling special or meaningful to you.

2 Read your poem aloud until you decide on a rhythm for the words. If the rhythm you like is too complicated to write down, have someone help you, or invent your own notation.

3 When the rhythm is set, start to sing or play a melody. Sometimes just humming a tune can get you started. When you have a melody you like, write it down in notation you have learned or some other way you invent.

4 Practice your composition. Perform it for someone. Make a recording of your composition.

Meet the Musician
ON NATIONAL RADIO!

Name: William MacMorran
Age: 14
Instrument: Bagpipes
Hometown: Bristol, Tennessee

Fourteen-year-old William MacMorran has already visited Scotland nine times and can't wait to go again. "It's the music that draws me there more than anything," he says. "It's just incredible!"

William has taken part in the Highland Games in Scotland, which celebrate Scottish heritage through athletic competitions, bagpipe playing, and dancing. "Highland Games are held in the United States too, but they're different in Scotland," explains William. "For one thing, they don't wear kilts over there—probably because they know they're Scottish and don't have to prove it!"

William's great-grandfather was born in Scotland, and his mom was the National Scottish Fiddling Champion. Celtic music is more than a family tradition: it's William's passion. In addition to playing the bagpipes, William plays Irish flute and Irish bouzouki. He also plays guitar in an ensemble called "Celtic Air."

When William's not immersing himself in Celtic culture, he enjoys playing baseball and tennis, skateboarding, and jamming with his high school bluegrass band.

 LISTENING   CD 10:30–31    **RECORDED INTERVIEW**

Tulloch Castle/Flowers of Red Hill
traditional Celtic songs

Listen to William's performance and interview on the national radio program **From the Top.**

Careers

"I wish they'd told us as children there were more choices in music besides teaching and performing," remarked Charlotte Lee, a classical music artist manager. Ms. Lee, a musician herself, started violin at age four and added the piano in fourth grade.

Ms. Lee majored in music performance and liberal arts in college. She then thought about entering law school, but it didn't seem right. Instead, she got an internship in the business side of music. Soon after joining the marketing department of a record company, Ms. Lee found she liked combining her passion for music with her business and people skills. She now books concerts, works closely with artists' managers to make sure tours run smoothly, and guides young artists' careers.

"I really like the challenges of my job," Ms. Lee explains, "but I also enjoy the opportunity to build relationships with these gifted artists and attend their amazing concerts for free."

Spotlight on Symphonic Bands

Did You Know?

Symphonic bands are made up of instruments in the woodwind, brass, and percussion families.

Symphonic bands are also called concert bands or wind ensembles. Symphonic bands perform in concerts, while marching bands perform at athletic events or march in parades.

 LISTENING CD 11:1–2

Shepherd's Hey
by Percy Grainger

Early Light
by Carolyn Bremer

Listen to the sound of the concert band. Grainger based his *Shepherd's Hey* on an English folk song. American composer Bremer is a baseball fan. In her piece, listen for quotes from "The Star-Spangled Banner" and for the crack of the bat hitting the ball.

UNIT
6

The Road to Performance

The theater goes dark . . . a spotlight cuts through the darkness to reveal a lone performer on stage. A roar rises from the audience as the music starts. The crowd is on its feet applauding madly for the star of the show.

The road to stardom is long and arduous, and a life in show business can be filled with struggle and disappointment. It may start with a dream, but it takes time, talent, determination, hard work, and a lot of luck.

Coming Attractions

Perform Czech partner songs.

Dance and sing to Greek music.

Learn about the history of rock and roll.

The musical *A Funny Thing Happened on the Way to the Forum* was written by American composer Stephen Sondheim in 1962. "Comedy Tonight" is the first song in the show. The star of the show comes out to tell the audience to prepare to have fun. There will be no sad stories and no tragic scenes in the show. There will only be fun, laughs, and "Comedy Tonight!"

Sing "Comedy Tonight." How does the rhythm of the song convey the excitement of opening night?

COMEDY TONIGHT

CD 11:3

Words and Music by Stephen Sondheim

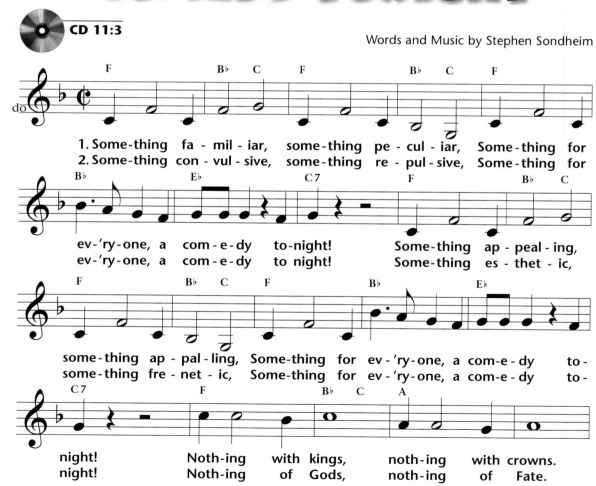

1. Some-thing fa - mil - iar, some-thing pe - cul - iar, Some-thing for
2. Some-thing con - vul - sive, some-thing re - pul - sive, Some-thing for

ev-'ry-one, a com - e - dy to-night! Some-thing ap - peal - ing,
ev-'ry-one, a com - e - dy to night! Some-thing es - thet - ic,

some-thing ap - pal - ing, Some-thing for ev - 'ry-one, a com-e-dy to-
some-thing fre - net - ic, Some-thing for ev - 'ry-one, a com-e-dy to-

night! Noth-ing with kings, noth-ing with crowns.
night! Noth-ing of Gods, noth-ing of Fate.

Nathan Lane and Whoopi Goldberg on Broadway in *A Funny Thing Happened on the Way to the Forum*

Bring on the lov - ers, li - ars and clowns!_ Old sit - u -
Weigh - ty af - fairs will just have to wait.___ Noth - ing that's

a - tions, new com - pli - ca - tions, Noth - ing por - ten - tous or po -
for - mal, noth - ing that's nor - mal. No re - ci - ta - tions to re -

lite:___ Trag - e - dy to - mor - row, com - e - dy to - night!
cite!___ O - pen up the cur - tains,

com - e - dy___ to night!_____

Taking the Long View

CONCEPT
METER
SKILLS
SING, LISTEN
LINKS
LANGUAGE ARTS

Standing atop a high mountain peak, looking out toward the distant horizon over the vast reaches of land, it seems like you can see forever!

"On a Clear Day" describes that feeling of limitless horizons. It was written by lyricist Alan Jay Lerner and composer Burton Lane for the 1965 musical *On a Clear Day You Can See Forever*.

Sing "On a Clear Day."

On a Clear Day

CD 11:6

Words by Alan Jay Lerner
Music by Burton Lane

The time signature for "On a Clear Day"— ¢ —is another way to indicate the $\frac{2}{2}$ time signature. It is also called **cut time** because it "cuts" the $\frac{4}{4}$, or c, time signature in half, becoming ¢, or $\frac{2}{2}$.

This new symbol indicates that there are two beats in each measure and that the half note is the unit of the beat. Cut time is sometimes called **alla breve**, an Italian musical term that, loosely translated, means "the half note gets the beat."

The origins of the c and ¢ go back centuries, to the beginnings of music notation. In those early days, time signatures were written as either circles or half circles. The half circle has come down to us today in the shape of a c.

Accent on Meter

Among the oldest and best-known English ballads is "Barbry Ellen."
It dates all the way back to Scotland in the mid-1600s. From the
British Isles it crossed the Atlantic with the settlers coming to the
New World. In this version, notice the changing meter.

See
music.mmhschool.com
to research English folk
songs/music.

Sing "Barbry Ellen."

CD 11:9

English Folk Song

1. All in the mer - ry month of ___ May, When the green buds
2. He sent his ser - vant to the ___ town To the place where
3. So slow - ly, slow - ly she got ___ up And ___ slow - ly
4. Oh yes, I'm low, I'm ver - y ___ low, And ___ death is
5. Oh yes, you're low and ver - y ___ low, And ___ death is

they were ___ swell - in', Young ___
she was ___ dwell - in', Say - in',
she came a nigh ___ him And ___ all
on me ___ dwell - in', No ___
on you ___ dwell - in', No ___

Wil - liam Green on his death bed ___ lay, For the love of
Mas - ter's sick and he sends for ___ you If your name is
she ___ said when ___ she got ___ there young ___ man I be -
bet - ter, no bet - ter I'll ev - er be If I can't wed
bet - ter, no bet - ter you'll nev - er be For you can't wed

Bar - bry ___ El - len.
Bar - bry ___ El - len.
lieve ___ you're ___ dy - in'.
Bar - bry ___ El - len.
Bar - bry ___ El - len.

In "Barbry Ellen" the meter changes several times. Its lines of text are written in varying lengths, and the meter changes accommodate these irregular phrases. If each measure had the same meter, the important words would not fall on the strong beats of the measure. By changing the meter, important words can be emphasized by having them occur on the stronger beats in each measure. What are some ways in which composers can emphasize words or notes in a piece of music?

MAP
NORTHERN IRELAND
SCOTLAND
IRELAND
ENGLAND
WALES

Words and Meter

The rhythm of words in poetry is also called **meter**. In the poem "Unfolding Bud" by Naoshi Koriyama, each line is a different length and rhythm. Write a rhythm for each line of the poem. Possible rhythms are given for the first few lines.

Unfolding Bud

by Naoshi Koriyama

One is amazed

By a water-lily bud

Unfolding

With each passing day,

Taking on a richer color

And new dimensions.

One is not amazed.
At a first glance,
By a poem,
Which is as tight-closed
As a tiny bud.

Yet one is surprised
To see the poem
Gradually unfolding,
Revealing its rich inner self,
As one reads it
Again
And over again.

THINK!
How does the changing meter reflect the words and meaning of the "Unfolding Bud?"

Unit 6 The Road to Performance   (209)

Music à la Mode

CONCEPT
MELODY
SKILLS
SING, PLAY
LINKS
HISTORY

As you have learned, major and minor scales are built on patterns of whole steps and half steps. Each scale has its own starting note, or **tonic**. For example, in the key of C major, C is the tonic note.

By using all the notes in a C major scale (the white keys on the piano keyboard), you can also create different types of scales, called **modes**. These modes use the same notes as a C major scale but are centered on a different tonic, or main note.

Two of these modes are the Dorian mode and the Mixolydian mode. Using just the white keys of the piano, the Dorian mode is centered on D, and the Mixolydian mode is centered on G.

The Dorian mode has qualities of both major and minor scales. The third note in the scale is a minor third above the tonic (a minor scale feature) and the sixth note in the scale is a major sixth above the tonic (a major scale feature). The Dorian mode is sometimes called the "bright minor" because it sounds predominantly minor but has some characteristics of a major scale.

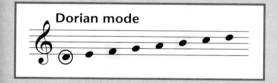

Dorian mode

"The Ship in Distress" tells of the hard and dangerous life of a sailor. Through high winds and heavy seas, this ship finally finds safe harbor. Sadly, that was not true for all ships, as this image shows. How does the sound of the Dorian mode convey the poignant story of the song?

Sing "The Ship in Distress." Does the song sound major or minor? Why?

The Ship in Distress

CD 11:12

English Ballad

1. You sail - ors bold who__ plough the o - cean. See
2. For four - teen days, heart - sore and hun - gry, see-ing
3. A full - dressed ship like the sun a - glit 'ring came

dan - ger lands - men__ nev - er know. It's not for ho - nor__
but wild wa - ter and__ bit - ter sky, Poor fel - lows, they stood__
bear - ing down__ to__ their re - lief. As soon as this glad__

or pro - mo - tion; No tongue can tell what they__ un - der - go. In the
in a tot - ter, A - cast - ing lots to which__ should__ die. The__
news was shout-ed, It ban - ished all their__ care and grief. The__

blus - t'rous__ wind and the gray dark wa - ter. Our
lot__ it__ fell on__ Rob - ert Jack - son whose
ship__ brought__ to, no__ long - er drift - ing, Safe

ship went drift - ing on the__ sea, Her hand-gear gone And her
fam - i - ly was so ve - ry__ great. "I'm free to die, but__
in St. Vin-cent, Cape Ver-de she gained. You sail - ors all who__

rud - der__ bro - ken which brought us to ex - tre - mi - ty.
oh, my__ com-rades, Let me keep look - out 'til break of day.
hear my__ stor - y pray you'll nev - er suf - fer the like a - gain.

More with Modes

Like the Dorian mode, the Mixolydian mode has qualities of both major and minor scales. Like major scales, the third note in the scale is a major third above the tonic. Like some minor scales, the seventh note in the scale is a minor seventh above the tonic.

Although the Mixolydian has a predominantly "major" sound to it, the lowered seventh gives it a somewhat haunting character.

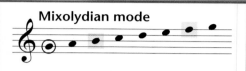

Dutch and English sailors began fishing for whales in the waters around Greenland early in the 1500s. "The Greenland Whale Fishery" came into being some time between then and the early 1700s. It has remained a great favorite and has been reprinted over and over the years in many versions.

Sing "The Greenland Whale Fishery." Which notes make the song sound major and which ones make it sound minor?

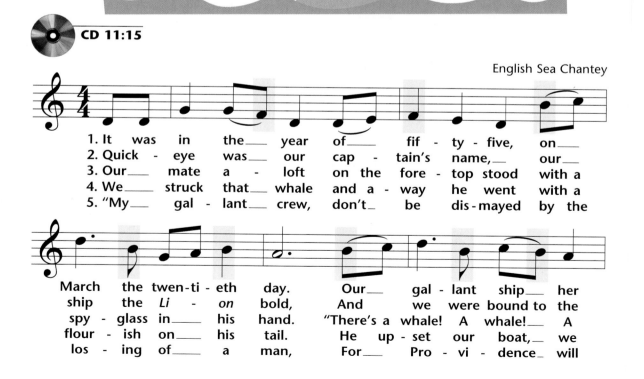

The Greenland Whale Fishery

CD 11:15

English Sea Chantey

1. It was in the year of fif - ty - five, on
2. Quick - eye was our cap - tain's name, our
3. Our mate a - loft on the fore - top stood with a
4. We struck that whale and a - way he went with a
5. "My gal - lant crew, don't be dis - mayed by the

March the twen - ti - eth day. Our gal - lant ship her
ship the Li - on bold, And we were bound to the
spy - glass in his hand. "There's a whale! A whale! A
flour - ish on his tail. He up - set our boat, we
los - ing of a man, For Pro - vi - dence will

Perform the accompaniment to "The Greenland Whale Fishery."

Playalong

THINK! The two songs in Dorian and Mixolydian mode use the same pitches. Why do they sound different from each other?

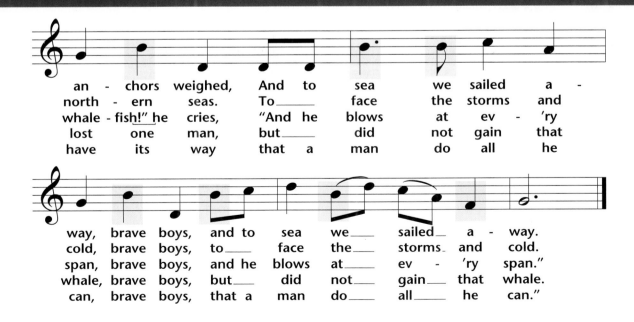

an - chors weighed,	And to	sea	we sailed a -
north - ern seas.	To___	face	the storms and
whale - fish!" he cries,	"And he	blows	at ev - 'ry
lost one man,	but___	did	not gain that
have its way	that a	man	do all he

way, brave boys,	and to	sea	we___ sailed___ a - way.
cold, brave boys,	to___	face	the___ storms_ and cold.
span, brave boys,	and he	blows	at___ ev - 'ry span."
whale, brave boys,	but___	did	not___ gain___ that whale.
can, brave boys,	that a	man	do___ all___ he can."

Greek Music, Greek Meters

CONCEPT
METER

SKILLS
LISTEN, PERFORM,
CREATE, MOVE

LINKS
SOCIAL STUDIES,
HISTORY

MAP
BULGARIA
ALBANIA
GREECE
TURKEY

In most of the music you have looked at, all the beats have been equal in length. In some regions and cultures, however, it is common for music to have two or more unequal beats. With a time signature of $\frac{5}{8}$, for example, there can be two uneven beats in each measure. The first beat could be three eighth notes long, and the second beat, two eighth notes long. Or the first beat could be two eighths and then three eighths for the second beat.

The uneven length of each beat in the measure creates a lilting hesitation. In many cultures and regions, rhythmic patterns of twos and threes or threes and twos are standard in vocal, instrumental, and dance music.

Much of the music from Greece is written in irregular meters like $\frac{5}{8}$, $\frac{5}{4}$, $\frac{7}{8}$, and $\frac{7}{4}$. It may seem difficult to dance to uneven beats, but once you feel the rhythm it is very natural and exhilarating.

"Tzakonikos" is a Greek circle dance in quick $\frac{5}{4}$ meter. It is said to originate from the ancient Greek myth about Theseus and Ariadne. Theseus learned the dance from Ariadne just before leaving the island of Delos, never to return.

Tzakonikos

CD 11:18   Greek Circle Dance

Listen to the Greek dance "Tzakonikos." It is written with a time signature of $\frac{5}{4}$. There are two main beats to each measure. Are the measures divided into groups of 3+2 or 2+3?

Perform $\frac{5}{4}$ meter by using words that have two or three syllables. For example:

2 + 3: "TELL ME ONE MORE TIME" or "AP-PLE CO-co-nut"

3 + 2: "WHO HAS MY PEN-CIL" or "CO-co-nut AP-ple"

Create your own phrases in five (2+3 and 3+2). Accompany them by tapping on the accented syllables.

Moving in $\frac{7}{8}$ Time

The time signatures of $\frac{5}{8}$ and $\frac{5}{4}$ have two beats of different length. To create meters with three uneven beats you can use meter signatures of $\frac{7}{8}$ or $\frac{7}{4}$ to create patterns of 3+2+2, 2+2+3, or 2+3+2.

Like many Greek songs, "Yerakina" uses the beat pattern of 3+2+2. This song is also used for a popular circle dance. The dancers sing and clap their hands as they circle around to the music.

Sing "Yerakina." Clap the main beats as you sing.

CD 11:19

Greek Folk Song

Greek: Kí - νη - σε ή Γε - ρα -
Pronunciation: ki ni se i ye ra
English: Yer - a - ki - na went for wa - ter, When she fell in to the

κί - να Γιά νε - ρό κρύ - ο νά
ki na yia ne ro kri o na
well and cried out, I ran to see. Then I heard her

φέ - ρη Τρούμ - τρούμ, τρούμ, τρούμ, τρούμ - τρούμ Τά - βρα -
fe ri droum droum droum droum droum droum ta vra
man-y brace-lets jan-gle droom droom droom droom droom."Yer-a-ki-na,

216

Clap to the main beats in this irregular rhythmic pattern of $\frac{7}{8}$. Say the words as you clap:

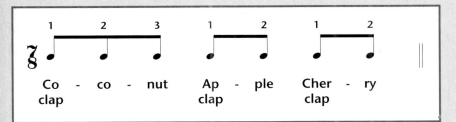

You have already practiced the most challenging part of the dance to "Yerakina"—the uneven beats. If you can move your feet to main beats you just clapped, you can do the dance.

Move to "Yerakina" in the dance pattern called a **grapevine**.

Measure 1
Beat 1 - Right foot steps right (count "one-two-three")
Beat 2 - Left foot crosses in front of right foot (count "one-two")
Beat 3 - Right foot steps right (count "one-two")

Measure 2
Beat 1 - Left foot steps in back of right foot (count "one-two-three")
Beat 2 - Right foot steps right (count "one-two")
Beat 3 - Left foot crosses in front of right foot (count "one-two")

Opera Is for Everyone!

CONCEPT
FORM
SKILLS
READ, LISTEN, SING
LINKS
DRAMA, CULTURES

Opera brings together all the performing arts—acting, singing, and dancing come together with staging, scenery, and costumes to create a world of fantasy. When American composer Libby Larsen was asked to write an opera for the 2002 Winter Olympics, she asked children to write and draw how they thought they would feel to be their favorite color. These writings and drawings were the inspiration for the characters in her opera, *Dreaming Blue*.

Read the poem aloud. Write your own ideas about being your favorite color.

(Untitled)
I asked a little child who cannot see,
"And what is color like?"
"Why green," said he,
"Is like the rustle when the wind blows through
The forest; running water, that is blue;
And red is like a trumpet sound; and pink
Is like the smell of roses; and I think
That purple must be like a thunderstorm;
And yellow is like something soft and warm;
And white is a pleasant stillness when you lie
And dream."
—*Anonymous*

▲ Scenes from
Dreaming Blue ▼

 LISTENING CD 11:23

There Was a Blue Flower from *Dreaming Blue* by Libby Larsen

The opera *Dreaming Blue* tells the story of a child who feels lost but has an adventure full of color, sound, and energy. The child's part is sung by a tenor.

Listen to "There Was a Blue Flower" in its original key. The song tells how the child (the blue flower) is lonely and sad. But by the end of the **aria**, or song, the child finds a new life and is no longer unhappy.

In performance, musicians may **transpose**, or change the key of, a piece of music. This is done so that the piece will fit the range of different instruments and voices. "There Was a Blue Flower" has been transposed down a fourth to make it easier for you to sing.

There Was a Blue Flower

CD 11:24

Words and Music by Libby Larsen

There was a blue flower a blue flower grow-ing all a-lone.

The flower was fright-ened,_ sad____ and fright-ened

he was the on - ly blue flower_____

grow-ing all a-lone. So he moved,_ he moved to a

place far a - way.__ Where am I go-ing he said

I'll go to the moun-tains I'll go to the moun-tains,

More

Listen to the transposed version of "There Was a Blue Flower" and follow the notation. Compare it to the recording of the original version.

"Get a Car/Polka Dot" is also from the opera *Dreaming Blue*. You will hear how the composer imitates the sounds of car horns and how she creates images of polka dots through her clever use of the syllables "pol-ka dot."

 LISTENING CD 11:27

Get a Car/Polka Dot from *Dreaming Blue*
by Libby Larsen

"Get a Car/Polka Dot" imitates nonmusical sounds from the world around us using instruments and voices. This tradition of music imitating real-world sounds goes back to the Renaissance.

Listen to "Get a Car/Polka Dot." Sing or play along with the rhythm when you hear *thudaduda ya hoo a eee a*. Then choose one syllable of "pol-ka dot" and listen to how it occurs in different places.

Meet the Musician

Libby Larsen (b. 1950) is one of America's most prolific and most performed living composers. She has written over 200 works in every genre—from chamber music and small vocal pieces to large orchestral, operatic, and choral scores. Her music has been praised for its dynamic, inspired, and vigorous representation of the contemporary American spirit.

CONCEPT
RHYTHM

SKILLS
CLAP, SING,
LISTEN

LINKS
CULTURE, FINE ART,
SOCIAL STUDIES

American culture is constantly enriched by the diversity of the many ethnic and national backgrounds of its people. These different cultures have all added to the arts in the United States and helped make them unique. The song "El Tambor" originated from Panama.

Clap the strong beat and snap the weak beat as you sing this song.

MAP
UNITED STATES

MEXICO   CUBA

COSTA RICA

PANAMA

El Tambor

The Drum

CD 11:28

Panamanian Folk Song
Spanish Words by José-Luis Orozco
English Words by MMH

Refrain

Spanish: El tam - bor, el tam - bor, el tam - bor de a - le - grí - a. Yo
Pronunciation: el tam bor el tam bor el tam bor ðe a le gɾi a yo
English: El tam - bor, el tam - bor, el tam - bor the drum of glad-ness, I

quie - ro que tú me lle - ves el tam - bor de a - le - grí - a.
kye ɾo ke tu me ye ßes el tam bor ðe a le gɾi a
want you to give me the_ drum, el tam - bor the drum of glad-ness.

Verse
Solo

O Jua - ni-ta o Jua-ni - ta, Jua-ni - ta a - mi - ga mí - a
o xwa ni ta o xwa ni ta xwa ni ta a mi ga mi a
Oh Jua - ni-ta, oh Jua-ni - ta, Jua-ni - ta my friend, a-mi - ga

D.C. al Fine

Group

Yo quie - ro que tú me lle - ves el tam - bor de a - le - grí - a.
yo kye ɾo ke tu me ye ßes el tam bor ðe a le gɾi a
I want you to give me the_ drum, el tam - bor the drum of glad-ness.

Review some of the rhythms you already know. Clap each of the following rhythmic building blocks.

Arrange the blocks, in any order you like, to accompany "El Tambor." The block that contains a quarter rest should be used for the last measure. This will give the accompaniment a feeling of completion.

Art Gallery

Kuna Indian Textile, Panama

Ceremonial musicians with flutes and maracas in traditional fiesta costumes

Unit 6 The Road to Performance

223

Global Voices

India

Bhangra is a lively form of music and dance that originated in the Punjab region of northern India. Bhangra may be more than 2000 years old. It began as a part of harvest festival celebrations and eventually became a part of other celebratory occasions, such as weddings and New Year celebrations.

LISTENING CD 12:1

Nach Nach Nach Punjabi song

"Nach Nach Nach" is a Bhangra song about a flirtation between a young boy and girl. The boy and girl alternate singing each verse of the song in Punjabi. *Soniye* is the boy's term of endearment for the girl. *Soniya* is the girl's term of endearment for the boy.

Art Gallery

Musicians and guests at a festival
Compare the musical instruments in this picture with the brass and percussion instruments in a symphony orchestra.

Listen to "Nach Nach Nach." Practice speaking the words of the song.

Verse 1 (man)
Nach nach nachke dikha soniye (2 times)
Ankh zara ankh se mila soniye
Meri behna ki shaadi hai
Mere naal bhangra paa soniye

English Translation:
Dance, dance, dance, O beautiful one!
Let our eyes meet, O beautiful one.
It is my sister's wedding.
Come and dance the Bhangra with me,
O beautiful one.

Verse 2 (woman)
Mere kareeb na aa soniya
Mujhse na yun takraa soniya
Chhod bhi de deewanapan
Aise na baat badha soniya

Don't come close to me, O beautiful one.
Don't come so near, O beautiful one.
Leave this madness.
Don't let things turn out this way,
O beautiful one.

Form two groups and improvise movement patterns for one of the verses. Perform your movements for the other group.

In the past 30 years, Bhangra has become popular around the world, often joined with other music styles such as hip-hop and reggae.

MAP

PAKISTAN
CHINA
PUNJAB
NEPAL
INDIA
BANGLADESH

Damdama Sahib Temple

To learn more about traditional Indian instruments, use the *World Instruments* **CD-ROM.**

Czech Melodies and Rhythms

CONCEPT
HARMONY
SKILLS
SING, LISTEN
LINKS
HISTORY,
SOCIAL STUDIES

The Czech people have kept their rich culture, including beautiful songs and dances, despite past centuries of occupation by different foreign governments.

Sing "Jede, jede, poštovský panáček." Sing the chord roots first, and then sing the melody with a neutral syllable, such as *la*, or with the text.

Jede, jede, poštovský panáček

Riding, Riding, Is Mr. Postman

Czech Folk Song

CD 12:2

Czech:	Je - de,	je - de	poš - tov - ský	pa - ná - ček,
Pronunciation:	yɛ dɛ	yɛ dɛ	posh tov ski	pa na chɛk
English:	Rid - ing, rid - ing,		Post - Man is	rid - ing

je - de,	je - de	poš - tov - ský	pán,
yɛ dɛ	yɛ dɛ	posh tov ski	pan
rid - ing, rid - ing,		is Mis - ter	Post.

1. Vpře - du - má tru - bič - ku, vza - du má truh - lič - ku,
   fpř̄ʒɛ du ma tř̄u bich ku vza du ma tu hlich ku
2. Má vra - ny ko - ni - čky ja - ko dvě ry - bi - čky,
   ma vř̄a ni ko nyi chki ya ko dvyɛ ř̄i bich ki
   Blow - ing his horn, he calls, Bear - ing the trunk he hauls,

je - de,	je - de	poš - tov - ský	pán.
yɛ dɛ	yɛ dɛ	posh tov ski	pan
je - de,	je - de	do Ro - ky - can.	
yɛ dɛ	yɛ dɛ	do ř̄o kɪ tsan	
rid - ing rid - ing		is Mis - ter	Post.

226

Partner songs are songs that are separate and distinct from each other but can be performed together. Although different in subject, they fit together harmonically and melodically.

Although it can stand on its own, "Jede, jede, poštovský panáček" can be sung as a partner song with "Já do lesa nepojedu."

Perform "Já do lesa nepojedu." When you know it well, sing it and "Jede, jede, poštovský panáček" together. Notice that the chord roots are the same.

MAP
GERMANY
POLAND
CZECH REPUBLIC
AUSTRIA   SLOVAKIA

Já do lesa nepojedu

To the Woods I Will Not Go

CD 12:6

Czech Folk Song

Czech: **Já do le - sa ne - po - je - du, já do le - sa ne - pu - du,**
Pronunciation: ya do lɛ sa nɛ po yɛ du ya do lɛ sa nɛ pu du
English: **To the woods I will not go now, to the woods I will not go.**

kdy - by na mě haj - ný při - šel, on by mi vzal se - ky - rú
gdi bɪ na myɛ hai ni pr̝ɪ shɛl on bɪ mi vzal sɛ ki r̝u
If the ran - ger should come near me, he would take my ax a - way.

Se - ky - ra je za dva zla - tý, a to - půr - ko za to - lár
sɛ ki r̝a yɛ za dva zla ti a to puř ko za to lař
What a loss! I need my ax and I would rath - er save my coins.

kdy - by na mě haj - ny při - šel, on by mi to všec - ko vzal.
gdi bɪ na myɛ hai ni pr̝ɪ shɛl on bɪ mi to vshɛts ko vzal
If the ran - ger should come near me, he would take my ax a - way.

Unit 6 The Road to Performance

227

Partner Songs

Now you are ready to add the third song to this group of partner songs. Practice "Neviděli jste tu mé panenky?" in the same manner you learned the first two songs. When you are ready, sing all three songs together.

Neviděli jste tu mé panenky?

Have You Not Seen My Dear Daughters?

CD 12:10

Czech Folk Song

Czech: Ne - vi - dě - li jste tu mé pa - nen - ky? šla do le - sa
Pronunciation: nɛ vi dyɛ li stɛ tu mɛ pa nen ki shlɑ do lɛ sa
English: Oh, have you not seen my dear-est daugh-ters? to the woods they

na ma - len - ky, ne - vi - dě - li jste tu mé pa - nen - ky,
na mɑ lɛn ki nɛ vi dyɛ li stɛ tu mɛ pa nɛn ki
went for ber - ries. Oh, have you not seen my dear - est daugh - ters

šla do le - sa trá - vu žit; šla do le - sa, by - la ro - sa,
shlɑ do lɛ sa tɾa vu ʒit shlɑ do lɛ sa bɪ la ɾo sa
cut - ting grass up to the woods? When they left home, it was morn - ing;

zá - blo ju to, by - la ro - sa, ne - vi - dě - li jste tu
za blo yu to bɪ la ɾo sa nɛ vi dyɛ li stɛ tu
bare-foot roam - ers, I am mourn - ing. Oh, have you not seen my

mé pa - nen - ky? šla do le - sa trá - vu žit.
mɛ pa nɛn ki shlɑ do lɛ sa tɾa vu ʒit
dear - est daugh - ters cut - ting grass up to the woods?

In the 19th century, composers became more and more aware of the folk music traditions from their native countries. One of the more important musical styles, called **nationalism**, used these folk music melodies and rhythms in large-scale orchestral works. Czech composer Bedřich Smetana was a leader in this new national style.

 LISTENING CD 12:14

From Bohemia's Forests and Meadows from *Má Vlast* by Bedřich Smetana

The best-known of Smetana's orchestral works is the cycle of symphonic poems called *Má Vlast* (My Country). It is a set of six pieces that paint "sound pictures" of the natural world of the Czech countryside. "From Bohemia's Forests and Meadows" is one movement from the cycle.

Follow the listening map for "From Bohemia's Forests and Meadows." What pictures of the natural world does the music evoke?

Listening Map for From Bohemia's Forests and Meadows

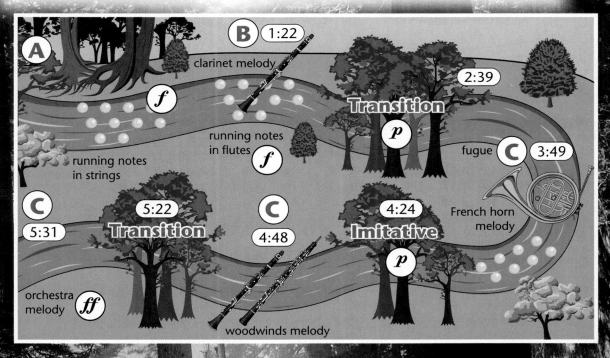

Sing, Play, Dance—Perform!

CONCEPT
FORM
SKILLS
SING, MOVE, PLAY
LINKS
SOCIAL STUDIES

As you have seen, music can serve many functions. It can be sung, danced to, listened to, or played. Some music can be used in more than one way. "Troika," a Russian folk song, is also used to accompany the traditional dance of the same name. In Russia, a *troika* is a three-horse carriage or sleigh.

The dance is performed in a circle of trios, like spokes of a wheel. Notice how the dancers represent the three side-by-side horses that pull the sleigh through the snow and how the rhythm echoes the movement of the horses as they pull the troika.

Sing "Troika." Notice the key.
Is it major or minor?

MAP

RUSSIA

CHINA

INDIA

CD 12:15

Words and Music by Dave and Jean Perry
Based on a Traditional Russian Folksong

Verse

1. Through the night the wind is blow - ing, swirl - ing 'round the
2. Swift - ly, now the sleigh is fly - ing; From the for - est
3. In the hall the peo - ple danc - ing; Sounds of laugh - ter

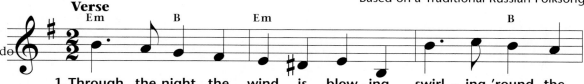

fall - en snow, Rid - ing high up - on the troi - ka,
to the town, Can - dles burn with cheer - ful bril - liance;
ev - 'ry - where. Play the bal - a - lai - kas to the

Refrain

to the vil - lage we must go.
Voic - es ring in fes - tive sound. } Hur - ry, coach - man,
beat - ing rhy - thms in the air.

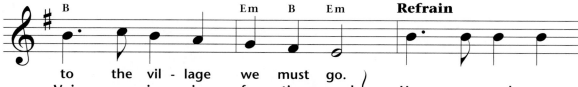

Move to "Troika" by doing the steps to the dance. Practice each section separately, and then put them all together.

Verse:

Formation:	Large circle of trios (each trio is like the spoke of a wheel)
16 counts:	Run forward (counter-clockwise) (holding inside hands)
8 counts:	Dancer on right runs under arch (formed by other 2 dancers' arms) and returns to place.
8 counts:	Dancer on left runs under arch (formed by other 2 dancers) and continues run to form trio circle.

Refrain:

Formation:	Small trio circles (each trio makes its own circle)
12 counts:	Run clockwise in trio circle
4 counts:	Three stamps while reversing facing
12 counts:	Run counterclockwise in trio circle
4 counts: 3	Stamps: open circle, return to beginning line

THINK!

In "Troika," how does the dance reflect the verse/refrain form of the music?

with the troi - ka, hur - ry, hors - es, through the snow,

To the win - ter cel - e - bra-tion, to the vil - lage far be - low.

Turkish Delight

"Dere Geliyor" is an old and popular Turkish folk song written in the Turkish **karsilama** dance rhythm of $\frac{9}{8}$. Each measure is divided into four beats of uneven length. The eighth notes are grouped in units of 2+2+3+2. This catchy rhythm gives "Dere Geliyor" a memorable, lilting feeling.

Sing "Dere Geliyor." "Dere" is the Turkish word for "river." Notice the way the irregular rhythm echoes the flow of a river as it overflows its banks and carries sand down to the sea.

MAP

BULGARIA

TURKEY

GREECE

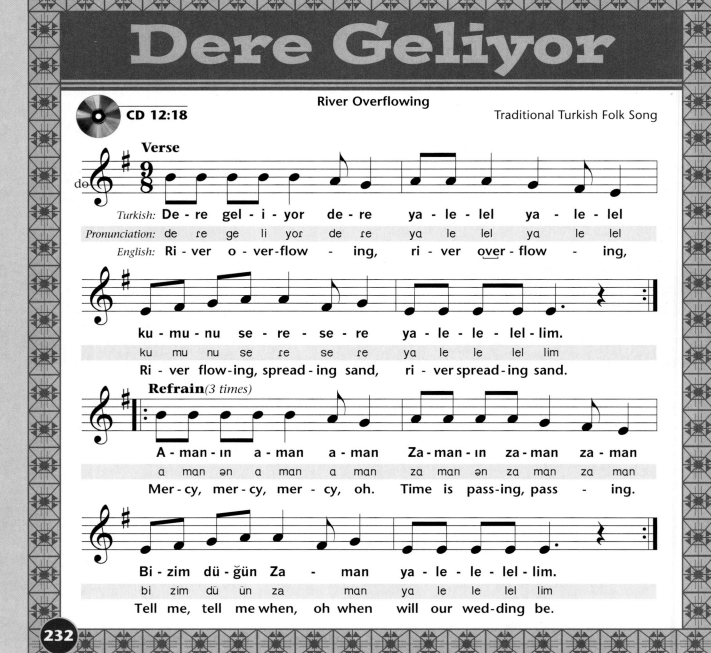

Dere Geliyor

CD 12:18

River Overflowing

Traditional Turkish Folk Song

Verse

Turkish: De - re gel - i - yor de - re ya - le - lel ya - le - lel
Pronunciation: de ɾe ge li yoɾ de ɾe ya le lel ya le lel
English: Ri - ver o - ver-flow - ing, ri - ver over - flow - ing,

ku - mu - nu se - re - se - re ya - le - le - lel - lim.
ku mu nu se ɾe se ɾe ya le le lel lim
Ri - ver flow-ing, spread - ing sand, ri - ver spread-ing sand.

Refrain (3 times)

A - man - ın a - man a - man Za - man - ın za - man za - man
a man ən a man a man za man ən za man za man
Mer - cy, mer - cy, mer - cy, oh. Time is pass-ing, pass - ing.

Bi - zim dü - ğün Za - man ya - le - le - lel - lim.
bi zim dü ün za man ya le le lel lim
Tell me, tell me when, oh when will our wed-ding be.

232

Although you may not have authentic Turkish instruments in your classroom, you can create an accompaniment using the instruments you do have.

Improvise three ostinatos to accompany "Dere Geliyor." Practice them one at a time. Use tambourine and finger cymbals for a Turkish flavor.

You can create a dance for "Dere Geliyor" in the form of the song. Use these guidelines to help you choreograph your dance:

• Imitate the song's form—verse/refrain.

• Start in a single group formation, then split into two groups.

• Add changes of direction and body facing to a simple walk.

Now put it all together. Sing, play, and dance to "Dere Geliyor."

LESSON
8

CONCEPT
FORM

SKILLS
SING,
ANALYZE

LINKS
HISTORY

Rock, Roll, and Stomp

Have you ever wondered where the term "rock and roll" came from? Read on to find out. Then sing "Rock Around the Clock." What are some of the things that make it appealing?

Learn About Rock and Roll

The phrase `rock and roll` was first coined in 1951 by Cleveland radio announcer Alan Freed. He used it to describe a new type of American music that combined the traditions of rhythm and blues and country and western music.

In 1954 Bill Haley formed a band called Bill Haley & His Comets. They recorded the first big rock and roll hit—"Rock Around the Clock." It heralded a new sound in music.

Haley had experimented earlier with this new style of music, but it was "Rock Around the Clock," written by a 63-year-old postal worker named Max Freedman, that started the popularity of rock and roll. Bill Haley & His Comets sold over 25 million copies of "Rock Around the Clock."

ROCK AROUND THE CLOCK

CD 12:22

Words and Music by
Max C. Freedman and Jimmy DeKnight

One, two, three o'-clock, four o'-clock, rock, five, six, sev-en o'-clock,

eight o' - clock rock, nine, ten e - lev-en o'-clock,

twelve o'-clock rock, we're gon-na rock a-round the clock to-night. Well get your

Create different ways to perform "Rock Around the Clock." For example, try dividing the beginning into four sections, with one singer each singing one phrase of the introduction and then everyone singing the verses together.

Bill Haley & His Comets

glad	rags	on		join	me,	Hon,___	we're gon-na
clock	strikes	two,		three	and	four,___	and___ the
chimes	ring	five		six	and	sev - en	we'll be
eight,	nine,	ten,	e -	lev -	en	too,___	I'll___ be
clock	strikes	twelve,	we'll	cool	off,	then,___	start___ a -

have	some	fun	when the	clock	strikes	one,___	
band	slows	down	we'll___	yell	for	more,_	
rock - in'	up	in___		sev - enth	heav'n_	we're gon - na
go - ing'	strong	and___		so	will	you,___	
rock - in'	'round	the___		clock	a - gain,_	

rock a-round the clock to - night,_ we're gon-na rock, rock, rock, 'til

broad day-light,_we'regon-na rock, gon-na rock a-round_ the clock_ to-night_

When the
When the
When it's
When the

Traditions of Today's Music

Another early rock and roll hit was "Blue Suede Shoes." Carl Perkins was only 23 years old when he wrote this smash hit song.

Meet the Musician

Carl Lee Perkins (1932–1998) was one of the founding fathers of rock and roll music. He grew up in Tennessee and was influenced by the country, gospel, and blues music he heard there. As a teenager, he formed a group called the Perkins Brothers. He went on to a career as a songwriter and performer that spanned over fifty years. In 1987 Carl Perkins was inducted into the Rock and Roll Hall of Fame.

Analyze "Blue Suede Shoes" and "Rock Around the Clock." What similarities do they share?

BLUE SUEDE SHOES

 **CD 12:25**

Words and Music by Carl Lee Perkins

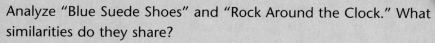

Well, it's one for the mon-ey, two for the show, three to get read-y, now

go, cat, go! But don't you step on my Blue Suede Shoes.

Well you can do an-y-thing but lay off of my Blues Suede Shoes.

236

Spotlight Your Success!

REVIEW

1 Which note equals one beat in cut time?

    a. ♩   **b.** ♩   **c.** ♩.

2 What is the syllable name of the tonal center for the Dorian mode?

    a. *re*   **b.** *do*   **c.** *la*

3 Which composer is an American living today?

    a. Libby Larsen   **b.** Bedřich Smetana   **c.** Carl Perkins

4 Which dances are often in $\frac{5}{8}$ or $\frac{7}{8}$ meter, with uneven beats?

    a. Russian folk dances
    b. dances with rock and roll music
    c. Greek folk dances

READ AND LISTEN

1 **Read** these rhythms. Then listen. Which rhythm has uneven beats?

    a.

    b.

    c.

2 **Read** these rhythms. Then listen. Which rhythm do you hear?

    a.

    b.

    c.

3 **Read** these melodies. Then listen. Which melody has *re* as its tonal center?

a.

b.

c.

4 **Read** these melodies. Then listen. Which melody has *so,* as its tonal center?

a.

b.

c.

THINK!

1 What are the skills and personal qualities needed to be a performer?

2 Make a list of two- and three-syllable words in a category of your choice. Use the words to create word chains illustrating meters of 5 and 7 with uneven beats. Play the rhythms of your word chains on a drum.

3 What kind of musical activity is your personal favorite? Choose an experience from this unit and **write** about what made this activity satisfying.

CREATE AND PERFORM

In a small group, choose a song or dance with uneven beats. Review and practice your selected piece. Then develop a percussion accompaniment. Write it down and put the piece together. Perform your piece for your classmates or another audience.

Spotlight on Music Reading

Spotlight on Music Reading

Spotlight on Music Reading

Basic Pitches and Rhythms

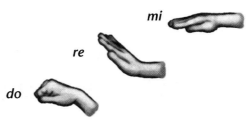

do   re   mi

Rhythms are created with combinations of notes and rests. In $\frac{4}{4}$ meter,

a quarter note = one sound to a beat.

Two eighth notes = two sounds to a beat.

A quarter rest = one beat of silence.

A half note = a sound lasting two beats.

A half rest = two beats of silence.

Read the pitches and rhythms in this spiritual.

GOOD NEWS

CD 12:29

African American Spiritual

do

Good   news!   Char - i - ot's   a - com - in',

Good   news!   Char - i - ot's   a - com - in',

Good   news!   Char - i - ot's   a - com - in',

And   I   don't want   it   to   leave   me   be - hind.

Practice with Pitches and Rhythms

This spiritual has a first, second, and third ending. The *D.C. al Fine* directs us to the beginning of the song and to the third ending, marked *Fine*.

Read and sing this *do-re-mi* song.

Roll de Ole Chariot Along

CD 12:32

African American Spiritual
Adapted by René Boyer-Alexander

Sing a Pentatonic Song

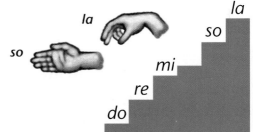

do re mi so la

Read the song using hand signs.

la
so
mi
re
do

I'm Going to Georgia

CD 12:35

North Carolina Folk Song

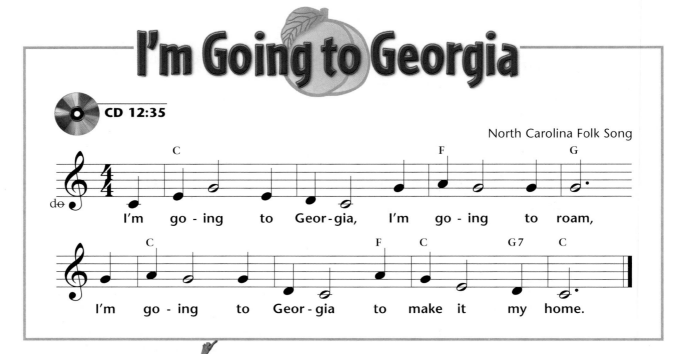

I'm go - ing to Geor - gia, I'm go - ing to roam,

I'm go - ing to Geor - gia to make it my home.

What is the main rhythm pattern in the song?

A dotted half note ♩. = a sound that lasts for three beats.

Identify the dotted half notes ♩. and sing the song again.

UNIT 1 READING

CONCEPT
MELODY
SKILLS
READ, SING

Sing Low *So* and Low *La*

What type of scale is used in the song?

Read and sing the song.

More Pentatonic Practice

Identify low *so* and low *la*. **Read** the song with pitch syllables.

Shoes of John

CD 13:4

Southern Highlands Folk Song

1. I am stand - ing in the shoes of John.
2. If they fit me, I will put them on.

I am stand - ing in the shoes of John.
If they fit me, I will put them on.

I am stand-ing, stand-ing, stand-ing, I am stand-ing, stand-ing, stand-ing,
If they fit me, fit me, fit me, If they fit me, fit me, fit me,

I am stand - ing in the shoes of John.
If they fit me, I will put them on.

Play or say this ostinato with the song.

Stand-ing in old shoes, worn out, leath - er shoes.

Improvise a rhythm ostinato for the song.

Sing Sixteenth Notes

In **2/4** meter, four sixteenth notes ♪♪♪♪ = one beat.

Read the song and identify the ? pitch at right.

?
ti
la
so
fa
mi
re
do

Salamanca Market

CD 13:7

Words and Music by Mary Goetze

I must go to Sal - a - man - ca Mar - ket,

Sal - a - man - ca Mar - ket in the morn - ing.

There's no place like Sal - a - man - ca Mar - ket,

Sal - a - man - ca Mar - ket all the day.

Read the rhythm, then listen for this pattern in the concerto.

LISTENING CD 13:12

Concerto Grosso, Opus 6, No. 11
by George Frideric Handel

High *Mi Re Do*

Identify high *mi re do* in this song.

Scraping Up Sand

CD 13:13

New England Folk Song

Create a pentatonic melody that includes high *mi re do*.

Play your melody on resonator bells to use as an introduction or as a B section for this song.

CONCEPT
RHYTHM
SKILLS
READ, SING

Sing in ¾ Meter

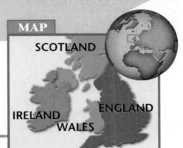

MAP
SCOTLAND
IRELAND   ENGLAND
WALES

Conduct in ¾.

Derry Ding Dong Dason

CD 13:19

English Canon

Der-ry ding dong da-son, I am John Ches-ton. We
weed-on, we wod-den, we weed-on, we wod-den, Bim-
bom, Bim-bom, Bim-bom, Bim-bom.

Lonesome Dove

CD 13:16

Tennessee Folk Song

1. Down in some lone - some, pin - ey grove,
2. I once, like you, I had a mate,

Down in some lone - some, pin - ey grove,
I once, like you, I had a mate,

My lit - tle dove, she sits and moans.
But now, like you, I'm des - o - late.

Sixteenth-Note Rhythms

A beat can be divided in the following ways:

Find these rhythms.

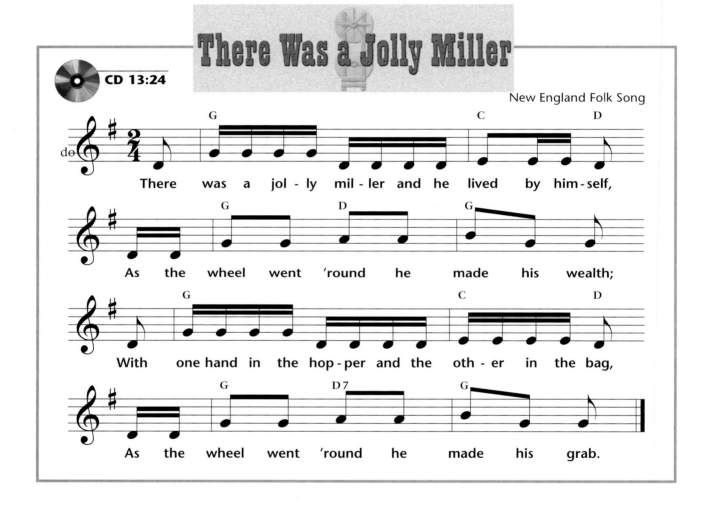

There Was a Jolly Miller

CD 13:24

New England Folk Song

There was a jol-ly mil-ler and he lived by him-self,

As the wheel went 'round he made his wealth;

With one hand in the hop-per and the oth-er in the bag,

As the wheel went 'round he made his grab.

More Practice with Sixteenth Notes

Sing this Southern folk song.

CD 13:27

Southern Folk Song

Sugar in the Gourd

1. Met her on the road, she danced on the board,
2. Had a lit - tle chick-en, she had a wood-en leg,
3. I_____ went_ down in the old clay_ field,

Played a lit - tle tune called "Sug - ar in the Gourd."
Best_ lit - tle chick-en that ev - er laid an egg.
Black - snake_ grabbed me by_ the_ heel.

Sug - ar in the gourd_ and I can't get it out,
Laid more eggs than an - y hen a - round the_ farm,
I_____ turned a - round_ just to do my_ best, And

Way to get the sug - ar out is roll the gourd a-bout.
Have to keep that chick - en and her eggs from an - y harm.
drove_ my_ head in - to a hor - net's_ nest.

Way to get the su - gar out, can't get it out.

Create your own rhythm ostinato using sixteenth-note patterns.

CONCEPT
MELODY
SKILLS
READ, SING

Sing with *Fa*

do re mi fa so la

fa

la
so
fa
mi
re
do

OH, HOW LOVELY IS THE EVENING

CD 13:31

English Round

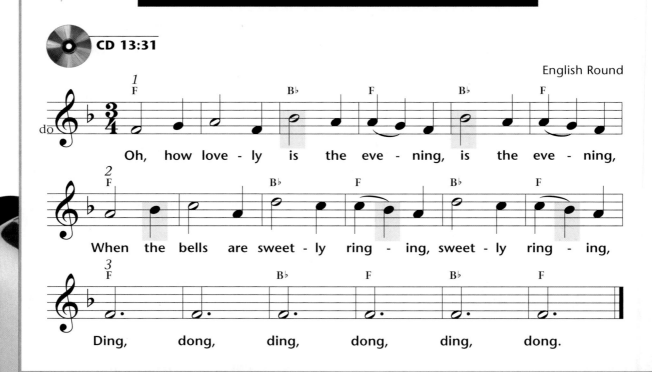

do

1 F   B♭   F   B♭   F

Oh, how love - ly is the eve - ning, is the eve - ning,

2 F   B♭   F   B♭   F

When the bells are sweet - ly ring - ing, sweet - ly ring - ing,

3 F   B♭   F   B♭   F

Ding, dong, ding, dong, ding, dong.

In $\frac{3}{4}$ meter, there are three beats per measure, with one quarter note getting the beat.

252

More Practice with *Fa*

Find *fa* in this song.

Old Jim John

American Folk Song

CD 13:34

Identify the sixteenth-note rhythm pattern in the song.

Find *fa* in this melody. Pat the rhythm, then read the melody with pitch syllables.

🔘 **LISTENING** CD 13:37

Cortège by Lili Boulanger

Cortège for violin and piano has *fa* and  rhythms. Lili Boulanger was the younger sister of Nadia Boulanger. Both were highly regarded composers.

Listen to Cortège and raise a hand when you hear the melody you read above.

Music Reading   **253**

CONCEPT
MELODY
SKILLS
READ, SING

Sing with *Ti*

do so la ti do' re' mi'

ti

Find *ti* in these songs.

Pauper sum ego

I Am Poor

CD 13:38

Latin Canon
English Words by Linda Worsley

Latin: Pau - per sum e - go.   Ni - hil ha - be - o.   Cor me - um da - bo.
Pronunciation: pɑu pɛr sum ɛ go   ni il ɑ bɛ o   kɔr mɛ um dɑ bo
English: Though I may be poor,   noth-ing can I give,   but my hum-ble heart.

Pick a Bale of Cotton

CD 13:42

African American Folk Song

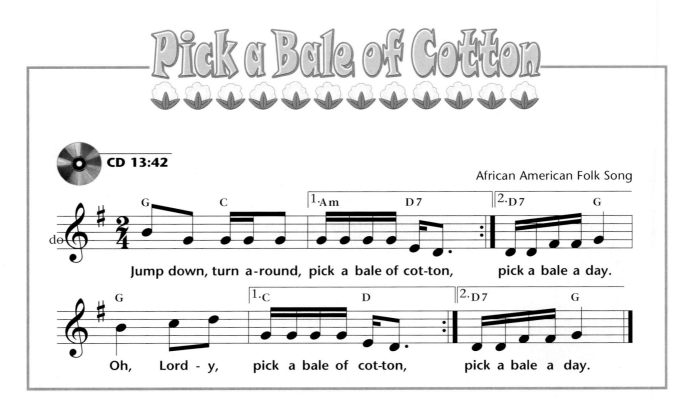

Jump down, turn a-round, pick a bale of cot-ton,   pick a bale a day.

Oh, Lord - y,   pick a bale of cot-ton,   pick a bale a day.

CONCEPT
MELODY, RHYTHM
SKILLS
READ, SING

Practice Pitches and Rhythms

Find *ti* in this song. Find the ♩♪ pattern.

Hotaru Koi

Come, Firefly

Japanese Folk Song
English Version by MMH

CD 13:45

Japanese: ほ　　ほ　　ほ　た　ろ　てい
Pronunciation: ho　　ho　　ho　ta　ɾu　koi
English: **Ho!　　Ho!　　Fire - fly, please come!**

あっ　ち　の　み　ず　は　に　が　い＿＿＿＿　ぞ
at　chi　no　mi　zu　wa　ni　ga　i＿＿＿＿　zo
You will find the wa - ter bad o - ver＿＿＿＿ there.

こっ　ち　の　み　ず　は　あ　ま　い　ぞ
kot　chi　no　mi　zu　wa　a　ma　i　zo
All of the wa - ter's good here, near to me!

ほ　　ほ　　ほ　た　ろ　てい
ho　　ho　　ho　ta　ɾu　koi
Ho!　　Ho!　　Fire - fly, please come!

や　ま　み　ち　てい　　あん　ど　の
ya　ma　mi　chi　koi　　an　do　no
On the moun - tain road, Come once a -

ひ　か　り　で　ま　た　て　い　てい
hi　ka　ɾi　de　ma　ta　ko　i　koi
gain and bring your ti - ny lan - tern light!

CONCEPT
TONALITY

SKILLS
READ, SING

Major Scale

A major scale is a succession of tones that ascend in the following order: whole step, whole step, half step, whole step, whole step, whole step, half step.

D E F♯ G A B C♯ D'

Sing the green phrase.
What do you notice about it?

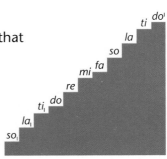

MAP

SWITZERLAND
ITALY
FRANCE
ALBANIA
GREECE

Canon

CD 14:1

Music by Luigi Cherubini
Traditional English Words

Do do so la mi fa so, Oh sing a song, You can sing it loud and long and you nev-er will go wrong, if you sing, *"La ti ti do."* The ga-mut you will run, and then your song is done. *Ti do so mi so do.*

Sing the song in canon.

CONCEPT
TONALITY
SKILLS
READ, LISTEN

Melodic Motion of a Major Scale

Read and hum this melody from *Madama Butterfly*.

LISTENING CD 14:6

Humming Chorus from *Madama Butterfly*
by Giacomo Puccini

Giacomo Puccini composed a portion of his famous opera *Madama Butterfly* to be sung without words. A chorus, accompanied softly by a muted orchestra, hums this background melody at the close of Act II.

Listen for the stepwise melodic motion in the "Humming Chorus."

Describe the mood created by the music.

Music Reading 257

Sing Dotted Rhythms

A dotted quarter note ♩. = ♩ + ♪

Clap these rhythm patterns.

Cape Cod Chantey

CD 14:7

New England Sea Chantey

Verse

Solo / Group

1. Cape Cod girls they have no combs,
2. Cape Cod boys they have no sleds,
3. Cape Cod men they have no sails,
4. Cape Cod wives they have no pins,

Heave a - way, heave a-way.

Solo / Group

They comb their hair with cod-fish bones,
They slide down-hill on cod-fish heads,
They sail their boats with cod-fish tails,
They pin their boats with cod-fish fins,

We are bound for Aus - tra - lia!

Refrain

All

Heave a-way my bul - ly, bul - ly boys, Heave a - way! Heave a - way!

Heave a-way and don't you make a noise, We are bound for Aus - tra - lia!

258

CONCEPT
TONALITY
SKILLS
READ, SING

Practice a Major Scale

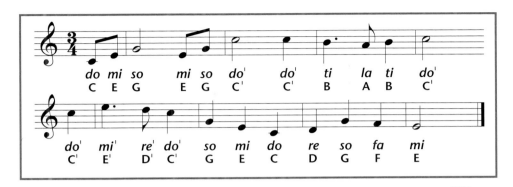

do mi so mi so do' do' ti la ti do'
C E G E G C' C' B A B C'

do' mi' re' do' so mi do re so fa mi
C' E' D' C' G E C D G F E

Wachet auf

Waken Now

MAP
DENMARK
NETHERLANDS
POLAND
GERMANY
BELGIUM
CZECH REPUBLIC
FRANCE
AUSTRIA
SWITZERLAND

CD 14:10

Words and Music by Johann Jakob Wachsmann
English Words by MMH

German: **Wach - et   auf,   Wach-et   auf   es   kräh - te   der   Hahn,**
Pronunciation: va xət ɑʊf va xət ɑʊf ɛs kʀe tə deʀ han
English: **Wak - en   now,   Wak-en   now,   proud   chan - ti - cleer   cries,**

die   Son - ne   be - tritt___ die   gol - de - ne   Bahn.
di zɔ nə bə tʀɪt di gɔl də nə ban
The   gold - en   sun   fol - lows   its   path through the   skies.

Sing and play the song on a keyboard.

Identify the ♩. ♪ rhythm in the song.

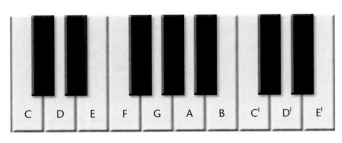

C D E F G A B C' D' E'

Syncopation

In syncopation, rhythmic stresses occur between beats or on a beat that is normally weak. The rhythmic emphasis of eighth-note pairs is changed when the second and third eighth notes are tied

Clap these syncopated rhythm patterns.

Which syncopated patterns do you find in the song?

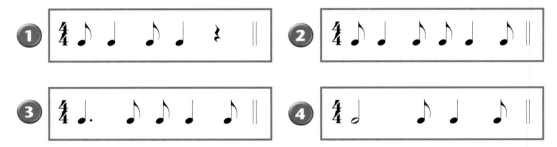

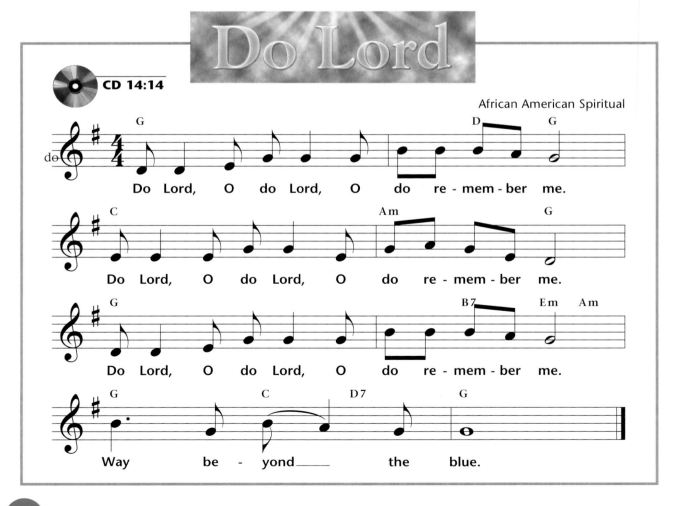

CD 14:14

African American Spiritual

Do Lord, O do Lord, O do re - mem - ber me.

Do Lord, O do Lord, O do re - mem - ber me.

Do Lord, O do Lord, O do re - mem - ber me.

Way be - yond___ the blue.

Another Dotted Rhythm

You've learned the ♩. ♪ rhythm. Syncopation occurs when the dotted rhythm pattern is reversed to ♪ ♩. This is another form of syncopation.

Charlotte Town

CD 14:17

American Folk Song

1. Char - lotte Town's burn - ing down,
2. Black them boots and make them shine,
(3.) old cow died and how I cried,

Good - bye, good-bye, The

Burn - ing down to the ground,
Black them boots and make them shine,
old cow died and how I cried,

Good-bye, Li - za Jane.

Ain't ya' might - y sor - ry?
Go - in' down to Cai - ro,
Oh, ___ how I loved her.

Good - bye, good - bye,

Ain't ya' might - y sor - ry?
Go - in' down to Cai - ro,
Oh, ___ how I loved her.

Good - bye, Li - za Jane.

1., 3. Fine | 2.
G | G

Jane. 3.The

Identify the other dotted rhythm pattern.

More Practice with Syncopation

Clap and sing the syncopated pattern created by the ties.

MAP
CENTRAL AFRICAN REPUBLIC
UGANDA
DEMOCRATIC REPUBLIC OF THE CONGO
KENYA
RWANDA
TANZANIA

Kakokolo

CD 14:20

Words and Music by Samite

Luganda: Ka - ko - ko - lo gwe ka - ko - ko - lo,_____
Pronunciation: ka ko ko lo gwe ka ko ko lo
English: *Ka - ko - ko - lo,* hey! *Ka - ko - ko - lo,*_____

ka - ko - ko - lo kwa - ta_en - ton - go - li yo._____
ka ko ko lo kwa tan ton go li yo
Ka - ko - ko - lo, oh,__ take up your gui - tar!_____

N - de - ter - a, maa - ma, n̯de - ter - a. Agen - da - no__ mu - lun - gi ta - la - ga.
n de te ɾa ma ma nde te ɾa agen da no mu lun gi ta la ga
Bring it to me, Ma - ma, play a song. Don't tell me__ you are go - ing a - way.

Refrain

Kyi maa - ma kyi nya - bo jang - u_e - no nga_o - yim - ba.
chi ma ma chi nya bo yang we no ngo yim ba
Hey, Ma - ma, pret - ty one, Come a - way, sing a song.

Repeat refrain last time only

Kyi maa - ma kyi nya - bo jang - u_e - no nga_o - yim - ba.
chi ma ma chi nya bo yang we no ngo yim ba
Hey, Ma - ma, pret - ty one, Come a - way, sing a song.

CONCEPT
RHYTHM

SKILLS
READ, LISTEN, ANALYZE

Rhythm Patterns You Know

Read and **sing** these patterns.

Pan - thers, pan - thers, pan - thers, pan - thers!

Bears and ti - gers!

 LISTENING CD 14:24

Panda Chant II by Meredith Monk

Meredith Monk is known for her use of innovative rhythms.

Listen to the music. Listen for the rhythms you just sang.

Meet the Musician

Meredith Monk (b. 1942) was born in Lima, Peru. She is a composer, singer, choreographer, and conductor. Among her many creations are films, mixed media, operas, and pieces for musical theater. Her unique approach combines vocal music with movement, objects, sound, and light. She created a vocal technique that treats the voice as an instrument. Meredith Monk has been widely honored for her creative achievement in music, dance, film, and musical theater. She is the recipient of a MacArthur "Genius" award, three Obie awards, and sixteen ASCAP awards.

$\frac{6}{8}$ Rhythms

There are two ways of counting $\frac{6}{8}$ meter. One way is to count the eighth note as the beat. The other way is to count the dotted quarter note as the beat.

Risseldy, Rosseldy

CD 14:25

Texas Folk Song

Verse

1. I mar-ried my wife in the month of June, Ris-sel-dy, ros-sel-dy,
2. She combed her hair but once a year, Ris-sel-dy, ros-sel-dy,
3. She kept her shoes on the pan-try shelf, Ris-sel-dy, ros-sel-dy,

Mow, mow mow.
I car-ried her off in a sil-ver spoon,
With ev-'ry rake she shed a tear,
If you want an-y-more you can sing it your-self,

Ris-sel-dy, ros-sel-dy, Mow, mow, mow.

Refrain

Ris-sel-dy, ros-sel-dy, hey bom-bas-sit-y, Nick-et-y, nack-et-y,

Ret-ric-al qual-i-ty, Wil-low-by, wal-lo-by, Mow, mow, mow.

Read this melody in $\frac{6}{8}$ meter.

 LISTENING CD 14:28

Barcarolle (Belle Nuit) from *Tales of Hoffman*
by Jacques Offenbach

Listen to "Barcarolle" and follow the listening map, raising a hand when you hear the melody you just read.

Listening Map for Barcarolle

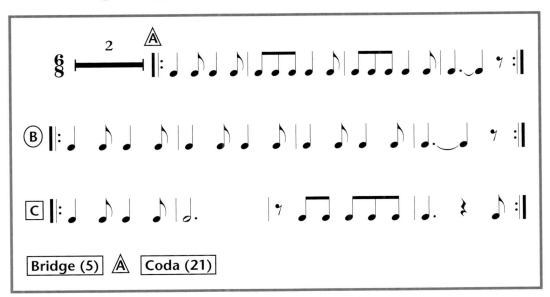

Sing a $\frac{6}{8}$ Song

A horse marine is someone who feels as out of place as a soldier riding a horse on the deck of a ship.

Look through this song.

In $\frac{6}{8}$ meter, a ♩. or ♫♪ get one beat. Find rhythm patterns that equal one beat in $\frac{6}{8}$ meter.

In $\frac{6}{8}$ meter, one beat can also have ♫♫♫ That's two sixteenth notes for every eighth note.

Sing the song.

CD 14:29

Traditional Dance Tune

Captain Jinks

Verse

1. I'm Cap - tain Jinks of the Horse Ma - rines, I feed my horse
2. I joined my corps when twen - ty one, Of course I thought
3. The first day I went out to drill, The bu - gle made
4. My tail - or's bills came in so fast, Forced me one day
5. Cap - tain Jinks came home last night, Pass your part -

on corn and beans, And of - ten live be - yond my means,
it cap - i - tal fun, When the en - e - my came, of course I run,
me feel quite ill, At the bal - ance step, my hat it fell,
to leave at last, And la - dies, too, no more did cast
ner by the right, Swing your neigh - bor so po - lite,

Though a cap - tain in the Ar - my. I teach young la - dies
For I'm not cut out for the Ar - my. When I left home, Ma -
And that would - n't do for the Ar - my. The of - fi - cers they
sheep's eyes at me in the Ar - my. My cred - i - tors at
For that's the style in the Ar - my. All join hands and

Play this ostinato with "Captain Jinks." Then, make up your own words to it and sing it with the Refrain.

how to dance, how to dance, how to dance, I teach young la - dies
ma, she cried, Ma-ma, she cried, Ma-ma, she cried, When I left home, Ma-
all did shout, all cried out, all cried out, The of - fi - cers they
me did shout, at me did shout, at me did shout, My cred - i - tors at
cir - cle left, cir - cle left, cir - cle left, All join hands and

how to dance, For I'm the star of the Ar - my.
ma, she cried, "He's not cut out for the Ar - my!"
all did shout, "Oh, that's the cure for the Ar - my!"
me did shout, "Why, kick him out of the Ar - my!"
cir - cle left, For that's the style of the Ar - my.

Refrain
I'm Cap - tain Jinks of the Horse Ma - rines,

I feed my horse on corn and beans, And of - ten live

be - yond the means of a Cap - tain in the Ar - my.

$\frac{6}{8}$ Music from Mexico

The Speckled Bird

MAP
UNITED STATES
MEXICO
GULF OF MEXICO
PACIFIC OCEAN
BELIZE
GUATEMALA
HONDURAS

CD 14:32

Mexican Folk Song
English Version by MMH

Spanish: Y es - ta - ba la pá - ja - ra pin - ta sen - ta - da en su
Pronunciation: yes ta βa la pa xa ɾa pin ta sen ta ðaen su
English: A bright speck - led bird__ was sit - ting up - on a green

ver - de li - món.__ Con el pi - co re - co - ge las flo - res,
βeɾ ðe li mon kon el pi ko ɾe ko xe las flo ɾes
lem - on branch.__ With her beak__ she gath - ered flow - ers,

Con el pi - co re - co - ge el a - mor. Ay, ay, ay, ay!__
kon el pi ko ɾe ko xel a moɾ ai ai ai ai
with her beak__ she gath - ered love, Ay, ay, ay, ay!__

¿En dón - de la en - cuen - tro yo?__ Con el pi - co re - co - ge las
en don de laen kwen tro yo kon el pi ko ɾe ko xe las
Then tell me where will it be?__ With her beak__ she gath - ered

flo - res, Con el pi - co re - co - ge el a - mor.__
flo ɾes kon el pi ko ɾe ko xel a moɾ
flow - ers, with her beak__ she gath - ered love.__

CONCEPT
RHYTHM

SKILLS
READ, SING

A Civil War Song in $\frac{6}{8}$

Pat the rhythm of the green pattern in the refrain.

CD 15:2

Civil War Marching Song

Verse

1. Sit - ting by the road - side on a sum - mer day,
2. Just be - fore the bat - tle the Gen - 'ral hears a row,___ He
3. Now our song has last - ed al - most long e - nough,___ The

Chat - ting with my mess - mates, pass - ing time a - way.
says, "The Yanks are com - ing, I hear their ri - fles now!"___ He
sub - ject's in - ter - est - ing, but rhymes are might - y rough.

Ly - ing in the shad - ow un - der - neath the trees,
turns a - round in won - der and what d'you think he sees?___ The
When the war is o - ver, then free from rags and fleas,___ We'll

Good - ness how de - li - cious! Eat - ing goo - ber peas!
Ten - nes - see Mi - li - tia eat - ing goo - ber peas!
kiss our wives and sweet - hearts and gob - ble goo - ber peas!

Refrain

Peas, peas, peas, peas, Eat - ing goo - ber peas!

Good - ness, how de - li - cious! Eat - ing goo - ber peas!

Minor Scales

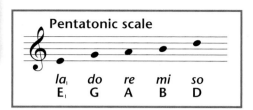

Pentatonic scale

la͵ do re mi so
E͵ G A B D

Minor scale

la͵ ti͵ do re mi fa so la
E͵ F#͵ G A B C D E

la
so
fa
mi
re
do
ti
la

Practice singing and playing these scales.

Read the pitches in this song. **Identify** the scale in which "I Got a Letter" is written.

I Got a Letter

CD 15:6

South Carolina Singing Game

Em
Solo   Group

do

1. I got a let-ter this morn-ing,
2. I wrote a let-ter this morn-ing,   Oh,   yes;
3. I mailed a let-ter this morn-ing,

Em
Solo   Group

I got a let-ter this morn-ing,
I wrote a let-ter this morn-ing,   Oh,   yes.
I mailed a let-ter this morn-ing,

A Spiritual in a Minor Key

Sing a major scale, then a minor scale. How does the tonality of this song support the mood of the words?

Sometimes I Feel Like a Motherless Child

CD 15:9

African American Spiritual

1. Some-times I feel like a moth-er-less child,
2. Some-times I feel like I'm al - most gone,

Some-times I feel like a moth-er-less child,
Some-times I feel like I'm al - most gone,

Some-times I feel like a moth-er-less child,
Some-times I feel like I'm al - most gone,

A long way from home, _____

A long way from home.

A Dance Song in Minor

Identify the scale of this song.

Tsing Chun U chü

Youth Dance Song

CD 15:13

Taiwanese Folk Song
Collected and Transcribed by Kathy B. Sorensen

Mandarin: 太 陽 下 山 明 朝 依 舊 爬 蹤 來
Pronunciation: tai yang sia shan ming jau yi jiu pa shang lai
English: **Though the sun has dis - ap - peared in - to the___west,**

花 兒 謝 了 明 年 還 是 一 樣 的 開 美 麗 小 鳥 一 去
hua ɹɛ siɛ liau ming niɛn hai shi yi yang di kai me li shiau niau yi tsu
Still the sun will rise a - gain each morn - ing at dawn. Though the flow - ers wilt and___

無 蹤 影 我 的 青 春 小 鸟 一 樣 不 回 來
wu ying jung wɔ di tsing chun shiau niau yi yang bu hue lai
die in___ fall, there will be new blos - soms when the spring comes___on.

我 的 青 春 小 鸟 一 樣 不 回 来 別 的 那 呀 哟
wɔ di tsing chun shiau niau yi yang bu hue lai biɛ di na ya yo
There will be new blos - soms when the spring comes___on. But the bird that flies___

別 的 那 呀 哟 我 的 青 春 小 鸟 一 樣 不 回 来
biɛ di na ya yo wɔ di tsing chun shiau niau yi yang bu hue lai
nev - er will re - turn. So it is when youth has flown a - way, it is gone.

CONCEPT
HARMONY
SKILLS
READ, SING

Sing F Major Chord Roots

What is the letter name of the flat in the key signature below?

Identify the roots of the I and V chords below.

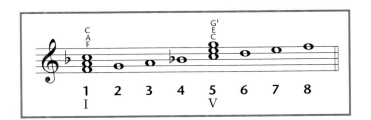

Find the chord markings in the song.

Identify the chord pattern in the song.

MAP

CHINA

RUSSIA

NORTH KOREA

SOUTH KOREA   JAPAN

Hae Wa Be

Sun and Rain

CD 15:17

Korean Children's Song
Collected and Transcribed by Kathy B. Sorensen

CONCEPT
RHYTHM

SKILLS
READ, SING

More Syncopated Patterns

Clap this rhythm.

Never Sleep Late Anymore

CD 15:23

American Folk Song

Identify any sharps or flats in the key signature.

Fun with Rhythms

Tying a note over to the next beat is a kind of syncopation that creates a jazzy feel.

Read these rhythms, practicing them first without the ties. Clap and say the rhythm with syllables of your choice.

Practice the rhythms with the ties added.

Every Mornin' When I Wake Up

CD 15:30

Words and Music by Avon Gillespie

Ev-e-ry morn-in' when I wake up I have a new song to sing, my chil-dren,

Ev-e-ry morn-in' when I wake up I have a new song to sing.

Improvise a syncopated ostinato using body percussion.

Use What You Know

"**M**erecumbé" is named for two dance rhythms of the Caribbean region; "mere" (from merengue) and "cumbe" (from cumbia).

Identify the syncopated rhythm figure in this song from Puerto Rico.

Sing or play a chord root accompaniment with the song.

MAP
UNITED STATES
MEXICO   CUBA
JAMAICA
HAITI
CENTRAL
AMERICA   PUERTO
RICO
DOMINICAN   SOUTH
REPUBLIC   AMERICA

Merecumbé

CD 15:26

Puerto Rican Children's Game Song
Arranged by Alejandro Jimenez
English Words by Linda Worsley

Spanish: El Juez le di-jo_al cu-ra. El cu-ra le di-jo_al juez.
Pronunciation: el xwes le ði xoal ku ɾa el ku ɾa le ði xoal xwes
English: The judge said to the pa-dre, The pa-dre said to the judge,

A dón-de_es-tá ese rit-mo, ca-ram-ba del me-re-cum-bé, ¡eh!
a ðon des ta ese ɾit mo ka ɾam ba ðel me ɾe kum be e
Where did we get this rhy-thm, *ca-ram-ba?* The *me-re-cum-bé,* eh!

Che qui mo-re-na, che qui. Che qui mo-re-na, ¡eh!
che ki mo ɾe na che ki che ki mo ɾe na e
Che qui mo-re-na, che qui! Che qui mo-re-na, eh!

A - dón-de es-tá ese rit-mo ca-ram-ba del me-re-cum-bé.
ɑ ðon des tɑ ese ɾit mo kɑ ɾɑm bɑ ðel me ɾe kum be
You can't re-sist the rhy-thm, *ca-ram-ba!* This *Me-re-cum-bé!*

Un pa-si-to pa-ra a'lan-te, un pa-si-to pa-ra a-trás,
un pɑ si to pɑ ɾɑ lɑn te un pɑ si to pɑ ɾɑ at tɾɑs
Take a step, a small step for-ward, Take a step, a small step back-ward,

dan-do que dan-do la me-dia vuel-ta, ¿quién se que-da-rá? ¡eh!
ðɑn ðo ke ðɑn do lɑ me ðyɑ βwel tɑ kyen se ke ðɑ ɾɑ e
Now turn a lit-tle, a half turn 'round, Now you know how it's done! eh!

I, IV, and V Chords

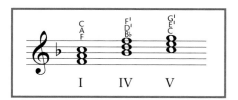

I   IV   V

Identify the chord roots for this song.

What is the key of the song?

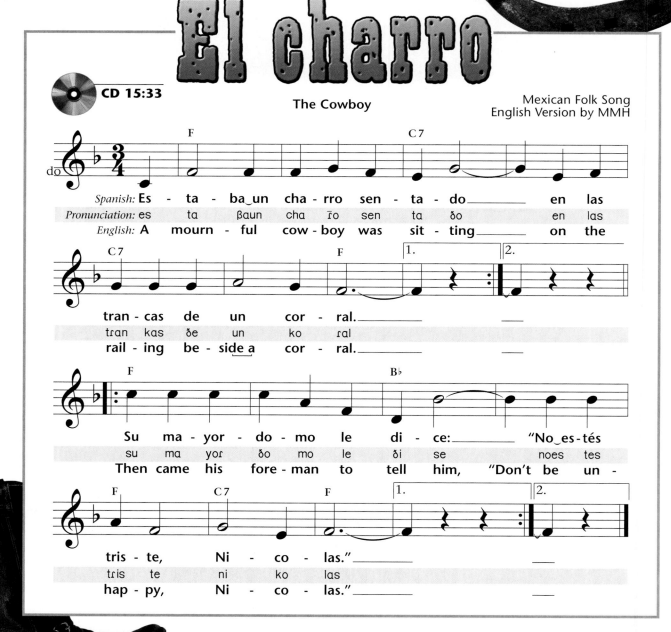

El charro

CD 15:33

The Cowboy

Mexican Folk Song
English Version by MMH

F   C7

Spanish: Es - ta - ba un cha - rro sen - ta - do _____ en las
Pronunciation: es ta βaun cha ɾo sen ta ðo en las
English: A mourn - ful cow - boy was sit - ting _____ on the

C7   F   1.   2.

tran - cas de un cor - ral. _____ ___
tɾan kas ðe un ko ɾal
rail - ing be - side a cor - ral. _____ ___

F   B♭

Su ma - yor - do - mo le di - ce: _____ "No es - tés
su ma yor ðo mo le ði se noes tes
Then came his fore - man to tell him, "Don't be un -

F   C7   F   1.   2.

tris - te, Ni - co - las." _____ ___
tɾis te ni ko las
hap - py, Ni - co - las." _____ ___

Sing or play a chord root accompaniment.

278

More Practice with Chords

Identify the I, IV, and V chords, then sing them with the song.

The refrain of this Liberian song is syncopated throughout.

Clap the rhythm of the refrain.

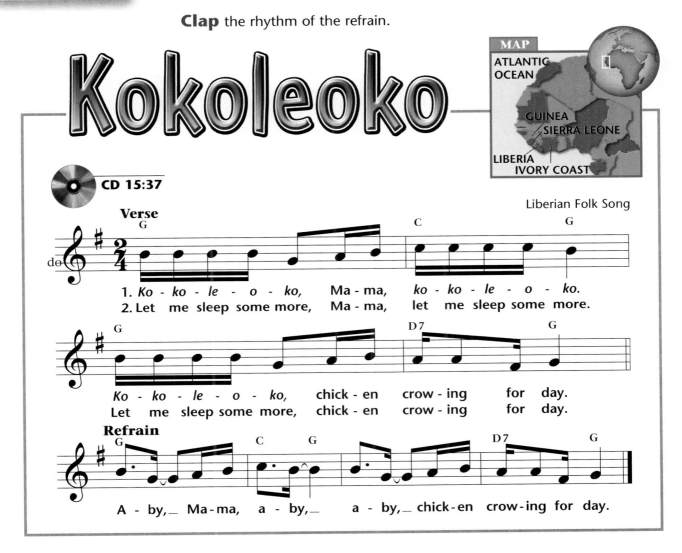

Play these parts with "Kokoleoko."

Chord Roots in a Minor Key

Identify the chord roots for the i and V chord in E minor.

MAP
POLAND
LITHUANIA
RUSSIA
BELARUS
UKRAINE

Bulbes

'Taters

Yiddish Folk Song
English Words by Jacob Sloan

CD 15:40

Sing a Minor Song

Sing this canon in a minor key.

Come and Sing Together

CD 16:1

Traditional Hungarian Melody

mp
Dm

If you'd dance then you must have boots of shin-ing leath-er,
Mon-ey in your pock-et-book, in your hat a feath-er.

Dm

But if you would sing with me, you don't need a

Dm *f*

cent, you see, So come and sing to-geth-er!

mf Dm *p*

If you'd dance then you must have boots of shin-ing leath-er!

More Practice with Minor Keys

Identify the name of the scale below.

Sing the song.

la₁ ti₁ do re mi fa so la
E₁ F#₁ G A B C D E

MAP
GERMANY
POLAND
CZECH REPUBLIC
SLOVAKIA
AUSTRIA

CD 16:5

Bohemian Folk Song

Wondering

1. Where are the clouds that were here last night?
2. How far a - way is the dis - tant sky?

Why does the moon give a sil - v'ry light?
How do we know which is you or I?

Who can tell? Who can say?

When will to - mor - row be yes - ter - day?
How man - y miles would be far a - way?

Sing or **play** a chord root accompaniment with the song.

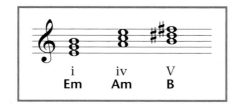

i   iv   V
Em   Am   B

282

Sing in $\frac{3}{2}$ Meter

Often songs that have three beats to a measure are in $\frac{3}{4}$ meter.

$\frac{3}{2}$ meter, like $\frac{3}{4}$ meter, has three beats per measure.

The difference is that in $\frac{3}{2}$ meter the half note ♩ gets the beat.

Wayfaring Stranger

CD 16:8

Southern Folk Hymn

I am a poor, way - far - ing stran - ger___
A-wand-'ring through this world of woe. But there's no sor - row,
toil, nor dan - ger___ in that bright land to which I go:
I'm go - ing there to see my Fa - ther,___ I'm go - ing there
no more to roam. I'm just a - go - ing o - ver Jor - dan,___
I'm on - ly go - ing o - ver home.

Two Mixolydian Songs

Sing these two songs based on the mixolydian scale.

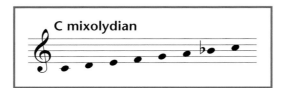

C mixolydian

Git Along, Little Dogies

CD 16:11

American Cowboy Song

Verse

1. As I was a - walk - ing one morn - ing for plea - sure,
2. Now ear - ly in spring-time we round up the do - gies,
3. It's whoop - ing and yell - ing and driv - ing the do - gies,

I spied a cow - punch - er a - rid - ing a - long.
We mark them and brand them and bob off their tails.
Oh, how I wish you_____ would go right a - long.

His hat was thrown back and his spurs were a - jing - lin',
We drive up our hors - es and load the chuck wag - on,
It's whoop - ing and punch - ing, git on, lit - tle do - gies,

And as he ap - proached he was sing - ing this song:
Then throw_____ the do - gies out on - to the trail.
You know that Wy - o - ming will be your new home.

Identify the mixolydian scale this song uses.

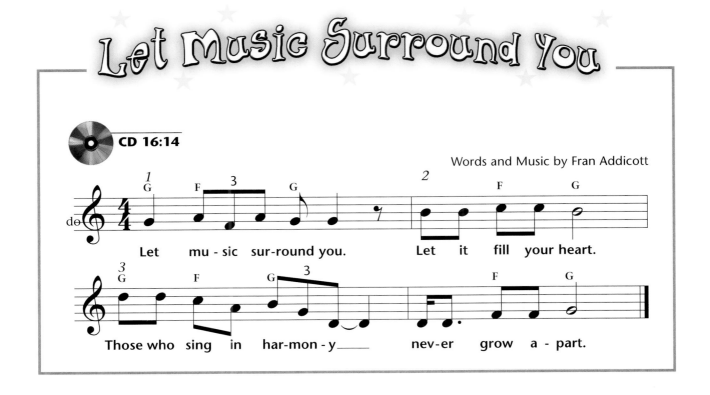

Words and Music by Fran Addicott

Let music surround you. Let it fill your heart.

Those who sing in har-mon-y____ nev-er grow a-part.

Another Tonal Center

Clap this pattern.

Identify the tonal center in this song.

Shady Grove

CD 16:17

Southern Appalachian Folk Song

Refrain

Shad - y Grove, my lit - tle love, Shad - y Grove, I know,

Shad - y Grove, my lit - tle love, Bound for Shad - y Grove.

Verse

1. Cheeks as red as the bloom - ing rose, Eyes of the deep - est brown,
2. Went to see my__ Shad - y Grove, She was stand - ing in the door,
3. Wish I had a__ big, fine horse, Corn__ to feed him on,
4. Shad - y Grove,__ my lit - tle love, Shad - y Grove, I say,

You are the dar - ling of my heart, Stay 'til the sun goes down.
Shoes_ and stock - ings in her hand, Lit - tle bare_ feet on the floor.
Pret - ty lit - tle girl,__ stay at home, Feed him_ when I'm gone.
Shad - y Grove,__ my lit - tle love, Don't wait 'til the Judg - ment Day!

CONCEPT
RHYTHM

SKILLS
READ, LISTEN

A Waltz in Five!

Practice these three patterns in $\frac{5}{4}$ meter.

 LISTENING CD 16:20

Five-Step Waltz by Edward Roland

Edward Roland (1803–1894) was an African American musician in the nineteenth century. He was one of the core members of the Philadelphia-based Francis Johnson band, which toured Europe, including England. While in England, it is said that they performed for Queen Victoria.

Listen for the rhythm patterns above in "Five-Step Waltz."

Tower of London

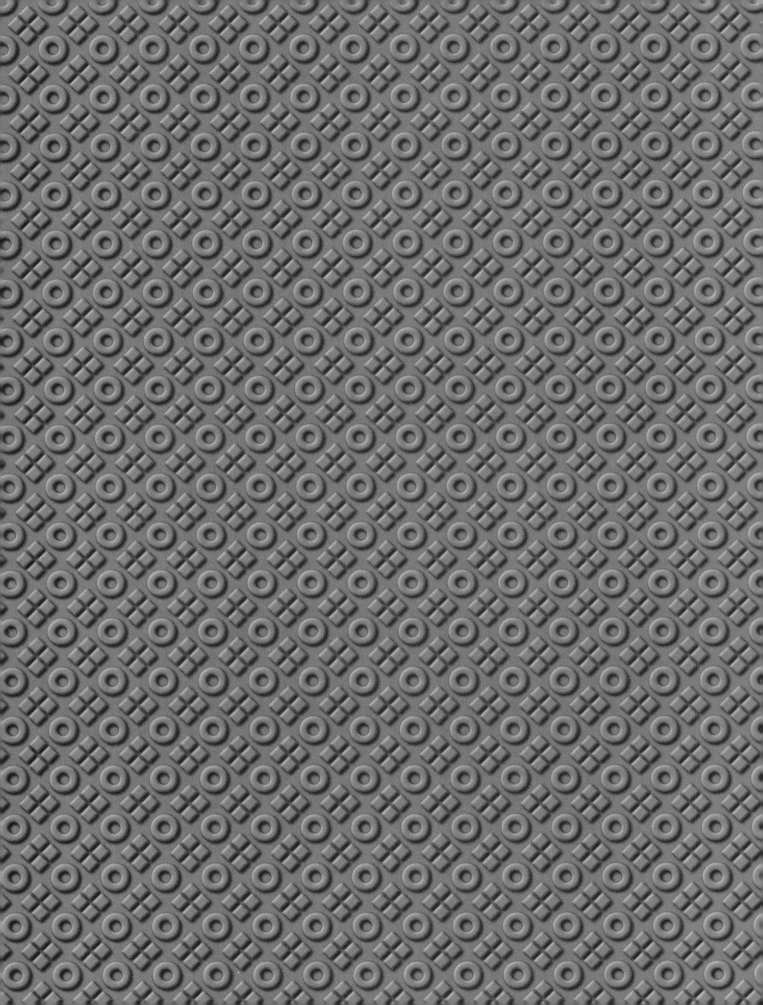

Spotlight on
Performance

Spotlight on Performance

Spotlight on Performance

Broadway For Kids

MTI's BROADWAY junior

ONCE ON THIS ISLAND JR.

Mini musicals specifically designed for classroom study and presentation, featuring scenes and songs from the musical Once On This Island Junior

Book and Lyrics by Lynn Ahrens

Music by Stephen Flaherty

Based upon the novel *My Love, My Love* **by Rosa Guy**

Musical Numbers

Waiting for Life

Mama Will Provide

Why We Tell the Story

ADMIT ONE 0596033

Once On This Island Junior,
Enrico Fermi Middle School,
Yonkers, NY

Libretto/Vocal Book

(In darkness, we hear the sounds of a violent storm. LIGHTS UP. A group of STORYTELLERS are huddled together around a fire. The storm frightens a LITTLE GIRL. The adults tell her a story in order to soothe her.)

STORYTELLER 1: *Once On This Island* is a mythical folktale set in the French Antilles.

STORYTELLER 2: It tells the story of Ti Moune, a little girl who was orphaned in a terrible storm.

STORYTELLER 3: Taking shelter in a tall tree, she was found by an old peasant couple, Mama Euralie and Tonton Julian.

STORYTELLER 4: While food and money were scarce, they took her in and raised her as their own.

STORYTELLER 1: And it wasn't long before Ti Moune grew from a small girl in a tree to a beautiful young woman.

STORYTELLER 2: A beautiful young woman with many dreams.

(STORYTELLERS now begin to work in the field.)

STORYTELLER 3: And one day, as Ti Moune worked in the fields with the other peasants, she saw the handsome Daniel Beauxhomme drive by in a beautiful car. Daniel was one of the wealthiest grand hommes, and Ti Moune had never seen anything ...

STORYTELLER 4: ... or anyone ...

STORYTELLER 1: ... so wonderful.

(TI MOUNE begins to sing as the PEASANTS gather around her.)

About the Script

CHARACTER NAMES are colored **RED**

DIALOGUE is colored **BLUE**

STAGE DIRECTIONS are colored *GREEN*

Waiting for Life

Music by Stephen Flaherty
Words by Lynn Ahrens

CD 16:21

A stran-ger in white in a car,_____ go-ing some-where,_____ go-ing_ far._____ How it must feel_ to go rac--ing wher-ev - er you please,

Storytellers
Oo la, oo la, oo la, oo la.

fly-ing as free_ as a bird_ with its tail_ in the breeze.

Oo la, oo la,

Girl 2
Ev - en the fish_ in the sea_ must be long - ing to

oo la, ooo.___

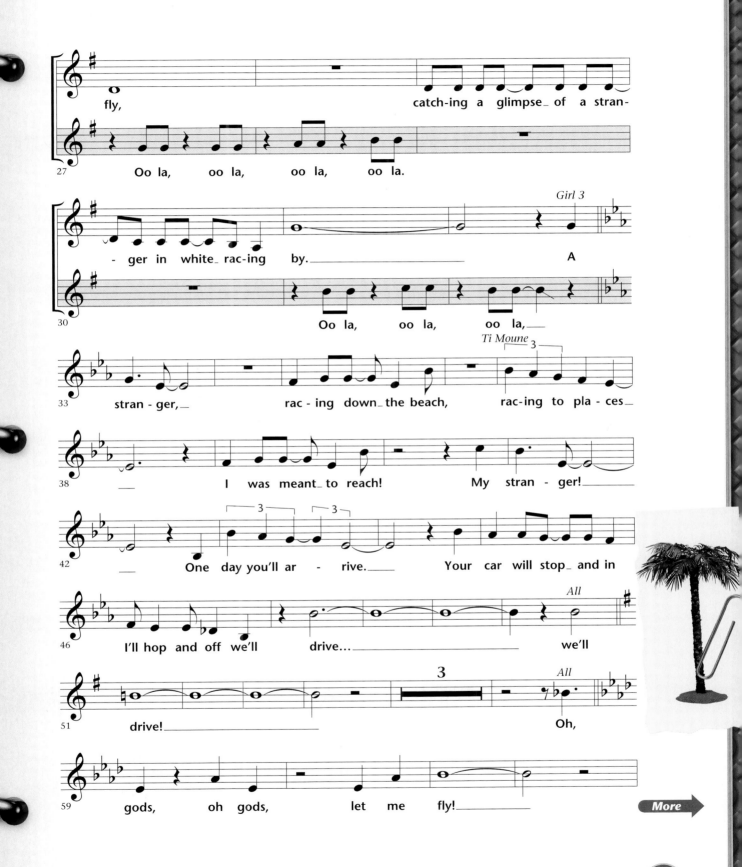

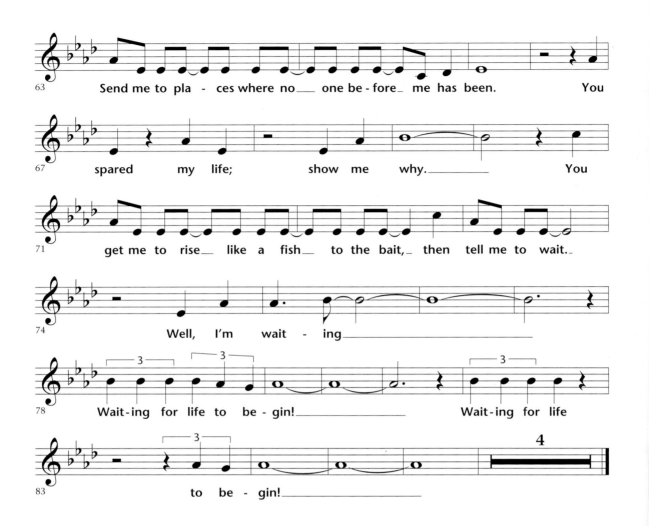

63 Send me to pla - ces where no___ one be - fore___ me has been. You

67 spared my life; show me why.___ You

71 get me to rise___ like a fish___ to the bait,___ then tell me to wait.___

74 Well, I'm wait - ing___

78 Wait - ing for life to be - gin!___ Wait - ing for life

83 to be - gin!___

Once On This Island Junior, Enrico Fermi Middle School, Yonkers, NY

Once On This Island Junior,
Enrico Fermi Middle School,
Yonkers, NY

STORYTELLER 1: The mythical rulers on the island heard her prayer, and laughed!

(ASAKA, AGWE, and PAPA GE burst into raucous laughter, looking down at the sleeping TI MOUNE. ERZULIE puts her arms around them.)

STORYTELLER 2: They argued which was more powerful, love or death.

STORYTELLER 1: They decided to create a terrible storm, resulting in a collision that would change two lives forever and test the powers of love.

STORYTELLER 2: Ti Moune discovered an unconscious Daniel lying in the road, his beautiful car smashed.

(We see TI MOUNE call for help.)

STORYTELLER 4: Ti Moune's long vigil began—

STORYTELLER 1: Until the Beauxhommes took Daniel back to their fine hotel, with its high iron gates, on the other side of the island.

(We see a recovering DANIEL being led off by a well-dressed BUTLER. They EXIT as TI MOUNE calls after them.)

STORYTELLER 3: Ti Moune begged her parents for permission to follow Daniel.

STORYTELLER 4: Knowing she could not be stopped, Tonton and Mama reluctantly gave their blessing.

STORYTELLER 3: So Ti Moune set off into the world, leaving behind the ones who loved her. And as she traveled, on every side was the terrible devastation of the storm.

Mama Will Provide

Music by Stephen Flaherty
Words by Lynn Ahrens

CD 16:22

Storyteller 1
But on this is - land, the

Storyteller 2
earth sings as soon as a storm ends. And as Ti

Moune set out, she real - ized she was walk-ing with old friends.

Storyteller 3
The birds...

Group 1
Coo coo, coo coo, coo coo coo

Group 3
Coo coo, coo coo, coo coo coo Sha sha sha - aah!

Storyteller 1
The trees...

Group 3
Sha sha sha sha - aah!

Group 4
Bum bum bum!

Storyteller 2
The frogs...

Group 4
Bah - um, bum, bum

Storyteller 3
And the bree - zes...

Group 2
Ooh Ooh

296

More

all a - lone in a world that may seem too wide.

But sit on Ma-ma's lap and I will draw a map

Girls

and what - ev - er you need, Ma - ma will pro - vide!

Asaka   *Group 1, 2*   *Group 3, 4*

I'll pro - vide you: Moss!   To soft - en the road!

Group 1, 2   *Group 3, 4*   *Group 1, 2*   *Group 3, 4*

Rocks!   To sit on!   Trees!   To sleep un - der - neath!

Group 1, 2 Group 3, 4   *Group 1, 2*   *Group 3, 4*

Sand!   Fun for your toes!   Plan - tain!   To fill up your bel - ly!

Group 1, 2   *Group 3, 4*   *Group 1, 2*   *Group 3, 4*

Breeze!   To fan your face!   Grass!   For mak -

Group 1, 2   *All*

- ing your bed!   Mos - quit - os?!   Ha!!

Asaka/All

Bugs will bite, lit - tle girl, and the night will fall.

More

299

All a-lone in the dark, you'll be ter - ri - fied.

But you will make it through, 'cause I am lik - ing you!

And what - ev-er you need, Ma - ma will...

Pro - vide!!!

STORYTELLER 1: At last Ti Moune arrived at the gates of the Hotel Beauxhomme, and went off in search of her Daniel.

(She spies DANIEL and runs to embrace him.)

STORYTELLER 2: But she found that while Daniel loved her ...

(DANIEL gently breaks the embrace, and presents a beautiful, well-dressed woman to TI MOUNE.)

STORYTELLER 3: ... her journey would not end as she had hoped.

DANIEL: Andrea and I have been promised to each other since we were children. Our parents are old friends.

TI MOUNE: But, Daniel!

DANIEL: This is how things are done, Ti Moune. It's expected.

TI MOUNE: Daniel, please.

DANIEL: Ti Moune, I thought you understood. We could never marry.

(TI MOUNE falls to the floor and weeps.)

STORYTELLER 4: And Papa Ge appeared to Ti Moune, and gave her the chance to trade Daniel's life for her own. She could say the word, Daniel would die, and life would go on as if she had never loved at all.

(PAPA GE stands over TI MOUNE, who sadly shakes her head "no" and turns away, crying even harder.)

ERZULIE: But even in the face of rejection, Ti Moune could not betray her love.

(PAPA GE looks over to the others, who join him and surround TI MOUNE.)

AGWE: And we began to cry tears of compassion for the orphan Ti Moune, who proved that love could withstand the storm and cross the earth.

PAPA GE: And survive, even in the face of death.

Once On This Island Junior,
Enrico Fermi Middle School,
Yonkers, NY

(The gods lift her up, spread her arms wide, and adorn her with beautiful leaves and branches.)

ASAKA: And then we blessed her, and transformed her into ...

ALL EXCEPT TI MOUNE: ... a tree!

STORYTELLER 1: A tree that sprang up and cracked the walls of the Hotel Beauxhomme, so that its gates could never close again.

STORYTELLER 2: A tree that lived forever, sheltering peasants and grand hommes alike.

STORYTELLER 3: A tree that watched over Daniel for his lifetime.

STORYTELLER 4: A tree in which his children played.

(Song introduction begins.)

ERZULIE: And one day, as Daniel's young son sat in the shade of the tree, he noticed a beautiful young peasant girl high in its branches looking out at the world. And the spirit of Ti Moune touched their hearts and set them free to love.

(The PEASANT GIRL climbs out of the tree.)

Once On This Island Junior, Enrico Fermi Middle School, Yonkers, NY

Why We Tell the Story

CD 16:23

Music by Stephen Flaherty
Words by Lynn Ahrens

Group 1

Group 2
Ooh, _____ ooh-way ___ ooh. ___

Ooh, _____ ooh-way ___

Ti Moune
___ ooh. _____ And she stands a-gainst ___ the light-

Daniel
- ning and ___ the thun - der, ___ And she shel-ters and ___ pro-tects

Group 1

Group 2
___ us from ___ a - bove, and she fills us with ___ the pow-

- er and ___ the won - der ___ of ___ her love. _____

And this ___ is why we tell the sto - ry,

why ___ we tell the sto - ry. _____ Why

we tell the sto - ry, why ___ we tell the sto - ry.

More

303

Group 1

So I hope that you will tell this tale to-mor-row.

Group 2

It will help your heart re-mem-ber and re-live.

It will help you feel the an-ger and the

Ti Moune

p

All

sor - row.... And for - give. For

out of what we live and we be - lieve.

Our lives be - come the sto-ries that we

slower

2

3

weave. Why we tell the

3

rit. e dim.

3

sto - ry... Why we tell the sto - ry.

Meet the Musicians

Lynn Ahrens and Stephen Flaherty

Besides *Once On This Island*, Lynn Ahrens and Stephen Flaherty cowrote the score to the Broadway smash hit, *Ragtime*. *Ragtime* won four 1998 Tony Awards, including Best Score and Best Musical. The two composers have been working together for many years and have written several Broadway musicals, including *Lucky Stiff, My Favorite Year,* and *Seussical.*

Ahrens and Flaherty also wrote the score for the animated film *Anastasia* in 1997. Ms. Ahrens is well known for the songs she wrote for the television series *Schoolhouse Rock!* Mr. Flaherty is a graduate of the Cincinnati College Conservatory of Music.

The Spirit of Broadway

Thousands of young singers, dancers, and actors dream of going from middle and high school productions to performing on Broadway. After they graduate, many come to New York City full of anticipation and hope. They often have only a few dollars in their pockets and the feeling of "That Great Come and Get It Day."

VOICE BUILDER: Project!

When you sing an exciting, up-tempo song like "That Great Come and Get It Day," your body language communicates the meaning of the song as well as your voice. As you sing, stand tall and project energy and confidence, as if you were standing on a Broadway stage. Project your instrument—your voice—and your facial expressions to the very back row of the balcony.

That Great Come and Get It Day

CD 17:1

from the musical *Finian's Rainbow*

Music by Burton Lane
Words by E.Y. Harburg

On that great come and get it day, won't it be fun when wor-ry is done and mon-ey is hay?

CONCEPT
RHYTHM

SKILLS
SING

Before Frank Loesser composed one of the most famous Broadway shows ever, *Guys and Dolls*, he composed the smash hit *Where's Charley?* It included this song with the very, very, very long title!

SKILL BUILDER: Steady Beat

Since this song is a march, **practice** maintaining a steady beat by marching in place as you sing the exercise below. Stay in exact step with your fellow singers and marchers.

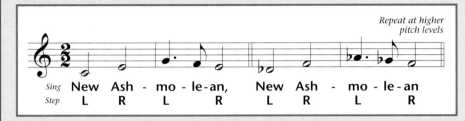

Repeat at higher pitch levels

Sing	New	Ash - mo - le - an,	New	Ash - mo - le - an
Step	L	R L R	L	R L R

The New Ashmolean Marching Society and Students Conservatory Band

from the musical *Where's Charley?*

CD 17:5

Words and Music by Frank Loesser

1. Here they come with the sun-light on the
2. Though they march on-ly slight-ly out of

trum-pets.   Here they come with the ban-ners fly-ing high.
tem-po,   though they play just a tri-fle out of tune,

In my throat I've a lump-y sort of feel-ing
though there's just a sug-ges-tion in the o-boe

and the bright gleam of pride is in my eye.
of the sound of a hound be-neath the moon;

Here they come with the clar - i - nets a - wail - ing.
though the trom - bone's a lit - tle in - de - pen - dent

Here they come rath - er brave - ly up the square.
and the drum - mer is not ex - act - ly choice,

And I know in a mo - ment I'll be cheer - ing
still the old col - lege spir - it is up - on me,

and my fine Sun - day hat will be high in the
and I shout ev' - ry time at the top of my

air for The New Ash - mo - le - an March - ing So -
voice for The New Ash - mo - le - an March - ing So -

ci - e - ty and Stu - dents Con - serv - a - to - ry Band.
ci - e - ty and Stu - dents Con - serv - a - to - ry Band.

1.   2   2.

Yes, The New Ash -

mo - le - an March - ing So - ci - e - ty and

Stu - dents Con - serv - a - to - ry Band.

CONCEPT
MELODY
SKILLS
SING

Broadway musicals often bring classic stories and imaginary legends to life. The legend of King Arthur and Camelot is just the kind of tale that can become real on a Broadway stage!

VOICE BUILDER: Melodic Leaps

Practice singing melodic leaps with this exercise.

Sing on pitch syllables first, then add the text using crisp diction.

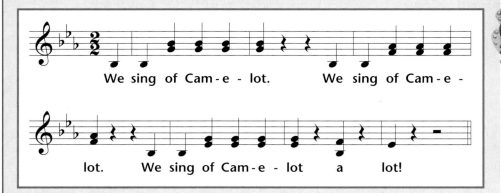

We sing of Cam-e-lot. We sing of Cam-e-lot. We sing of Cam-e-lot a lot!

CAMELOT

from the musical *Camelot*

CD 17:8

Music by Frederick Loewe
Words by Alan Jay Lerner

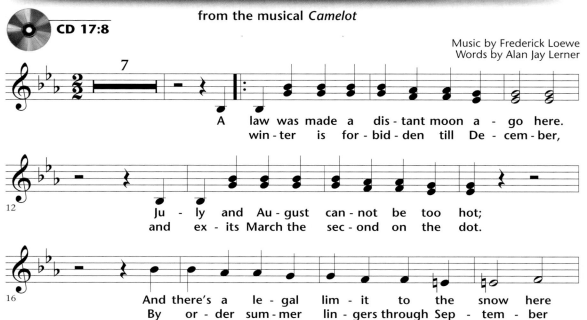

A law was made a dis-tant moon a-go here.
win-ter is for-bid-den till De-cem-ber,

Ju-ly and Au-gust can-not be too hot;
and ex-its March the sec-ond on the dot.

And there's a le-gal lim-it to the snow here
By or-der sum-mer lin-gers through Sep-tem-ber

in Cam - e - lot. The

in Cam-e-lot. Cam-e-lot!

Cam-e-lot! I know it sounds a bit bi - zarre,

But in Cam-e-lot, Cam-e-lot,

that's how con-di-tions are. The

poco rit.

rain may nev - er fall till af - ter sun - down. By

eight the morn-ing fog must dis-ap-pear. In

short, there's sim - ply not a more con - gen - ial

spot for hap-p'ly - ev - er - aft - er - ing than here

a tempo

in Cam - e - lot!

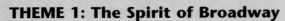

THEME 1: The Spirit of Broadway

CONCEPT
HARMONY
SKILLS
SING: POSTURE

Set in the 1800s during the Gold Rush, the musical *Paint Your Wagon* tells the story of people flocking to California with visions of gold. Even when the riches didn't pan out and all seemed lost, they kept right on singing. Their American spirit lived on.

VOICE BUILDER: Sitting and Singing

Good posture and proper breathing are crucial to excellent vocal sound and intonation. This is true whether you stand or sit while singing. When sitting and singing:

- Sit with a relaxed, but firm, body position.
- Sit forward on your chair with your back straight and feet flat on the floor.
- Hold your chest high and keep your shoulders relaxed and down.

They Call the Wind Maria

from the musical *Paint Your Wagon*

CD 17:12

Music by Frederick Loewe
Words by Alan Jay Lerner

A - way out here they got a name for
fore I knew Ma - ri - a's name and

wind and rain and fi - re.
heard her wail and whin - in',

The rain is Tess, the
I had a girl, and

With their real-life excitement, stories from history often make wonderful Broadway shows. In 1997, composer Maury Yeston helped bring the tragic story of the *Titanic* to Broadway with great lyrics and a beautiful musical score.

Doing the Latest Rag

from the musical *Titanic*

CD 17:16

Words and Music by Maury Yeston

Ev'-ry-one up__ and out,
Young Mis-ter Hart - ley is

fol - low the band__ and shout, "Is - n't it a love - ly day!" Yes!
play-ing quite smart - ly in rhy-thm that could nev - er

Watch-ing all the la - dies in Pa - ri - sian fash-ion on dis - play.

lag! It's a mu - si - cal treat__ to hear a

band with a beat__ per-form-ing their lat - est rag! Come on and

CONCEPT
HARMONY
SKILLS
SING, READ

Giuseppe Verdi's opera *Aida* has appeared on countless stages around the world since it debuted in 1871. In 2000, Tim Rice and Elton John created a modern adaptation of this great work. With its modern rock arrangements, the show was soon the toast of Broadway.

SKILL BUILDER: Consonance and Dissonance

Harmony, two or more notes sounding at the same time, can either be **consonant** or **dissonant**. Pitches sounded in consonant harmony are found together in a major or minor chord (*do-mi-so* or *la-do-mi*). Pitches sounded in dissonant harmony are not found together in a major or minor chord. Examples of dissonant intervals are *do-re* or *fa-ti*.

Sing these two patterns found in "Fortune Favors the Brave." **Read** the second measure of each example. Which interval is consonant and which one is dissonant?

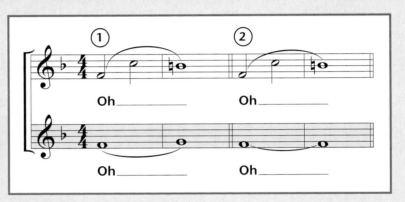

FORTUNE FAVORS THE BRAVE

from the musical *Aida*

CD 17:20

Music by Elton John
Lyrics by Tim Rice

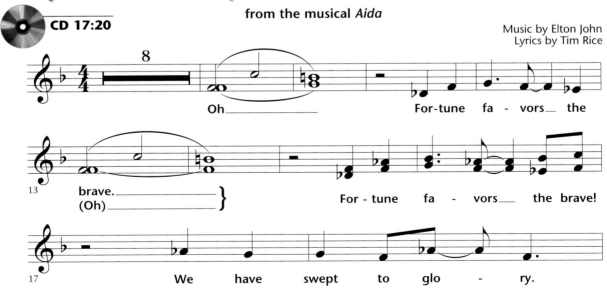

Adventures at Sea

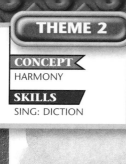

Crashing waves, pounding storms, salty air, enormous whales, ruthless pirates, wide-open waters—the ocean has many opportunities for adventure. The four songs in this theme tell exciting tales of the high seas that will definitely have you dreaming of the life of a sailor.

VOICE BUILDER: Diction

Sing *ta* and *teh* first and then sing the words below. Pronounce the *k* of "mark" and the *t* of "what" with crisp and precise diction.

ta	teh	ta	ta	ta	teh
Mark	well	what	I	do	say.

 LISTENING CD 17:24

Whup! Jamboree English Sea Chantey

Listen to the men of the Robert Shaw Chorale perform "Whup! Jamboree," an exciting sea chantey from England. Though the singers perform with lots of energy and heartiness, you can hear their careful phrasing and vowel production through the entire piece.

Robert Shaw

During their long, lonely days at sea, sailors often passed the time by singing songs called "sea chanteys." These songs helped sailors get through grueling, backbreaking tasks such as raising sails and swabbing the deck. Life on board the ship was not easy, but songs like "A-Rovin'" made it seem better for a little while.

A-Rovin'

CD 17:25

Sea Chantey
Adapted and Arranged by Emily Crocker

With energy

mf

1. In Am - ster - dam there lived a maid, mark well what I do
2. He took this fair maid for a walk, mark well what I do

mf

1. In Am - ster - dam there lived a maid, mark well what
2. He took this fair maid for a walk, mark well what

say.   In Am - ster - dam there lived a maid, and for her smiles a
say.   He took this fair maid for a walk, and they had such a

I do say. In Am - ster - dam there lived a maid.   And
I do say. He took this fair maid for a walk,

sai - lor stayed.   I'll rove no more with you, fair
love - ly talk.

I will go no more a - rov - in' with you, my fair

More

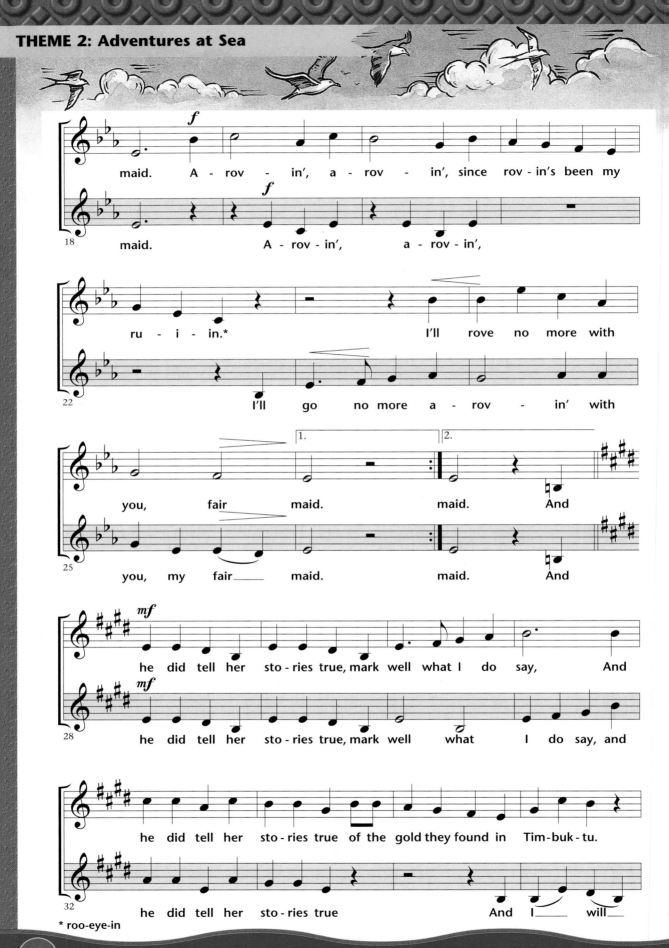

maid. A - rov - in', a - rov - in', since rov - in's been my

18 maid. A - rov - in', a - rov - in',

ru - i - in.* I'll rove no more with

22 I'll go no more a - rov - in' with

1. 2.
you, fair maid. maid. And

25 you, my fair maid. maid. And

he did tell her sto - ries true, mark well what I do say, And

28 he did tell her sto - ries true, mark well what I do say, and

he did tell her sto - ries true of the gold they found in Tim - buk - tu.

32 he did tell her sto - ries true And I will

* roo-eye-in

320

More

Music can build the mood of a story like nothing else. And when it comes to spooky stories, music can turn them into truly frightening experiences.

VOICE BUILDER: Dynamics

To practice dynamics, hold your hands out with your palms facing one another. As you sing, move your hands apart and together according to the numbers and directions below.

① Palms about 1 inch apart (*piano*)

② Palms about 1 foot apart (*mezzoforte*)

③ Palms about 2 feet apart (*forte*)

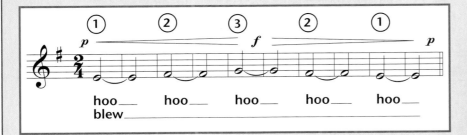

THE GHOST SHIP

🔘 **CD 17:29**

Words and Music by
Don Besig and Nancy Price

1. Now   lis - ten   well   as   a   tale   I   tell   of   a
(2.)   then   I   spied off the   star - board   side   a____

night   I   shook   with   fear.____   We were   sail - ing   west   on   the   o - pen
strange,   mys - ter - ious   sight.____   I____   froze   with   fear   as   it   drift - ed   **More**

21 sea, head-in' home from a long, long year._____ I was stand-ing
near like a ghost in the dark__ of night._____ I could see a

27 watch all a-lone that night when I heard a wail-ing cry._____
sail on a bro-ken mast and de-sert-ed decks be-low._____

33 ___ As I strained to see what the sound could be, some-thing
___ From__ all a-round came a mourn-ful sound, but I

38 flashed and caught__ my eye._____ And the cold wind
saw not a liv-ing soul!_____ } And the cold wind

f   *p*

44 blew,_____

1.   *mf*

54 ___ and the cold wind blew._____ 2. 'Twas

2.   *mf*   *f*

And the cold wind blew._____ Well,

mp

60 ___ and the cold wind blew._____

CONCEPT
HARMONY

SKILLS
SING

Just like stories or poems, song lyrics often use metaphors to strengthen their message. At first, the words to "Ride on the Wind" seem like a simple tale about a young sailor. If you look for metaphors in the lyrics, you might discover different meanings.

VOICE BUILDER: Singing in Tune

Practice singing in tune with this exercise based on the C major scale. **Sing** first on pitch syllables and then on the vowels *oo* or *ah*. **Listen** carefully to those around you so that the final C major chord is in tune.

Part 1

do re mi fa so la ti do¹

Part 2

do re mi fa so la ti do¹ ti la_____ so

Part 3

do re mi fa so la ti do¹ ti la so fa_____ mi

Ride on the Wind

CD 17:33

Words and Music by Mark Patterson

Moderately flowing

All - Unison
mp

Ride on the wind,__ young sail - or, ride on the wind__ of your dreams._

cresc.

As you find your way__ on the o - pen sea__ let your heart set the course,__ set your

14 spir-it free_ as you ride on the wind,_ the wind of your dreams.

mf
19 Ride on the wind,_young sail-or, ride up-on_ your_ dreams.

24 Find your way_ on the o-pen sea,_then set the course,_set your spir-it free._

28 Ride on the wind,_ ride on the wind, the wind of your dreams.

f
32 When you find the clear, blue wa-ters of the o-pen sea,

cresc.
36 Let your sail un-furl and you can go an-y place that you

,mf
dream. Ride on the wind,_____ ride on the wind,_____

mf
39 dream. Ride on the wind,_ ride on the wind._ **More**

CONCEPT
MELODY

SKILLS
SING

In the 1600s and 1700s, any mention of the Barbary Coast would strike fear in the hearts of people on the shores of Europe. Pirates based on the Barbary Coast along northern Africa were known for being both fearless and evil. As you sing "The Coasts of High Barbary," imagine your boat is slipping along the coast hoping to avoid the dreaded Barbary pirates!

VOICE BUILDER: Hold That Syllable!

Sometimes you have to sing a single word or syllable on several notes. This happens in "The Coasts of High Barbary" on the word "High-o." As you sing the *oh* vowel, repeat the *oh* sound on each separate note. This technique is called "repeating the vowel." It will help your lips stay rounded while you keep vertical space inside your mouth to produce a good vocal sound.

Sing twice and then repeat at the next higher pitch.

High - o!

The Coasts of High Barbary

CD 18:1

Sea Song
Arranged by Jeanne Julseth-Heinrich

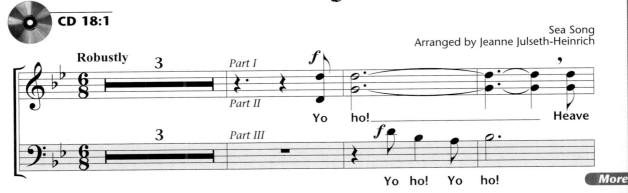

More

blow____ ye winds____ High - O!_____ High -

blow____ ye winds____ High - O!_____ High -

O!_____ Heave ho! Heave ho! Heave

O!_____ For broad - side, for broad - side they

ho! Heave ho! Blow high,

fought all on the main! Blow high!_____ Blow

blow low, and so____ sail - ed we! Un -

low,_____ and so____ sail - ed we! Un -

CONCEPT
MELODY

SKILLS
SING: VOCAL BLENDING

Festival of Voices

Whether you sing in the shower, on the way to school, in your bedroom, or with your headphones on, singing always feels good. When you join your voice together with others in a choir, you can take this feeling to a whole new level. Celebrate the power of vocal music as you learn and sing the following five uplifting songs.

VOICE BUILDER: Blending Your Voice

Vowels are the basis for a good choral tone. Always sing vowels with a relaxed jaw, vertical mouth shape, and space inside the mouth. This helps produce a full and free sound that blends well with other voices.

Sing the exercise below and work to achieve the full and free sound that results from blended voices and pure vowels.

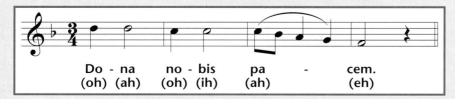

Do - na   no - bis   pa - cem.
(oh) (ah)   (oh) (ih)   (ah)   (eh)

Dona Nobis Pacem

CD 18:6

Latin Hymn

Latin: Do - na no - bis pa - cem, pa - cem.
Pronunciation: dɔ na nɔ bis pɑ chɛm pɑ chɛm

Do - na___ no - bis pa - cem.

Do - na no - bis pa - cem.

Do - na no - bis pa - cem.

Do - na no - bis___ pa - cem.

Do - na no - bis pa - cem.

CONCEPT
HARMONY
SKILLS
SING

"**A**ll Ye Who Music Love" is a **madrigal** written by Baldassare Donato, an Italian composer who lived in the 1500s. Madrigals were the love songs of their time. Composers of madrigals often used famous poetry for the song lyrics. Imagine a Shakespeare poem set to rock and roll!

VOICE BUILDER: Melismas

Music from the Renaissance era often features **melismas**, or groups of notes sung on a single word or syllable. As you sing the exercise below, concentrate on sustaining a continuous flow of air.

Sing first on the syllable *ta*. Then connect the slurred notes on the eighth notes. Finally, sing on the text. Apply what you have learned when you sing "All Ye Who Music Love."

Repeat at higher pitch levels

ta   ta ta   ta ta   ta   ta   ta
ta   ta___   ta___   ta   ta   ta
All   ye___   who___ mu - sic   love.

All Ye Who Music Love

CD 18:7

Words by Thomas Oliphant
Music by Baldassare Donato

Allegro   *mf*

1. All   ye who mu - sic,   All
2. Come, lads and lass - es,   Come,

mf

1. All   ye who mu - sic,   All
2. Come, lads and lass - es,   Come,

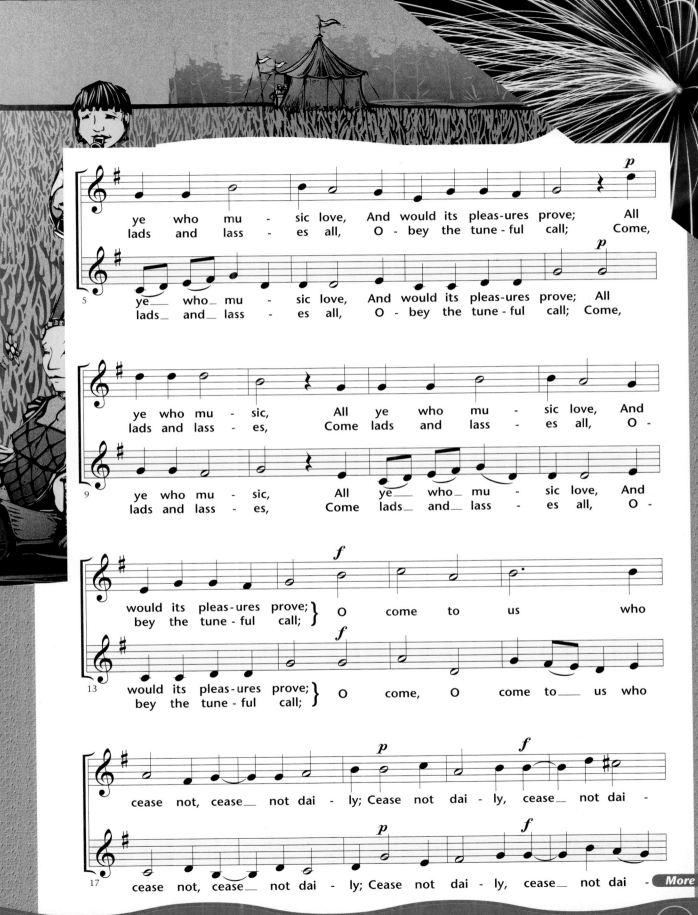

CONCEPT
HARMONY

SKILLS
SING

"N'kosi sikelel' iAfrika" was written in 1897 by a South African composer named Enoch Mankayi Sontonga. For many years, this song was a symbol of the movement for racial equality in South Africa. It represented so much that it was adopted as the national anthem there.

SKILL BUILDER: Harmony

Sing these three-part chords to practice the harmony in this song.

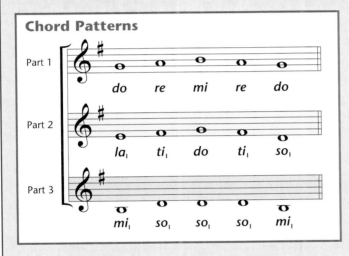

Chord Patterns

Part 1: do re mi re do

Part 2: la, ti, do ti, so,

Part 3: mi, so, so, so, mi,

MAP
NAMIBIA
BOTSWANA
SWAZILAND
SOUTH AFRICA LESOTHO

N'kosi sikelel' iAfrika

Lord Bless Africa

CD 18:11

Words and Music by
E. M. Sontonga
Arranged by Cheryl Lavender

Zulu: N'ko-si si-ke-lel' i - Af - ri - ka. Ma-lu-pha-ka-nyi-sw'u -
Pronunciation: ṇko si si ke lel i af ɾi kɑ mɑ lu pɑ kɑ nyi swu

N'ko-si si-ke-lel' i - Af - ri - ka. Ma-lu-pha-ka-nyi-sw'u -
ṇko si si ke lel i af ɾi kɑ mɑ lu pɑ kɑ nyi swu

N'ko-si si-ke-lel' i - Af - ri - ka. Ma-lu-pha-ka-nyi-sw'u -
ṇko si si ke lel i af ɾi kɑ mɑ lu pɑ kɑ nyi swu

More ➡

CONCEPT
MELODY

SKILLS
SING

Franz Schubert was a great European composer. He wrote many songs like "The Trout" that were meant to be performed by a singer and a pianist. He often created piano accompaniments that imitated the sounds referred to in the lyrics. Listen to the accompaniment before you sing the song. What do you think the piano is imitating?

SKILL BUILDER: Intervals

The distance between two pitches is called an **interval**. Some intervals, like the ones in the pattern below, can be tricky to sing accurately. **Practice** this melody from "The Trout." Begin slowly and gradually increase the tempo.

en-tranced   me   as___ I___ stood
so   crys - tal   clear_ I___ thought

The Trout

CD 18:17

Words and Music by Franz Schubert
Arranged by Ed Harris

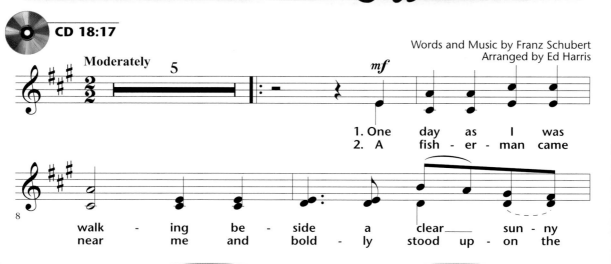

Moderately   5   *mf*

1. One   day   as   I   was
2. A   fish - er - man   came

walk   -   ing   be - side   a   clear____ sun - ny
near   me   and   bold - ly   stood up - on the

stream,   I   spied   a   trout   so   dash - ing,   an
shore.   He   had   a   string   of   fish,   yet   he

ar - row__ he   did   seem.   This   quick,   mag - nif - i - cent__
hoped   to__ catch   one   more.   I   looked   in - to__ the__

crea - ture   en - tranced   me   as__ I__ stood,   such
wa - ter   so   crys - tal   clear__ I__ thought,   my

beau - ty   found   in   na - ture   is   all   so   fair   and__
trout   is   free   for - ev - er,   my   trout   can - not   be__

mp

good,   such   beau - ty   found__ in - na - ture   is
caught;   my   trout__ is   free__ for - ev - er,   my

3

all   so   fair   and__ good.
trout   can - not   be__ caught.

mp

This   fish - er   was   no   sports - man.

More ▶

CONCEPT
MELODY
SKILLS
SING, READ

Many cultures around the world have a story about a huge flood that completely covered all the land. "Didn't It Rain" is an African American spiritual that tells the biblical story of a great flood.

SKILL BUILDER: Minor and Major

In "Didn't It Rain," the refrain is in a major key and the verse is in a minor key. **Practice** the two patterns below to help you sing the pattern accurately and in tune. Begin slowly and gradually increase the tempo.

Find other examples of these patterns in the song.

Major

Did - n't it rain,_____ chil - dren

Minor

Well, it rained for - ty days and it rained for - ty nights

Didn't It Rain

CD 18:22

Traditional Spiritual
Adapted and Arranged by Emily Crocker

With energy

All - Unison
mf

Did-n't it rain,_____ chil-dren

God's gon-na 'stroy this world with wa-ter, now did-n't it

rain, my Lord, now did-n't it rain, rain,_ rain._ Well, it

More

rained for - ty days and it rained for - ty nights, there

was - n't no land no - where in sight. ____

mf
God sent a ra - ven to car - ry the news, He

spread his wings and a - way he flew. ____

Part I *f*
Did - n't it rain, ____ chil - dren,

Part II *f*
Did - n't it rain,

God's gon - na 'stroy this world with wa - ter, now did - n't it

did - n't it rain, did - n't it rain,

rain, my Lord, now did-n't it rain, rain,_ rain._

rain, rain, did-n't it, did-n't it rain, rain,_ rain._ Well, it

For-ty days, for-ty nights,

rained for-ty days 'n' for-ty nights with-out stop-pin',

he was glad when the rain stopped drop-pin'._

No-ah was glad when the rain stopped drop-pin'._

Sent a rain-bow, sent a sign, no wa-ter, but fire_ next_

God sent No-ah a rain-bow sign, said "No more wa-ter, but fire next time!"_

time!_ Did-n't it rain,_ chil-dren,

Did-n't it rain,

More

Reflections

Reflections in music are different than reflections in sight. They can occur in music in many different ways—when lyrics or melodies repeat, or when thoughts and feelings are written into the lyrics. Why do you think music is such an effective way to express a person's reflections? Does music help you reflect on things in your life? How?

VOICE BUILDER: Spanish Vowels

As with English, singing Spanish lyrics requires paying close attention to vowel production. Knowing the five basic singing vowels—*ah, eh, ee, oh,* and *oo*—is very important when singing in Spanish. It helps you pronounce Spanish correctly and forms the basis of a blended choral sound.

Sing this exercise with a relaxed jaw, vertical mouth shape, and space inside the mouth.

Ah, ah, ah, pa - lo - ma

"Huainito" is a folk song that comes from Argentina, a country in South America. In Argentina, a *huainito* is a type of folk song that often tells a sad love story. Argentina has many enchanting styles of music, from folk songs like "Huainito" to the *tango*, a dance music that is now popular all over the world.

CD 19:1

Argentinian Folk Song
Arranged by Victoria Ebel-Sabo

Slowly

Spanish: Dos pa - lo - mi - tas se la - men - ta - ban llo - ran - do;
Pronunciation: dos pa lo mi ta se la men ta βan ʒo ɾan do
English: Two lit - tle doves were sit - ting to - geth - er, cry - ing so;

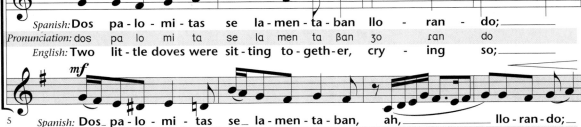

Spanish: Dos pa - lo - mi - tas se la - men - ta - ban, ah, llo - ran - do;
Pronunciation: dos pa lo mi ta se la men ta βan a ʒo ɾan do
English: Two lit - tle doves were sit - ting to - geth - er, ah, cry - ing so;

More

The waterfront in Tierra del Fuego, Argentina

mf

y la_u-na_a la_o-tra se con-so-la-ban di - cien - do:
i lau na lao tra se kon so la ßan di syen do
One to the oth - er in con-so-la-tion mur - mured low:

mf

y la_u-na_a la_o-tra se_con - so-la-ban, ah,_____ di - cien - do:_
i lau na lao tra se kon so la ßan a di syen do
One to the oth - er in_con-so-la-tion, ah,_____ mur-mured low:_

mf

¿Quién te_ha cor-ta - do tus be-llas a - las pa - lo - ma?
kyen tea koɾ ta ðo tus ße ʒas a las pa lo ma
Who could it be who's tak - en your soft wings, lit - tle dove?___

mf

¿Quién te_ha cor-ta - do tus be-llas a - las, ah,_____ pa-lo-ma?
kyen tea koɾ ta ðo tus ße ʒas a las a pa lo ma
Who_ could it be who's tak - en your soft wings, ah,_____ lit - tle dove?_

mf

¿Q'_al - gun fal - sa - rio ha sor - pren - di - do tu vue -
kal gun fal sa ɾyo a sor pɾen di ðo tu ßwe
Who is the false one who took ad - van - tage of your

mf

¿Q'_al - gun fal - sa - rio ha sor - pren - di - do, ah,_
kal gun fal sa ɾyo a sor pɾen di ðo a
Who is the false one who took ad - van - tage, ah,_____

lo?   Ah,   ah,   ah,   pa - lo -
lo   ɑ   ɑ   ɑ   pɑ   lo
love?   Ah,   ah,   ah,   lit - tle

tu vue - lo?___   Ah,_____   ah,_____
tu βwe lo   ɑ   ɑ
of your love?_   Ah,_____   a,_____

ma.   ¿Q'_al - gun fal - sa - rio ha sor - pren - di - do
mɑ   kɑl gun fɑl sɑ ɾyo ɑ soɾ pɾen di ðo
dove,   Who is the false one who took ad - van - tage

___ pa - lo - ma, ¿Q'_al - gun fal - sa - rio ha___ sor - pren - di - do
pɑ lo mɑ kɑl gun fɑl sɑ ɾyo hɑ soɾ pɾen di ðo
___ lit - tle dove, Who is the false one who_ took ad - van - tage,

tu   vue - lo?   Qui - so_el in - gra - to que yo mis a - las
tu   βwe   lo   ki swel in gɾa to ke yo mis ɑ lɑs
of   your   love?   It was a vil - lain to whom I gave my

ah,_____   tu vue - lo?___ Qui - so_el in - gra - to que yo mis a - las,
ɑ   tu βwe lo ki swel in gɾa to ke yo mis ɑ lɑs
ah,_____   of your love? It_ was a vil - lain to_whom I gave my,

More

de de-sen-ga-ño me mue-ro. Ah, ah,
ðe ðe seng ga nyo me mwe ɾo a a
he left me help-less here to die. Ah, ah,

de_de-sen-ga-ño, ah,_____ me mue-ro.__ Ah,_____
ðe ðe seng ga nyo a me mwe ɾo a
he_left me help-less, ah,_____ here to die.__ Ah,_____

ah, y lue-go a-ban-do-na-da
a i lwe go a ban do na ða
ah, sweet his words. When he'd de-ceived me,

_____ ah,_____ y lue-go. a-ban-do-na-da
a i lwe go a ban do na ða
ah,_____ sweet his words. When he'd de-ceived me,

de de-sen-ga-ño me mue-ro.
ðe ðe seng ga nyo me mwe ɾo
he left me help-less here to die.

de de-sen-ga-ño, ah,_____ me mue-ro.
ðe ðe seng ga nyo a me mwe ɾo
he left me help-less ah,_____ here to die.__

CONCEPT
MELODY
SKILLS
SING: BREATHING

"Dandansoy" is a song of the Visayan people of the Philippines, a country of beautiful islands in the Pacific Ocean with many different cultures, languages, and musical styles. The words to "Dandansoy" are a reflection on a journey the singer must take. They encourage those left behind to remain happy and upbeat.

VOICE BUILDER: Airflow

One aspect of good breath support is continuous airflow. As you sing long phrases, it is important to supply the vocal cords with a continuous stream of air. This allows them to vibrate freely.

Sing this melodic pattern from mm. 33–39 in "Dandansoy." This phrase is quite long, so you will need to use "staggered" breathing. This means that each singer should take a breath at a different time than his or her neighbor.

MAP
CHINA
VIETNAM
PHILIPPINES
MALAYSIA
INDONESIA

Traditional Visayan Folk Song

CD 19:9

yaw,_____ U - ga - ling kon i - kaw hid-la-
yau   u   ga   ling   kun   i   kau   hid la

won,_____ Ang Pa - yao i - mo lang lan-ta-
wun   ʌng   pa   yau   i   mo   lang   lan ta

won._____ Ah
wun   a

Dan-dan-soy ko - ni - mo Ah
dan dan soi   ku   ni   mu   a

Dan-dan - soy ko - ni - mo a - po - son,_____
dan dan soi   ku   ni   mu   a   pa   sun

More

A fish market in the Philippines

Mountains on the island of Bohol, Philippines

soy ba-ya-an ta i-kaw, _____ Pa-u-
soi ba ya an ta i kau pa u

li a-ko sa Pa-yao, _____ U-ga-
li a ko sa pa yau u ga

ling kon i-kaw hid-la-won, _____ Ang Pa-
ling kon i kau hid la wun ʌng pa

yao i-mo lang lan-ta-won. _____ Dan-dan-
yau i mo lang lan ta wun dan dan

soy, Dan - dan - soy. _____
soi dan dan soi

 **LISTENING** CD 19:14

Ti Ayat Traditional Filipino Folk Song

Listen to the Iskwelahang Pilipino Rondalla Ensemble of Boston perform "Ti Ayat." Like "Dandansoy," this piece is an example of *rondalla* music. The Ensemble, which formed in 1986, has toured the world and played before former Filipino Presidents Corazon Aquino and Fidel Ramos and for the United Nations in New York.

CONCEPT
TONE COLOR

SKILLS
SING

"Bashana Haba'ah" was written by Nurit Hirsh, a Jewish composer who has lived in Israel and the United States. Besides songs like "Bashana Haba'ah," she has written music for orchestras, scores for movies and television, and children's music.

VOICE BUILDER: The Changing Voice

As boys and girls grow into adolescence, their voices begin to mature. For boys, the voice changes in both pitch and tone quality, called **timbre**. Boys may find certain pitches that were once easy to sing are now out of their range, but that they are able to sing lower notes than they could sing before. Boys with changing or changed voices can continue to sing high notes by singing in their high voice, called **head voice**.

Girls' voices also go through a process of development. A girl's voice may become breathy and some notes that were easy to sing clearly may be more difficult.

All adolescent singers should use good posture, breath support, and vowel production to strengthen their vocal skills. **Sing** this exercise in head voice. Boys with changing voices can transition into their new, lower voice as needed. Drop out when you can no longer sing the notes.

MAP

ISRAEL
GAZA
WEST BANK
JORDAN
EGYPT
SAUDI
ARABIA

Bashana Haba'ah

CD 19:15

In the Year to Come

Music by Nurit Hirsh
Words by Ehud Manor
Arranged by V. Pasternak
Edited by Henry Leck

CONCEPT
EXPRESSION
SKILLS
SING, READ

Have you ever felt so cheerful you wanted to burst out singing? "Sing Hosanna" is the perfect piece for that feeling. Sing with brightness and energy and share your happiness with everyone around you.

VOICE BUILDER: Expression Marks

You can take your singing to the next level by accurately following the expression marks written in the music. Expression marks include dynamic marks like a *crescendo* or an accent mark; as well as articulation marks like phrases and *staccato*.

Identify and review all the expression and articulation marks in "Sing Hosanna" before you begin to sing.

CD 19:19

Words and Music by Michael Jothen

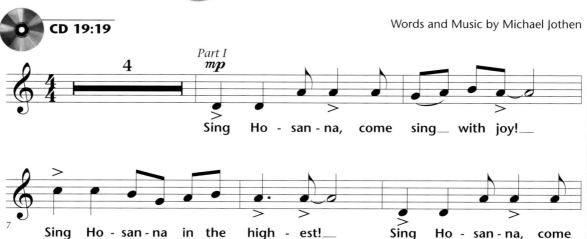

high - est!___ Sing Ho - san - na, come sing__ with joy!___

san - na, Sing Ho - san - na,

Sing Ho - san - na in the high - est!___ *cresc.* Now is the time__ to sing.

sing__ Ho - san - na, Sing Ho -

Lift up your voice, Lift up your voice now in song!

san - na, Al - le - lu - ia.

CONCEPT
RHYTHM/MELODY
SKILLS
SING, READ

"Jordan's Angels" is an example of a new composition that incorporates an older style, in this case a **spiritual**. African Americans created spirituals by combining elements of European music with the African musical styles of their ancestors.

SKILL BUILDER: Taking a Rest

Sometimes it's not what you sing, but what you don't sing that is important. In "Jordan's Angels" there are some very important rests in the melody.

Speak these words in rhythm taking care to observe the rests accurately. Find other places in the song where there are rests within a phrase.

Mm. 20-23

Some - day my soul   shall be free. I shall be free.

Mm. 36-39 (Part 2)

Some - day my soul   shall be   free. I shall be free.

Jordan's Angels

CD 19:22

Words and Music by Rollo A. Dilworth
Based on the Spiritual "All Night, All Day"

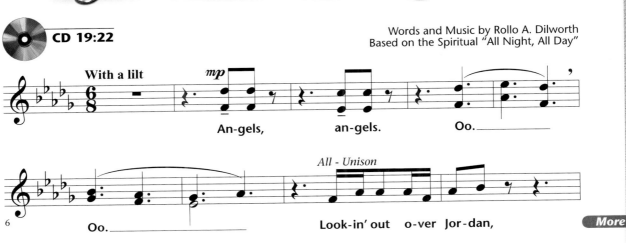

With a lilt

An-gels,   an-gels.   Oo.

All - Unison

Oo.   Look-in' out   o-ver Jor-dan,

More

Happy Days

Everybody lives for those wonderful days when everything seems to be going just right. It is no coincidence that music seems to be around on those days, too. Whether you're hanging out with your friends, relaxing at the park with your family, or taking a long trip in the car, music is always there to keep your spirits high.

Beginning with "Cum-ma-la Be-stay," the five songs in this theme will put a smile on your face and cheer you up even when you are having a bad day. Enjoy!

VOICE BUILDER: Articulators

In addition to vowel sounds, singing requires articulation to produce the consonants in the text. The articulators we use in singing are the lips, the teeth, and the tongue. **Practice** the exercise below to help you activate your articulators. Then apply this technique to the nonsense words in "Cum-ma-la Be-stay."

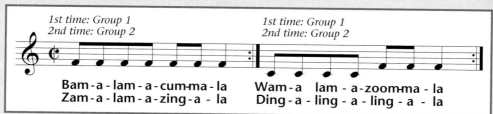

1st time: Group 1
2nd time: Group 2

Bam - a - lam - a - cum-ma - la
Zam - a - lam - a - zing - a - la

1st time: Group 1
2nd time: Group 2

Wam - a   lam - a - zoom-ma - la
Ding - a - ling - a - ling - a - la

Cum-ma-la Be-stay

CD 19:26

Words and Music by Donny Burke,
Jerry Vance, and Terry Philips
Arranged by Michael Jothen

Solo

to Coda ⊕
All

Bam-a-lam-a-cum-ma-la. Cum-ma-la be-stay. Bam-a-lam-a-cum-ma-la.

All

Bam-a-lam-a-cum-ma-la.

"Cripple Creek" is a classic American folk song that people have sung for generations. Folk songs like this are often arranged in new ways to keep them fresh and interesting. Over the years, musicians and singers have added many verses to this song.

After you have learned to sing "Cripple Creek," create a verse of your own and have your choir perform it.

VOICE BUILDER: *Ee* and *Eh*

Each of the five basic vowels we use in singing (*ah, eh, ee, oh,* and *oo*) require special techniques for good tone quality. To sing the *eh* and *ee* vowels properly, it is especially important to maintain an open space inside your mouth and to keep the corners of your mouth from spreading outward.

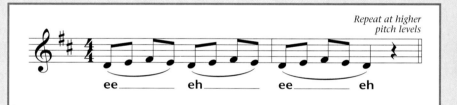

Repeat at higher pitch levels

ee____ eh____ ee____ eh

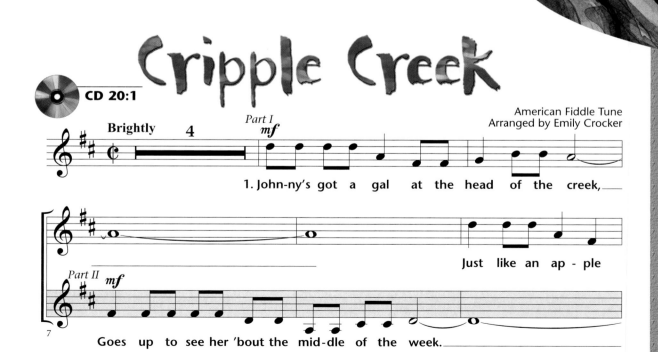

CD 20:1

Cripple Creek

American Fiddle Tune
Arranged by Emily Crocker

Brightly 4 *Part I* *mf*

1. John-ny's got a gal at the head of the creek,____

Just like an ap-ple

Part II mf

Goes up to see her 'bout the mid-dle of the week.____

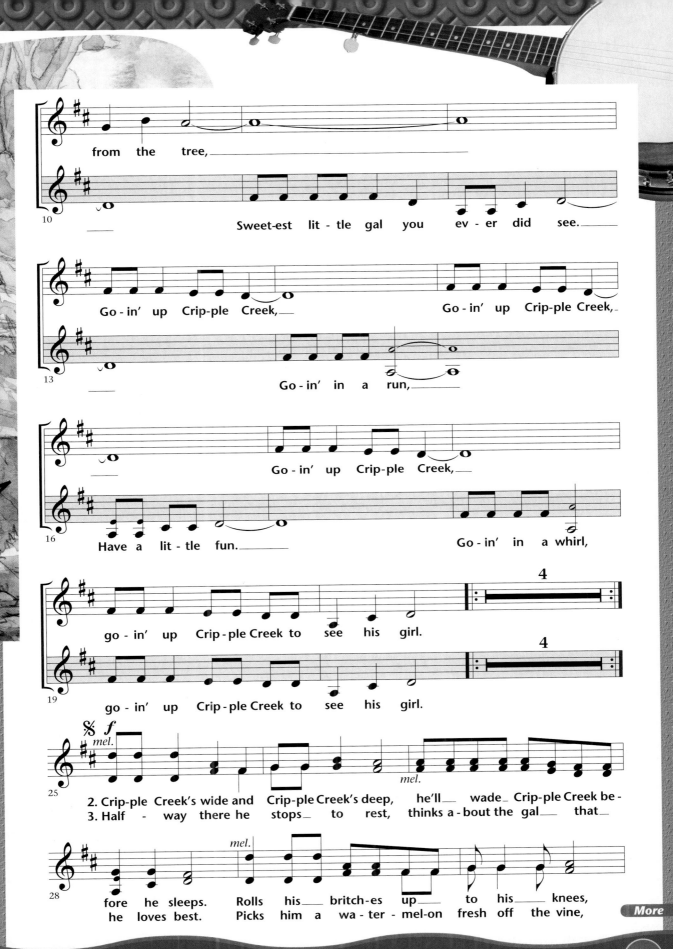

LISTENING CD 20:5

Cripple Creek American Folk Song

Listen to this instrumental version of "Cripple Creek" by the legendary bluegrass musicians Lester Flatt and Earl Scruggs. Earl Scruggs is credited with inventing the bluegrass style of banjo picking, which uses three fingers. In bluegrass, each instrument often plays the melody of the tune. Can you hear the melody of "Cripple Creek" as it passes from one instrument to the next?

CONCEPT
RHYTHM

SKILLS
SING: DICTION

"Leila" is a folk song from North Carolina. Each of the three vocal parts in this song has tricky rhythms that are full of repeating syncopation. When you perform your part with the other two, listen for the new and surprising rhythm patterns the parts create together.

VOICE BUILDER: *L*, *M*, and *N*

The consonants *l* and *n* are produced by the tip of the tongue while the consonant *m* is produced by the lips. Practice speaking these phrases very lightly and precisely. **Speak** each phrase three times.

- "The lips, the teeth, the tip of the tongue"
- "Fa la la la la"
- "Nine nimble noblemen"
- "Make mine macaroni"

Sing this exercise and articulate the consonants *l, m,* and *n* very lightly and precisely.

lay lay lay lay lay lay lah lah lah lah lah lah
nay nay nay nay nay nay nah nah nah nah nah nah
may may may may may may mah mah mah mah mah mah

Leila

CD 20:6

Folk Song from North Carolina

Lei-la, that's shoo my love, Lei-la, that's shoo my love.

2nd time only

Lei-la, that's shoo my love, Lei-la, shoo my love.

Lei - la, that's shoo my love, Lei - la, that's shoo my love.

13

Lei - la, that's shoo my love, Lei - la, shoo my love.

Solo   *Group*

Turn me in a cir - cle now. Shoo, Lei - la, shoo my love,

17

Shoo, Lei - la, shoo my love.

Solo   *Group*

Turn me in a cir - cle now. Shoo, Lei - la, shoo my love.

21

Shoo, Lei - la shoo my love.

Solo   1.   2.   **8**

Turn me in a cir - cle now, In a cir - cle cir - cle now.

Part I   **8**

Lei - la, that's shoo my love, Lei - la, that's shoo my love. shoo my love.

Part II   **8**

25

Lei - la that's shoo my love, Lei - la, shoo my love. shoo my love.

A visit to the doctor for a checkup is usually a not-so-pleasant experience. You sit in the waiting room, sit in the exam room, and sit on the exam table while the doctor sticks a tongue depressor in your mouth. On the other hand, what if you had an appointment with "Doctor Jazz"? Then it would be a whole lot more exciting!

VOICE BUILDER: Scat Singing

Jazz singers who improvise use "scat" or nonsense syllables for their improvisation.

Sing these notes from the G blues scale:

Now add rhythm and scat syllables.

Doc - tor Jazz__   Su - per en - er - giz - in'   Feel al - right__
Doot doo - wah__   doo - be doo - be doo - wah   doo dot dah__

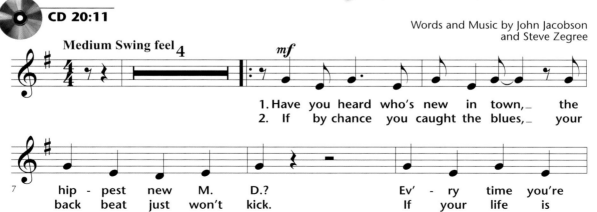

CD 20:11

Words and Music by John Jacobson
and Steve Zegree

Medium Swing feel   *mf*

1. Have you heard who's new   in   town,__   the
2. If   by chance you caught the blues,__   your

hip - pest new M. D.?   Ev' - ry time you're
back beat just won't kick.   If your life is

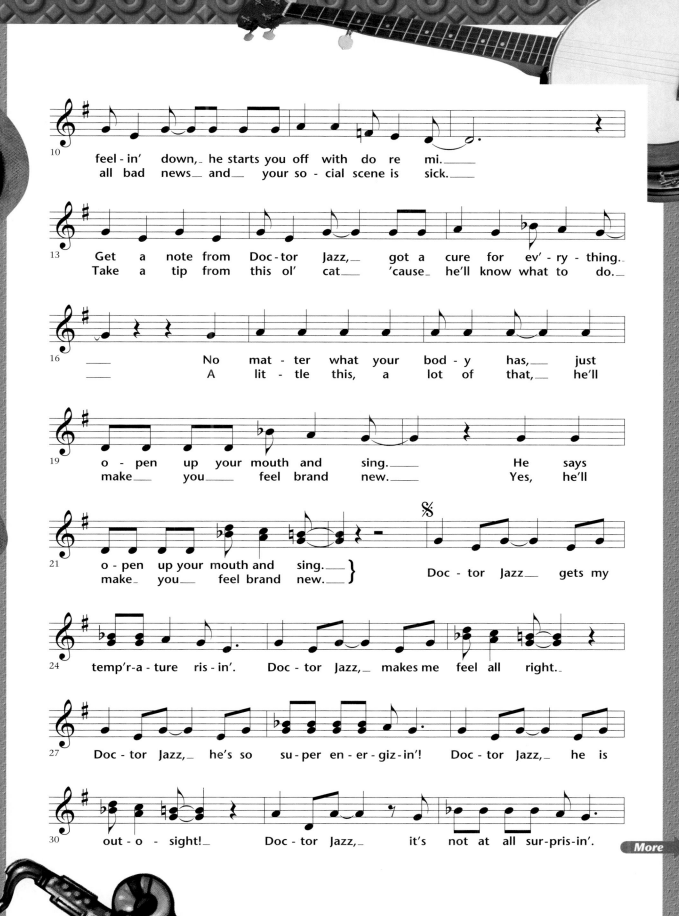

CONCEPT
HARMONY

SKILLS
SING

LA BAMBA

Traditional Mexican Folk Song
Adapted and arranged by Roger Emerson

CD 20:15

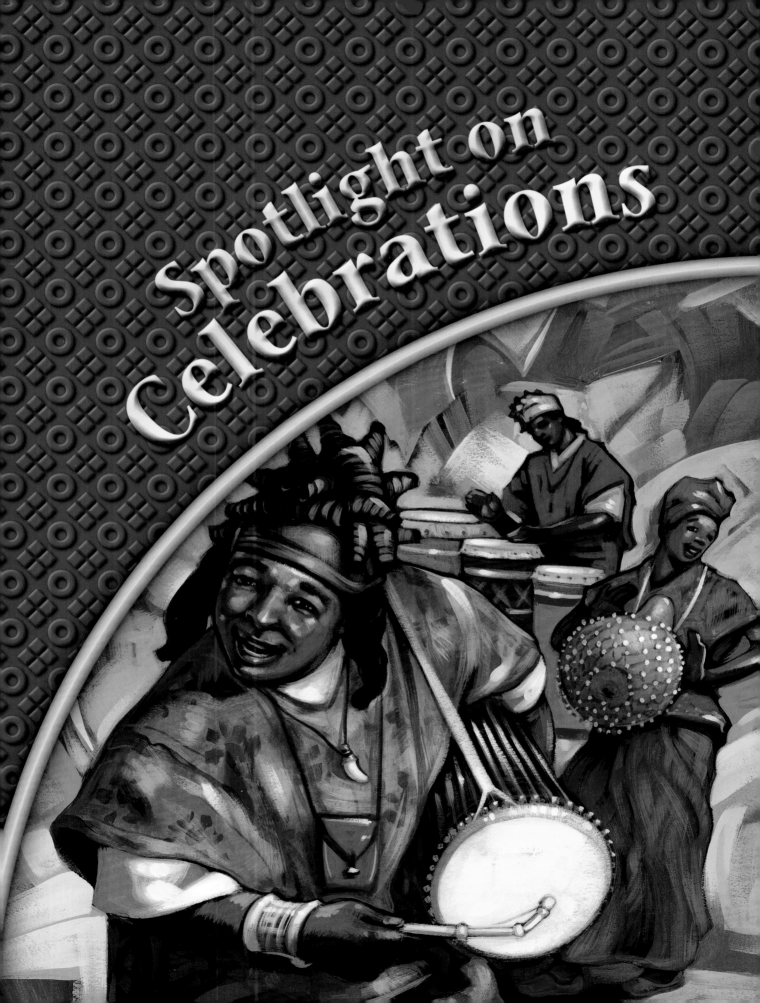

Spotlight on Celebrations

Spotlight on Celebrations

Spotlight on Celebrations

CONCEPT
METER

SKILLS
SING, DESCRIBE

During the War of 1812, Francis Scott Key was a prisoner on a British ship that was attacking Fort McHenry in Baltimore. When the battle was over and the smoke had cleared, Key saw the red, white, and blue flag still blowing in the breeze. This sight inspired him to write the words to "The Star-Spangled Banner." The words were later set to music and the song was declared the national anthem of the United States.

Clap the following pattern found in "The Star-Spangled Banner."

CD 20:21

Music Attributed to J.S. Smith
Words by Francis Scott Key

Oh, — say, can you see, by the dawn's ear - ly light,

What so proud - ly we hailed at the twi-light's last gleam-ing?

Whose broad stripes and bright stars, through the per - il - ous fight,

Describe what Francis Scott Key saw after the battle had ended.

CONCEPT
ARTICULATION
SKILLS
SING, LISTEN

Samuel Francis Smith wrote the lyrics to "America" in 1831, setting them to a tune that he found in a German school music book. He was most likely unaware that it was the same melody as "God Save the King!"—the British national anthem. "America" was introduced on July 4, 1831, in Boston, Massachusetts.

CD 21:1

Music by Henry Carey
Words by Samuel F. Smith

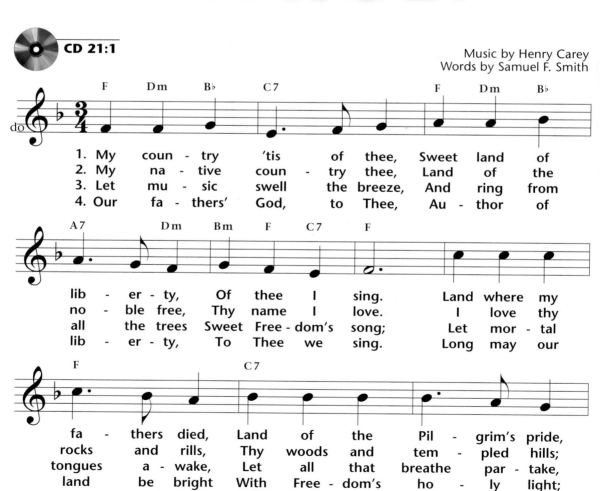

1. My coun - try 'tis of thee, Sweet land of
2. My na - tive coun - try thee, Land of the
3. Let mu - sic swell the breeze, And ring from
4. Our fa - thers' God, to Thee, Au - thor of

lib - er - ty, Of thee I sing. Land where my
no - ble free, Thy name I love. I love thy
all the trees Sweet Free - dom's song; Let mor - tal
lib - er - ty, To Thee we sing. Long may our

fa - thers died, Land of the Pil - grim's pride,
rocks and rills, Thy woods and tem - pled hills;
tongues a - wake, Let all that breathe par - take,
land be bright With Free - dom's ho - ly light;

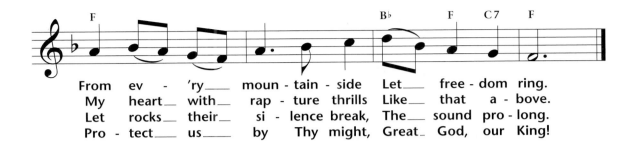

From ev - 'ry___ moun - tain - side Let___ free - dom ring.
My heart___ with___ rap - ture thrills Like___ that a - bove.
Let rocks___ their___ si - lence break, The___ sound pro - long.
Pro - tect___ us___ by Thy might, Great_ God, our King!

Create your own verse for "America." Include reasons why you love your country.

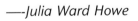

LISTENING CD 21:5

Battle Hymn of the Republic

Music by William Steffe, Words by Julia Ward Howe

This song is based on a poem written by Julia Ward, and music by William Steffe. This song has become one of the best-loved patriotic anthems.

The words to the song are as follows:

Mine eyes have seen the glory of the coming of the Lord;

He is trampling out the vintage where the grapes of wrath are stored;

He has loosed the fateful lightning of his terrible swift sword;

His truth is marching on.

Glory, Glory, Hallelujah! Glory, Glory, Hallelujah!

Glory, Glory, Hallelujah! His truth is marching on!

—*Julia Ward Howe*

CONCEPT
TEMPO
SKILLS
SING

"The Stars and Stripes Forever" was written by John Philip Sousa, a famous bandleader and composer of marches. Sousa composed this popular march on Christmas Day, 1896. In December 1897, it was named the official march of the United States of America.

Pat on the downbeats of "The Stars and Stripes Forever." Share where you have heard this familiar tune before.

The Stars and Stripes Forever

CD 21:9

Words and Music by John Philip Sousa

March time

Hur - rah for the flag of the free,_____ May it wave as our

stand-ard for-ev - er, The gem of the land and the sea,_____ The_

ban-ner of the right._____ Let des - pots re - mem - ber the

day_____ When our fa - thers with might - y en-deav -

or Pro-claimed as they marched to the fray,_____ That by their

might, and by their right, It waves for - ev - er!

Semper Fidelis by John Philip Sousa

John Philip Sousa (1854–1932) always wanted to join the circus when he was young. So he put his musical talents to work and became a famous composer of marches. When his career was on the rise he wrote "Semper Fidelis" which later was adopted as the official march of the Marine Corps. In Latin, the title means "always faithful."

Identify the instruments heard in "Semper Fidelis."

Hispanic Heritage Month

National Hispanic Heritage Month takes place between September 15th and October 15th. Hispanic Americans celebrate their history and culture with special foods, and also by dancing and singing songs about the love of their homeland.

Create an ostinato pattern to play with the Mexican song "El tecolote."

Play your pattern on a non-pitched instrument.

The Owlet

MAP
UNITED STATES
MEXICO   BELIZE
GUATEMALA

CD 21:13

Mexican Folk Song
English Words by Linda Worsley

Spanish: Te-co - lo-te de Gua-da - ña,   pá - ja-ro ma-dru-ga-dor. Te-co-
Pronunciation: te ko lo te ðe gwa ða nya   pa xa ɾo ma ðɾu ga ðoɾ te ko
English: Lit-tle owl of Gua-da-ña cries.   wak-ful-ly watch-ing the night, Lit-tle

lo-te de Gua-da - ña,   pá - ja-ro ma-dru - ga - dor. Quién tu-
lo te ðe gwa ða nya   pa xa ɾo ma ðɾu ga ðoɾ kyen tu
owl of Bua-da-ña flies.   And my poor heart would take flight. With your

vie - ra___ tus a - li-tas, quien tu-vie-ra___ tus a - li-tas, quién tu-
βye ɾa   tus a li tas kyen tu βye ɾa   tus a li tas kyen tu
wings I___would go fly-ing, With your wings I___ would go fly-ing, With your

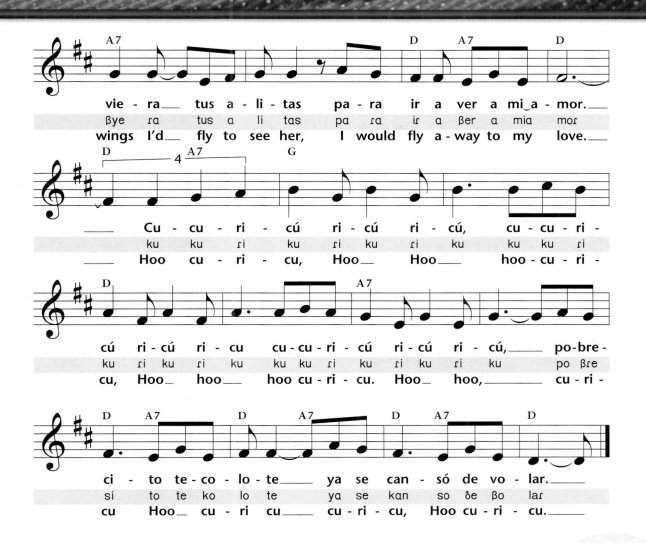

vie – ra__ tus a – li – tas pa – ra ir a ver a mi_a – mor.__
 βγe ɾa tus a li ɾas pa ɾa ir a βer a mia moɾ
wings I'd__ fly to see her, I would fly a – way to my love.__

__ Cu – cu – ri – cú ri – cú ri – cú, cu – cu – ri –
ku ku ɾi ku ɾi ku ɾi ku ku ku ɾi
__ Hoo cu – ri – cu, Hoo__ Hoo__ hoo – cu – ri –

cú ri – cú ri – cu cu – cu – ri – cú ri – cú ri – cú,__ po – bre –
ku ɾi ku ɾi ku ku ku ɾi ku ɾi ku ɾi ku po βɾe
cu, Hoo__ hoo__ hoo cu – ri – cu. Hoo__ hoo,__ cu – ri –

ci – to te – co – lo – te__ ya se can – só de vo – lar.__
si to te ko lo te ya se kan so ðe βo laɾ
cu Hoo__ cu – ri cu __ cu – ri – cu, Hoo cu – ri – cu.

🎵 **LISTENING** CD 21:17

Este son by Juan Carlos Ureña

Juan Carlos Ureña is one of the best known songwriters and singers of
Costa Rica. "Este son" describes the country Juan Carlos longs to be in.
The song also brings to mind different musical styles: Afro-Cuban, salsa,
and pop.

Identify the musical instruments you hear in "Este son."

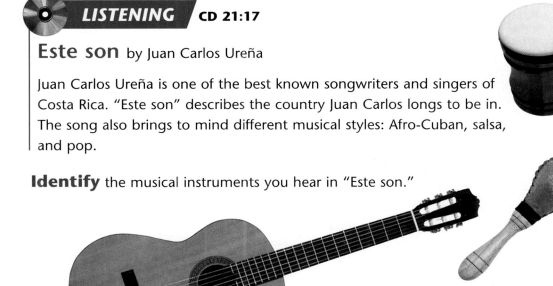

CONCEPT
METER
SKILLS
LISTEN, SING

The Hmong New Year in Laos is a time of rest from the harvest and work. It is a time when Hmong people start new lives along with a new year. Over a period of ten days, families celebrate by participating in a variety of New Year's celebration activities and by cooking a variety of dishes for meals. Sing this Hmong folk song.

Listen and watch for upward and downward movement in the song "Ua Txiab."

Ua Txiab

The Village

MAP
MYANMAR
LAOS
THAILAND
KAMPUCHEA VIETNAM

CD 21:18

White Hmong Folk Song
Collected, Transcribed and Arranged by Vilay Her
English Words by Linda Worlsey

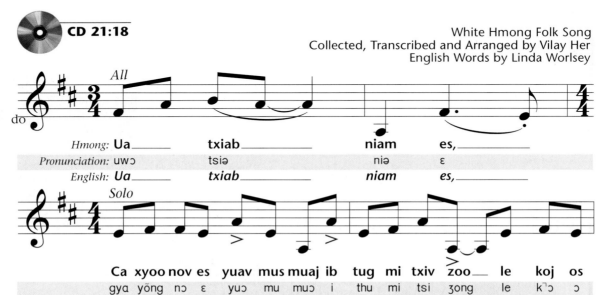

Hmong: **Ua** _____ **txiab** _____ **niam** **es,** _____
Pronunciation: uwɔ tsiə niə ɛ
English: **Ua** _____ **txiab** _____ **niam** **es,**

Ca xyoo nov es yuav mus muaj ib tug mi txiv zoo___ le koj os
gya yõŋ nɔ ɛ yuɔ mu muɔ i thu mi tsi ʒɔŋ le kʰɔ ɔ
1. This year I am thank-ful for a fa-ther like you,___good fa-ther,
2. This year I am thank-ful for a moth-er like you,___good moth-er,

All

ntuj es____ os.
thu ɛ ɔ
ntuj es____ os.
ntuj es____ os.

Solo

Ca xyoo nov es yuav mus muaj koj los khwv zaub mov__ rau peb noj
gya yŏng nɔ ɛ yuɔ mu muɔ kʰɔ lɔ ku ʒɑʊ mɔ dɑʊ beɪ nɔ
This year I am thank-ful you pro - vide us with food,__ good fa - ther,
This year I am thank-ful that you care for us all,__ good moth-er,

All

ntuj es____ os.
thu ɛ ɔ
ntuj es____ os.
ntuj es____ os.

Use *World Instruments* **CD-ROM** to learn more about Asian instruments.

Create movements with your arms to show the melodic direction as you listen again!

Girls and boys playing a traditional ball game during Hmong New Year.

CONCEPT
STRUCTURE
SKILLS
SING

Diwali Song

MAP
CHINA
PAKISTAN
NEPAL
INDIA
BANGLADESH

CD 21:22

Collected by Kathy B. Sorensen
As sung by Chhanda Chakroborti

Hindi: दी प ज ल ओ दि प ज ल ओ आ आ दी ठा ळी
Pronunciation: di pə ja ja o di pə ja la o a jə di wa li
English: **Light up your lamps, come light them to-day, the day of Di-wa-li**

रे दी प ज ला ओ दी प ज ला ओ
ɾe di pə ja la o di pə ja la o
Re._____ **Light up your lamps, come light them to-day. The**

Fine

आ ज दी टा ली रे खु शी खु शी स व ह स ते आओ
a jə di wa li ɾe ku shi ku shi sa va hă sə te ao
day of Di-wa-li Re. Ev-'ry-one smil-ing and hap-py, Ah-oh

आ ज दी टा ली रे आ ज दी वा ली
a jə di wa li ɾe a jə ki wa li
To-day, Di-wa-li___ Re, to-day, Di-wa-li,

D.C. al Fine

आ ज दी वा ली आ ज दी वा ली रे
a jə di wa li a jə di wa li ɾe
to-day, Di-wa-li, To-day, Di-wa-li Re._____

*D*iwali, the Indian festival of lights, marks the beginning of a new year. It is celebrated in almost all the regions of India. The celebration continues for five days, each day with its own meaning, with the retelling of myths, legends, and beliefs. Homes are decorated with *diyas*, or small lamps, to welcome *Lakshmi*, the goddess of wealth and prosperity.

On the first day of the Diwali festival people decorate their houses with rice powder. The designs are known as rangolis.

CONCEPT
TONALITY

SKILLS
SING, CREATE

The Loy Krathong Festival is one of the biggest festivals in Thailand. On the full moon in November, people celebrate by making wishes and launching small vessels called *krathongs* into rivers or swimming pools. Traditional krathongs are made from layers of the trunk and leaves of banana trees. They are filled with food, nuts, flowers and candles, which represent hope for the future.

People watch as their krathong floats away, hoping that the flame will not go out.

Thai dance is graceful, accompanied by a special orchestra of traditional Thai musical instruments. The costumes are rich in color and style and vary from region to region.

Pleeng Loy Krathong

Full Moon Song

CD 21:26

Thai Folk Song
Collected by Pomprapit "Ros" Phoasavadi
Transcribed by Patricia Shehan Campbell

Create your own imaginary krathong and make a wish about your future.

Seasonal Songs

Maybe you experience winter as a time to bundle up and enjoy the cold, brisk air and fun winter activities. Maybe you experience winter as a cold, wet season in which you have to bundle up, put up with freezing rain and slush, and stay indoors. Maybe you experience winter as a little bit of both!

Describe your perfect winter day to a friend.

A PERFECT WINTER DAY

CD 21:28

Words and Music by
Teresa and Paul Jennings

Sing 1st & 3rd times only

I
do

It was a - snow - in'.   The wind was

Sing 2nd & 3rd times

II
do

I   don't par - tic - u - lar - ly

blow - in'.   The snow was fall - in'   all a -

like   the win - ter.   I   al - ways get   (sniff) a

round me.   I was a - slid - in'.   My feet were

head   (sniff) cold.   (sniff)   I   think it's cold and wet and

glid - in'. It was a per - fect win - ter

mes - sy and slop - py. Just a per - fect win - ter

day! What a per-fect day to build a snow-man!

(sniff), if you like that sort of thing. I have a head - ache.

Build a snow-man! Build a snow-man! What a per-fect day to

My eyes itch. My nose is clogged. Oh,

build a snow-man! A per - fect win - ter

I feel crum - my on this per - fect win - ter

More

CONCEPT
FORM

SKILLS
SING, LISTEN

Random gleeful sounds

per - fect win - ter day!

Random sniffling, etc.

Group sneeze:

Per - fect win - ter day! Achoo!

Create movements to express the experiences that take place in "A Perfect Winter Day."

 LISTENING CD 22:1

Winter from *The Four Seasons*
by Antonio Vivaldi

This movement is from "Winter," one of the concertos for solo violin and strings. Vivaldi used special effects, such as playing close to an instrument's bridge, to represent a frozen landscape.

Identify the passages that sound like shivering in bitter winds, stamping icy feet, and teeth chattering from the cold.

CD-ROM

Use *Orchestral Instruments* **CD-ROM** to learn more about strings and keyboard instruments.

CONCEPT
RHYTHM
SKILLS
LISTEN, SING

Over 2000 years ago, a small group of Jewish people, called the Maccabees, defeated a powerful invading army. When they reopened their temple they had just enough lamp oil to last for one day, yet the flame burned for eight days! People today light the Hanukkah menorah on each of the holiday's eight nights.

 **LISTENING** CD 22:6

Hashual Israeli Folk Dance

A Hanukkah celebration often includes dancing and music. The dance "Hashual" (The Fox) is called a round dance.

Listen to sections A and B of this dance.

The Fox

Describe the differences between the two sections.

Ma'oz Tsur

MAP
ISRAEL
GAZA
WEST BANK
EGYPT
JORDAN
SAUDI ARABIA

CD 22:2

Jewish Folk Song

Hebrew: מָ עוֹז צוּר יְ שׁוּ עָ תִי לְ ךָ נָ אֶ ה לְ שַׁ בֵּ חַ

Pronunciation: mɑ oz tsuɾ yɛ shu a ti lɛ xa na e lɛ sha be ax

English: **Rock of ag - es, all our days, We fill the air with songs of praise.**

Hebrew: תִּ כּוֹן בֵּית תְּ פִ לָּ תִי וְ שָׁם תּוֹ דָה נְ זַ

Pronunciation: ti kon beit tɛ fi la ti vɛ sham to da nɛ za

English: **All our foes thou will as - sail. Thy strength and pow - er**

Hebrew: בֵּ חַ לְ עֵת תָּ כִין מַט בֵּ חַ מִ צָּר הַ נַּ

Pronunciation: be ax lɛ et ta xin mat be ax mi tsaɾ ha nɑ

English: **will not fail. We'll de - di-cate the al - tar, Faith will nev - er**

Hebrew: בֵּ חַ אָז אֶג מוֹר בְּ שִׁיר מִז מוֹר

Pronunciation: be ax az eg moɾ bɛ shir miz moɾ

English: **fal - ter. With our house of prayer re - stored,**

Hebrew: חַ נֻ כַּת הַ מִז בֵּ חַ בֵּ חַ

Pronunciation: xa nu kat ha miz be ax be ax

English: **Fill the air with hymns of praise. hymns of praise.**

405

CONCEPT
ARTICULATION
SKILLS
SING

A favorite pastime during the Christmas season is singing carols. This French carol has become one of the most popular songs of the holiday season.

Play this pattern on measures 3 and 4, and on measures 7 and 8.

Choose an appropriate tone color for your accompaniment.

Les Anges dans nos Campagnes

Angels We Have Heard on High

MAP

SWITZERLAND
FRANCE
ITALY
SPAIN

CD 22:7

Allegretto
Verse

French Carol

French: Les an-ges dans_ nos cam-pa-gnes ont en-ton-né l'hym-
Pronunciation: le ā ʒə dā nɔ kā pɑ nyə ō ā tɔ̃ nə lim
English: 1. An-gels we have_ heard on high,_ Sweet-ly____sing-ing_
2. Shepherds why this_ ju-bi-lee?__ Why your_ joy-ous__

ne des cieux, Et l'é-cho de nos mon-ta-gnes
nə de syö e le ko də nɔ mɔ̃ ta nyə
o'er the plains, And the moun-tains in re-ply____
strains pro-long? What glad tid-ings did you hear?__

re - dit ce chant mé - lo - di - eux:
rə di sə shã me lo di ö
Ech - o - ing their___ joy - ous strains:
Which in - spire your___ heav'n - ly song?

Refrain

descant

Glo - ri - a

Glo - ri - a

in ex - cel - sis De - o, Glo -

in ex - cel - sis De - o, Glo -

- ri - a in ex - cel - sis De - o.

- ri - a in ex - cel - sis De - o.

CONCEPT
METER

SKILLS
SING, LISTEN

The spirit of the Christmas season is expressed in this Irish folk song about a warm welcome to the weary traveler.

MAP

SCOTLAND

NORTHERN
IRELAND

ENGLAND

WALES

IRELAND

Carol from an Irish Cabin

CD 22:12

Music by Dale Wood
Words by Ruth Durand

1. The cold wind blows o - ver the heath - er, _____
2. The clean snow falls soft - ly, falls soft - ly, _____
3. So let there be no fear of dark - ness, _____

The salt wind blows o - ver the sea, _____ The __
The snow crys - tals cov - er the moor. _____ Let __
And let there be no fear of sea; _____ Let the

harsh wind blows down from the moun - tains, _____ And
wan - der - ers lost and grown wea - ry, _____ Find
star guide the lost and for - sak - en, _____ Safe

blows a white Christ - mas to me. _____
wel - come at my cab - in door. _____
o - ver the moor - lands to me. _____

LISTENING CD 22:15

Trepak from *The Nutcracker* by Piotr Ilyich Tchaikovsky

The ballet *The Nutcracker* is a Christmas tale. "Trepak" is a Russian dance, in which the dancers do high jumps and spins.

Listen to "Trepak" as you follow the map.

Listening Map for Trepak

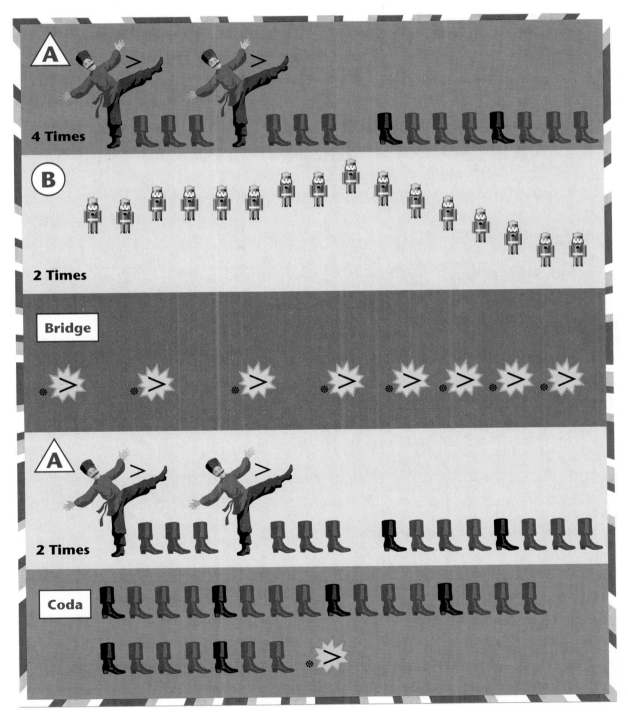

CONCEPT
RHYTHM
SKILLS
SING, IDENTIFY

The song "Mele Kalikimaka" went around the world on Bing Crosby's "White Christmas" album, and became a popular holiday song of the 1950s.

Identify the sound of the ukulele in this song.

Mele Kalikimaka

Merry Christmas

CD 22:16

Words and Music by R. Alex Anderson

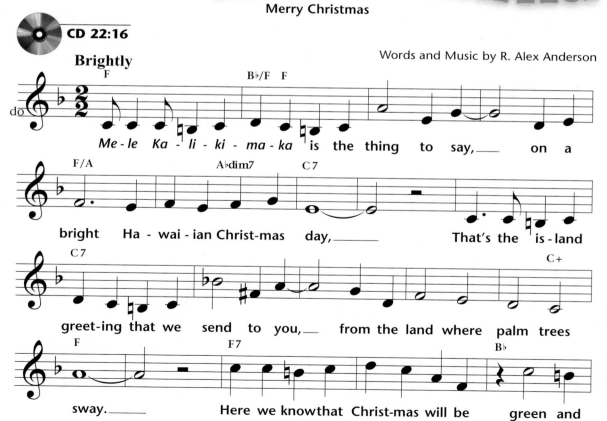

Me - le Ka - li - ki - ma - ka is the thing to say, ___ on a

bright Ha - wai - ian Christ-mas day, ___ That's the is - land

greet-ing that we send to you, ___ from the land where palm trees

sway. ___ Here we know that Christ-mas will be green and

bright, the sun will shine by day, and all the stars at night,

Me - le Ka - li - ki - ma - ka is Ha - wai - i's way to

say Mer-ry Christ-mas to you._____ you._____

R. Alex Anderson (1894–1995) was born in Honolulu, Hawaii. He had no formal musical training and did not speak Hawaiian, yet his songs capture the musical identity of the Hawaiian people. He was also a golf partner of Bing Crosby!

CONCEPT
STRUCTURE

SKILLS
SING

The song "Silent Night" was originally written in German, with the title "Stille Nacht, Heilige Nacht." It was written on Christmas Eve in 1818 by Franz Gruber, an Austrian organist and composer, and Josef Mohr, a clergyman. "Night of Stars" was composed to be a partner song with "Silent Night." Partner songs are songs that can be sung together to create harmony.

Night of Stars / Silent Night

CD 22:19

Words and Music by Linda Worsley
Music by Franz Gruber
Words by Josef Mohr

Sing 1st and 3rd times only

Night of won-der, night of stars, one bright-er star a-

Sing 2nd and 3rd times

Si - lent night, ho - ly night, All is calm,

bove. Lis - ten now to an - gels sing-ing.

all is bright 'round yon vir - gin moth - er and child.

Hear the joy - ful mes - sage ring-ing: Peace, peace to

Ho - ly in - fant so ten - der and mild, Sleep in heav - en-ly

CONCEPT
BACKGROUND
SKILLS
LISTEN

Kwanzaa is a unique African American celebration that focuses on the values of family, community, and responsibility. Families and friends gather together to remember their culture, history, and ancestors. Kwanzaa is based on seven guiding principles, one for each day between December 26th and January 1st. Kwanzaa uses words from Swahili, an African language. The word Kwanzaa means "first fruits of the harvest."

KWANZAA is...

Kwanzaa is a holiday,
but unlike most,
does not convey
a religious observation
nor does it celebrate our nation.

And though our nation gave it birth,
it celebrates the cultural worth
of a darker continent
and the people they were sent.

People of a darker hue,
People much like me and you,
People whose great history
has been cloaked in mystery.

So Kwanzaa is
the time and place to reflect and retrace
the history missing from the books,
a time for taking second looks.

Kwanzaa is the poured libation
spilled in reverent observation
of the past that paved the way
for your people here today.

Kwanzaa is "nguzo saba,"
the seven principles that we harbor,
beginning with the unity
that makes us strong and helps us see
in perspective proper light
the other six that we recite.

One day after Christmas comes,
we listen to the kwanzaa drums
and celebrate for seven days
our old customs and modern ways.

So Kwanzaa is our very own,
since 1966 it's grown
from a private observation
to one that's shared thoughout the nation.

—*Cedric McClester*

 LISTENING CD 22:23

Seven Principles

by Bernice Johnson Reagan

The Kwanzaa song "Seven Principles" is performed by Sweet Honey in The Rock. This ensemble of African American women perform arrangements of spirituals, hymns, gospel, jazz, and blues, as well as their original compositions.

Find ways to include the seven principles of Kwanzaa in your everyday routine.

See **music.mmhschool.com**
Research Kwanzaa on the Web.

CONCEPT
RHYTHM
SKILLS
IDENTIFY

The powerful speeches of Dr. Martin Luther King, Jr., defined the civil rights movement in the early 1960s. In the summer of 1963, Dr. Martin Luther King, Jr., delivered his "I Have a Dream" speech to over 200,000 Americans in Washington, D.C.

LISTENING CD 22:27

I Have a Dream
by Dr. Martin Luther King, Jr.

Dr. King was a powerful speaker. His words delivered a strong message reinforced by his expressive voice.

Identify changes of tempo in "I Have a Dream."

During the civil rights movement, African American people sang to stay strong and unified, and to express the ideals for which they were fighting. The words of the spiritual "I'm Gonna Sit at the Welcome Table" speak of the desire to have equal rights.

I'm Gonna Sit at the Welcome Table

CD 22:24

African American Spiritual

1. I'm gon-na sit at the wel-come ta-
2. I'm gon-na move those Jim Crow la-
3. I'm gon-na walk the streets of glo-
4. All God's chil-dren gon-na sit to-geth-

ble, lis-ten to me. I'm gon-na sit at the wel-come
bels, lis-ten to me. I'm gon-na move those Jim Crow
ry, lis-ten to me. I'm gon-na walk the streets of
er, lis-ten to me. All God's chil-dren gon-na sit to-

ta - ble one of these days, Hal - le - lu - jah. I'm gon-na
la - bels one of these days, Hal - le - lu - jah. I'm gon-na
glo - ry one of these days, Hal - le - lu - jah. I'm gon-na
geth - er one of these days, Hal - le - lu - jah. All God's

sit at the wel - come ta - ble. I'm gon-na
move those Jim Crow la - bels. I'm gon-na
walk the streets of glo - ry. I'm gon-na
chil-dren gon - na sit to - geth - er. All God's

1., 2., 3.

sit at the wel - come ta - ble one of these days. ____
move those Jim Crow la - bels one of these days. ____
walk the streets of glo - ry one of these days. ____
chil-dren gon-na sit to - geth - er one of these days. ____

4.

____ All God's chil - dren _____ gon - na sit to -

geth - er one of these days. _____

CONCEPT
TONALITY

SKILLS
SING

Valentine's Day is a time to celebrate love and friendship. How do you celebrate your friendships?

 LISTENING **CD 22:32**

You've Got a Friend by Carole King

Carole King's hit song, "You've Got a Friend," enjoyed popularity both through her 1971 recording and through her friend James Taylor's recording of the same year. Both artists have been inducted into the Grammy Hall of Fame, which honors recordings of historical significance and enduring quality that have thrived for twenty-five years or more.

Sing this traditional Scandinavian folk song about the importance of friends.

Vem Kan Segla

Who Can Sail?

CD 22:28

Folk Song from Åland, a Swedish-speaking Island of Finland.
English Words by Linda Worsley

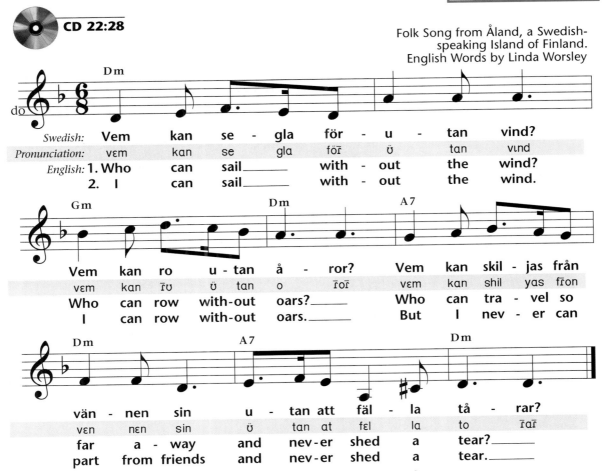

Dm

Swedish: Vem kan se - gla för - u - tan vind?
Pronunciation: vɛm kan se gla föɾ ʊ tan vɪnd
English: 1. Who can sail____ with - out the wind?
2. I can sail____ with - out the wind.

Gm   Dm   A7

Vem kan ro u - tan å - ror? Vem kan skil - jas från
vɛm kan ɾʊ ʊ tan o ɾoɾ vɛm kan shil yas fɾon
Who can row with-out oars?____ Who can tra - vel so
I can row with-out oars.____ But I nev - er can

Dm   A7   Dm

vän - nen sin u - tan att fäl - la tå - rar?
vɛn nɛn sin ʊ tan at fɛl la to ɾaɾ
far a - way and nev-er shed a tear?____
part from friends and nev-er shed a tear.____

Write a letter to a friend, expressing your gratitude for the friendship.

Noruz is the Iranian New Year's festival. It celebrates hope and renewal. Between the 19th and 21st of March, families gather at their homes and wait for the start of the new year. To celebrate the new year, relatives pay visits to each other and exchange gifts of coins and sweets.

Sing this song about Haji Firuz, one of the entertainers of Noruz. He wanders the streets and alleyways in his red costume, playing his tambourine, during the final weeks of the year.

Part of the Noruz celebration is planting *sabzeh,* usually wheat or lentil sprouts, representing rebirth. Apples represent health and beauty.

Haji Firuz

Persian Folk Song
As Collected and Sung by Hooshang Bagheri
English Version by MMH

CD 23:1

Pronunciation: hɑ ji fi ɾuz æm mæn sɔ li yɛ ɾuz æm mæn
English: Ha - ji Fi - ruz I am! Ev - 'ry year I come 'round.

hɑ ji fi ɾuz æm mæn sɔ li yɛ ɾuz æm mæn
Ha - ji Fi - ruz I am! Ev - 'ry year I come 'round.

Instrumental

sɔl e no vi ni ɔ mæd e di ke xɔx ti ɔ mæd
Cel - e - brate a fine new year, Cel - e - brate, the time is here.

sha di ko nid pɑ be ku bid dæst də zæ nid ke ɔ mæd
Stamp your feet, and clap your hands and Cel - e - brate the fine new year.

421

Seasonal Songs

In Finland, also known as *Suomi*, spring begins in early April.

Suomen Salossa

The Finnish Forest

MAP

NORWAY
FINLAND
SWEDEN
ESTONIA
RUSSIA
LATVIA

CD 23:5

Finnish Folk Song
English Words by Linda Worsley

Finnish: Hon - ka - en kess - kel - lä mök - ki - ni sei - soo,
Pronunciation: hon ka ɛn kɛs kɛl lœ mök ki ni sɛɪ so
English: Deep in the pines of the green leaf - y for - est,

Suo - me - ni so - re - as - sa sa - los - sa,
swɔ me ni so ɾe as sa sa los sa
There in Su - o - mi - land, my cot - tage stands.

Hon - ka - en vä - lil - tä siin - ta - vä sel - kä
hon ka ɛn vœ lil tœ sin ta vœ sɛl kœ
Light spark - 'ling 'round from the dawn soft - ly break - ing,

Vilk - ku - vi ko - it - te - hen va - los - sa. Hoi
vilk ku vi ko 'it tɛ hɛn va los sa hɔɪ
Here in Su - o - mi - land, the fair - est of lands. *Hoi*

laa - ri laa - ri laa, Hoi laa - ri laa - ri laa, Hoi
la ɾi la ɾi la hɔɪ la ɾi la ɾi la hɔɪ
laa - ri laa - ri laa, Hoi laa - ri laa - ri laa, Hoi

laa - ri laa - ri laa, Hoi laa - ri laa - ri laa,
laa - ri laa - ri laa, Hoi laa - ri laa - ri laa,

Kai - ku mun su - loi - nen Suo - me - ni maa!
Joy - ful the song of our fair na - tive land!

LISTENING CD 23:9

Introduction (excerpt) from *The Rite of Spring*

by Igor Stravinsky

Igor Stravinsky (1882–1971) wrote *The Rite of Spring* as a ballet score.
The piece begins with a very high bassoon solo, which is famous
among bassoonists for its difficulty!

Listening Map for Introduction

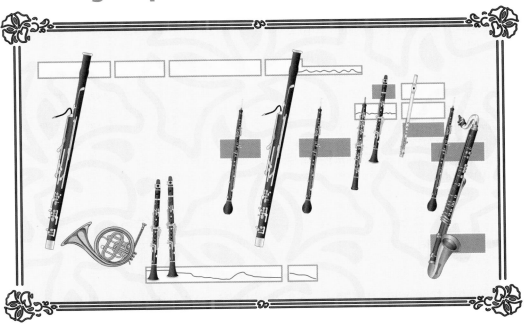

CONCEPT
RHYTHM
SKILLS
SING

Shavuot is a traditional Jewish festival that celebrates the spring harvest. In ancient times, farmers brought the first fruits of the harvest to Jerusalem to give thanks. In modern times, first fruits and vegetables are often donated to the poor. "Shibolet Basadeh" is a popular circle dance song that talks about the harvest.

Sing "Shibolet Basadeh," stamping your foot and clapping your hands on every beat.

Shibolet Basadeh

Wheat in the Field

CD 23:10

Words and Music by Matiyahu Shelem
English Words by Linda Worsley

Identify Section A and Section B in "Shibolet Basadeh."

Jewish Musicians in Jerusalem

This painting was created by Vladimir Mnev (b. 1950). Before he became an artist, Vladimir Mnev studied physics in Moscow. Now he lives in Jerusalem.

Write a story about the musicians in this painting.

Concerns about protecting the planet and preserving natural resources increased in the second half of the twentieth century. People began to take action to protect the environment. Earth Day was created more than thirty years ago to help raise public awareness of this issue.

"Earth Child" is a Native American song that celebrates the beauty and wonder of our planet.

Listen to "Earth Child" and point to the syncopated patterns whenever you hear them.

Earth Child

CD 23:14

Words and Music by Sharon Burch

Vocables: Hey yah way— oh high yoh hey— oh high yoh hen— nay

2 Fine

yen nah hen— nay yen nah hen— nay yen nah hen— nay yennah

English: I am an Earth chi - ld. I live in beau - ty all— a -

round me. Vocables: Hen— nay yen nah hen— nay yen nah hen— nay

yen nah   hen__ nay yen nah   *English:* I am   the Sun's

chi - ld.   I   do be - lieve_____   in love and

D.C. al Fine

peace,____ With all the beau-ty that__ sur - rounds me.

Powwow

Powwows are Native American social and cultural celebrations. The heart of every powwow is the powwow circle, set aside for singing, dancing, and drumming. The circle represents the cycle of the moon, sun, earth and life. Traditionally, the musicians have often been men, but nowadays more and more of the skilled drummers, flute players and singers are women.

Play this rhythm along with "O Hal'lwe." Follow the dynamics of the song.

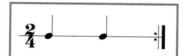

O Hal'lwe

Nanticoke Women's Honoring Song

 CD 23:18

Traditional Song of the Nanticoke Tribe

*First time through, begin **pp** and build to **ff**.*
*Last time through, begin **ff** and end **pp**.*

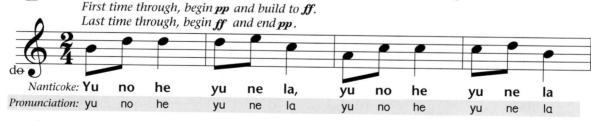

Nanticoke: **Yu no he yu ne la, yu no he yu ne la**
Pronunciation: yu no he yu ne la yu no he yu ne la

yu no he yu ne la yu no he yu ne la
yu no he yu ne la yu no he yu ne la

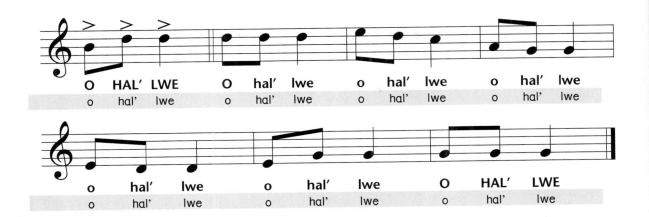

O HAL' LWE   O hal' lwe   o hal' lwe   o hal' lwe
o hal' lwe   o hal' lwe   o hal' lwe   o hal' lwe

o hal' lwe   o hal' lwe   O HAL' LWE
o hal' lwe   o hal' lwe   o hal' lwe

 LISTENING CD 23:22

Lakota Flute Song by Georgia Wettlin-Larsen

Georgia Wettlin-Larsen, also known as Whirling Cloud Woman, is a Sioux composer, performer and dancer. Wettlin-Larsen uses her voice to mimic the sound of the Plains flute.

Geraldine Barney

 LISTENING CD 23:23

Tsidii-Bird by Geraldine Barney

Geraldine Barney is a Navajo songwriter. Melodies from Plains and Navajo traditions inspired her to compose songs for flute, voice and guitar. *Tsidii* is the Navajo word for "bird."

Compare the two pieces of music.

Native American cedar flute

CD-ROM

Use *World Instruments* **CD-ROM** to learn more about Native American Instruments.

429

Playing the Recorder

Playing the Guitar

STANDARD TUNING

E A D G B E

Glossary of Instruments

A

---

accordion a keyboard instrument that is a kind of portable organ with keys, metal reeds, and a bellows. The bellows forces air past the reeds to produce sound. It is often played while standing, and is held by straps over the shoulders, **135 CD 25:10**

B

---

bagpipe a woodwind instrument that is made of a leather bag and pipes. It is played by blowing air through a blowpipe into the bag and then pressing the bag so that the air is forced out through the pipes, **CD 25:11**

banjo a string instrument that has a round body, a long neck, and five strings, played by plucking, **CD 25:20**

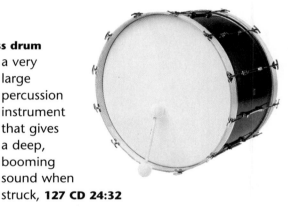

bass drum a very large percussion instrument that gives a deep, booming sound when struck, **127 CD 24:32**

bassoon a low-pitched woodwind instrument with a long wooden body attached to a smaller, curved metal tube with a double reed. It is played by blowing into the reed while covering fingerholes along the body. It is part of a woodwind quintet, **127 CD 24:15**

cello the second-largest instrument in the orchestral string family. It is held between the knees and played by bowing or plucking the strings. It is part of a string quartet or quintet, **CD 24:6**

clarinet a woodwind instrument that uses a single reed and is played by blowing into the mouthpiece while covering fingerholes along the body. It is part of a woodwind quintet, **148 CD 24:12**

conga a Latin American hand drum that has a low-pitched sound when struck and is usually played in pairs tuned a fifth apart, **7 CD 25:30**

cymbal a metal percussion instrument shaped like a plate that is played by hitting one against another or striking one with a stick or mallet to make a clashing sound, **CD 24:37**

djembe a West African drum usually made from pottery or wood and played with the hands, **CD 25:2**

double bass the largest instrument in the orchestral string family, held upright and played by bowing or plucking the strings, **CD 24:7**

flute a long, thin, woodwind instrument that is played by blowing across a hole at one end while covering holes along the body with fingers. It is part of a woodwind quintet, **CD 24:10**

French horn a brass instrument that is played by the buzzing of lips into the mouthpiece while pressing keys with fingers. It is part of a brass or woodwind quintet, **CD 24:20**

güiro a Latin American percussion instrument that is made from a gourd and has a bumpy surface that is scraped with a stick to make a sound, **7 CD 25:33**

guitar a string instrument with a long neck and usually six strings, played by strumming, plucking, or picking, **127 CD 25:13**

harp one of the oldest and largest instruments of the string family, in which the strings are set in an upright triangle-like frame with a curved top. It is played by plucking or strumming the strings with fingers, **127**
CD 24:8

koto a long, flat, Japanese string instrument that is played by plucking its 13 strings, **15**
CD 25:53

mandolin a string instrument that is similar to a small guitar but it has a different body shape and 8 metal strings,
CD 25:16

maracas a Latin American percussion instrument that is made from a gourd and is played by shaking, which produces a rattling sound. They are usually played in pairs, **7 CD 25:35**

oboe a high-pitched, double-reed woodwind instrument that is played by blowing into the reed while covering fingerholes along the body. It is sometimes part of a woodwind quintet,
CD 24:13

piano a keyboard instrument in the percussion family that is played by pressing keys on the keyboard. Its sound is produced by hammers hitting stretched strings, **32 CD 24:41**

piccolo a small woodwind instrument, similar to the flute, but playing higher pitches, **CD 24:11**

saxophone a woodwind instrument that is played by blowing into the mouthpiece while pressing keys along the body with fingers, **CD 24:16**

shekere an African percussion instrument that is a hollow gourd covered with a net of beads or seeds, **CD 25:8**

slit drum a percussion instrument that is found in Africa, Asia, and Oceania and is formed by hollowing a tree trunk through a slit on one side, **CD 25:9**

snare drum a percussion instrument with wires or strings stretched along the bottom. When the top of the drum is struck, the wires vibrate and give the drum a loud, slightly rattley sound, **CD 24:35**

spoon a common household object that is used as a percussion instrument by holding two together and striking them against the body. Musicians sometimes use an instrument created by fastening two spoons together with a wooden handle, **CD 25:23**

timpani also known as kettledrums, a set of percussion instruments consisting of two or more large kettle-shaped drums played with mallets, **CD 24:26**

taiko drum a barrel-shaped Japanese percussion instrument that is played with sticks, or *bachi*, **16 CD 25:51**

trombone a large, low-pitched instrument in the brass family. It is played by the buzzing of lips into the mouthpiece while moving the slide in or out. It is sometimes part of a brass quintet, **CD 24:21**

tambourine a percussion instrument that is a small, hand-held drum with metal disks attached loosely around the rim. It is played by either shaking or tapping with the hand, **CD 24:36**

trumpet the smallest, highest-pitched instrument in the brass family, played by the buzzing of lips into the mouthpiece while pressing keys with fingers. It is often used to play a fanfare to honor important people or to announce an important event, and is part of a brass quintet, **CD 24:18**

tuba the largest, lowest-pitched instrument in the brass family, played by the buzzing of lips into the mouthpiece while pressing keys with fingers. It is part of a brass quintet, **127 CD 24:22**

xylophone a percussion instrument that is made up of one or two rows of wooden bars of different lengths, played by hitting the bars with mallets, **127 CD 24:30**

viola a string instrument larger and lower-sounding than the violin. It is played by being held under the chin and bowing or plucking the strings. It is part of a string quartet or quintet, **CD 24:5**

violin the smallest of the orchestral string instruments. It is played by being held under the chin and bowing or plucking the strings. It is part of a string quartet or quintet, **127 CD 24:4**

Glossary of Terms

A

AABA form a four-part form with just two segments of music—one for each of the A sections and one for the B section, **168**

alla breve an Italian musical term that means "cut time," **207**

aria a solo song typically heard in an opera, **218**

arrangement a different version or adaptation of a musical composition, **50**

B

bass low in pitch, **146**

bhangra a lively form of music and dance that originated in northern India, **224**

blues a style of music in which a singer/songwriter shows his or her pain in a way with which we can understand and identify, **178**

C

canon a musical form in which a melody is imitated exactly in one or more parts, similar to a round, **49**

choir an organized group of singers, **46**

chord three or more pitches sounded together, **140**

choreography the art of making up a pattern of dance movements to go with specific music, **87**

clefs the symbols at the beginning of a staff that indicate the pitch of the notes, **132**

consonance the sounding of a combination of pitches that creates little tension, **68, 316**

countermelody a contrasting melody written to go with a song, **177**

cut time ¢ or 2/2 a meter signature in which there are two beats in each measure and the half note gets one beat, **207**

D

descant an accompanying melody that is sung above the main melody of a song, **52**

dissonance the sounding of a combination of pitches that creates harmonic tension and that sounds unfinished, **68, 316**

Dorian mode a scale using all the white keys of a keyboard from D to D, **104, 137**

drum circles music-making events where people sit or stand in a circle while playing world percussion instruments, **37**

E

enunciate to pronounce words clearly, **55**

F

figures a series of dance steps, **96**

form the order of phrases or sections in music, **27**

G

gigue a lively dance that was popular in the seventeenth century, **128**

grapevine a patterned dance step, **217**

H

head voice the voice young males use to sing high notes after their voices have started to change, **360**

I

interval the distance between two pitches, **342**

intonation singing or playing the correct pitch in tune, **48**

K

kokiriko an ancient Japanese percussion instrument that is made up of short lengths of thin bamboo; it makes a fast rippling sound when played, **145**

L

lyrics the words of a song, **150**

M

madrigal a song in which famous poetry is used for song lyrics, **336**

melismas groups of notes sung on a single word or syllable, **336**

melodic contour the upward or downward movement, or shape, of a melody, **25**

melody a pattern of pitches that moves upward, downward, or stays the same, **22**

meter the organization of beats within a measure, **182, 209**

modes another name for scales; for example, the Dorian mode, **210**

modulations transitions from a section of music based on one scale to a section based on a different scale, **61**

N

nationalism a style of music that uses folk music melodies and rhythms in large-scale orchestral works, **229**

O

overture an instrumental piece that begins an opera or other large musical work, **152**

P

parallel to move in the same direction, **58**

partner songs separate songs that sound good when sung at the same time, **227**

pentatonic a scale having only five pitches, **12**

R

ragtime a style of piano music in which the melody is strongly syncopated while the accompaniment keeps a steady beat, **110**

rhythm combinations of longer and shorter sounds and silences, **6**

rock and roll a style of music developed in the 1950s that combined the traditions of blues and country music, **234**

root the pitch on which a chord is built, **146**

round 1) a type of canon; a short song for two or more voices in which each voice begins at a different time; 2) a type of dance that is done in a circle, **98**

sixteen-bar blues a form of blues in which a 4-bar statement is made and repeated twice, and then a 4-bar response to the statement concludes the piece, **179**

solfège rehearsing a song using pitch syllables, **48**

spiritual an African American folk song, many of which began as religious songs, **365**

syncopation a type of rhythm in which stressed sounds occur on normally weak beats or between beats, **13**

taiko a kind of Japanese drumming music; the Japanese word *taiko* means "fat drum," **16**

texture the way melody and harmony combine to create layers of sound, **29**

timbre tone color, **65, 360**

tonic the starting note of each scale, **210**

transpose to change the key of a piece of music, **218**

triads chords of three pitches, each one of which is two steps away from the other, **140**

unison all performing the same part at the same time, **46**

upbeat tempo a quick and energetic speed to the beat, **13**

vibration rapid movement back and forth or up and down, **66**

Acknowledgments, continued

Every Mornin' When I Wake Up, Words and Music by Avon Gillespie. Copyright © by CPP/Belwin, Inc. All Rights Reserved. Used by Permission.

Fortune Favors the Brave, from Walt Disney Theatrical Productions' AIDA. Music by Elton John. Lyrics by Tim Rice. Copyright © 2000 Wonderland Music Company, Inc., Happenstance Ltd. and Evadon Ltd. All Rights Reserved. Used by Permission.

Ghost Ship, The, from REFLECTIONS OF A LAD AT SEA. Words by Don Besig and Nancy Price. Music by Don Besig. Copyright © 1982 by Shawnee Press, Inc. International Copyright Secured. All Rights Reserved. Reprinted by Permission.

Gonna Build a Mountain, from the Musical Production STOP THE WORLD - I WANT TO GET OFF. Words and Music by Leslie Bricusse and Anthony Newley. Copyright © Copyright 1961. (Renewed.) TRO Essex Music Ltd., London, England. TRO - Ludlow Music, Inc., New York, controls all publication rights for the U.S.A. and Canada. International Copyright Secured. All Rights Reserved Including Public Performance For Profit. Used by Permission.

Guitar Man, The, Words and Music by Audrey Snyder. Copyright © 1979 by Jenson Publications. International Copyright Secured. All Rights Reserved.

Heart, from DAMN YANKEES. Words and Music by Richard Adler and Jerry Ross. Copyright © 1955 FRANK MUSIC CORP. © Renewed 1983 LAKSHMI PUJA MUSIC LTD. and J & J ROSS MUSIC CO. All Rights Administered by THE SONGWRITERS GUILD OF AMERICA. All Rights Reserved. Used by Permission.

Huainito, Argentinian Folk Song. Arranged by Victoria Ebel-Sabo. Copyright © Shawnee Press, Inc. International Copyright Secured. All Rights Reserved. Reprinted by Permission.

If I Had a Hammer (The Hammer Song), Words and Music by Lee Hays and Pete Seeger. TRO - © Copyright 1958 (Renewed) and 1962 (Renewed). Ludlow Music, Inc., New York, NY. International Copyright Secured. All Rights Reserved Including Public Performance For Profit. Used by Permission.

It Don't Mean a Thing (If It Ain't Got that Swing), Words and Music by Duke Ellington and Irving Mills. Copyright © 1932 (Renewed 1959) and Assigned to Famous Music Corporation and EMI Mills Music Inc. in the U.S.A. Rights for the world outside the U.S.A. Controlled by EMI Mills Music Inc. (Publishing) and Warner Bros. Publications U.S. Inc. (Print). International Copyright Secured. All Rights Reserved.

Jordan's Angels, Words and Music by Rollo Dilworth. Incorporating "All Night, All Day" Traditional Spiritual. Copyright © 2002 by HAL LEONARD CORPORATION. International Copyright Secured. All Rights Reserved.

Kakokolo, Words and Music by Samite of Uganda. Copyright © by Samite Music. International Copyright Secured. All Rights Reserved.

Lean on Me, Words and Music by Bill Withers. Copyright © 1972 Interior Music Corp. (BMI). Copyright Renewed. All Rights Reserved. Used by Permission.

Let It Roll, Words and Music by Paul Kennerley. Copyright © 1983. RONDOR MUSIC LONDON) LTD. All Rights in the USA and Canada Controlled and Administered by IRVING MUSIC, INC. All Rights Reserved. Used by Permission.

Let Music Surround You, Words and Music by Fran Addicott. Copyright © by Fran Addicott. International Copyright Secured. All Rights Reserved.

Listen to the Music, Words and Music by Ed Robertson. Copyright © by Hinshaw Music, Inc. International Copyright Secured. All Rights Reserved.

Lullaby of Broadway, from GOLD DIGGERS OF 1935. Words by Al Dubin. Music by Harry Warren. Copyright © 1935. (Renewed.) WARNER BROS. INC. All Rights Reserved. Used by Permission.

Mama Will Provide, From MTI's Broadway Junior Broadway for Kids ONCE ON THIS ISLAND Junior. Lyrics by Lynn Ahrens. Music by Stephen Flaherty. Lyrics Copyright © 1991 Hillsdale Music. Music Copyright © 1991 by Stephen Flaherty. All Rights Reserved. Used by Permission.

Mele Kalikimaka (Merry Christmas), Words and Music by Alex Anderson. Copyright © 1949. UNIVERSAL – POLYGRAM INTERNATIONAL PUBLISHING, INC. Copyright Renewed. All Rights Reserved. Used by Permission.

Merecumbé, Puerto Rican Children's Song. Arranged by Alejandro Jimenez. Copyright © by Alejandro Jimenez. International Copyright Secured All Rights Reserved.

Morena de mi corazón (Dark Haired Lady of my Heart), Words and Music Cesar Rosas. Copyright © 1995. CEROS MUSIC (BMI)/Admin. by BUG MUSIC. All Rights Reserved. Used by Permission.

Mountain Music, Words and Music by Randy Owen. Copyright © 1980. Sony/ATV Songs LLC. All Rights Administered by Sony/ATV Music Publishing, 8 Music Square West, Nashville, TN 37203. International Copyright Secured. All Rights Reserved.

Mr. Scott Joplin's Ragtime Rag, Based on "Pineapple Rag" by Scott Joplin. Additional Words and Music by Mark Brymer. Copyright © 2002 by Brymark Publishing Co. International Copyright Secured. All Rights Reserved.

New Ashmolean Marching Society and Students Conservatory Band, The, from WHERE'S CHARLEY? by Frank Loesser. Copyright © 1948, 1950 (Renewed) FRANK MUSIC CORP. All Rights Reserved.

O, Desayo, Angolan Folk Song. English Words and Arrangement by Elliot Z. Levine. Copyright © 1995 by Plymouth Music Co., Inc. Used by Permission.

O, La Le! (Caribbean Praise), Words and Music by Hugh Davis. Copyright © 2004 by HAL LEONARD CORPORATION. International Copyright Secured. All Rights Reserved.

Old Barn Dance, The, Words and Music by Jan Reese. Copyright © 1987 by HAL LEONARD CORPORATION. International Copyright Secured. All Rights Reserved.

On a Clear Day (You Can See Forever), from ON A CLEAR DAY YOU CAN SEE FOREVER. Words by Alan Jay Lerner. Music by Burton Lane. Copyright © 1965 by Chappell & Co. and WB Music Corp. in the United States. Copyright Renewed. Chappell & Co. owner of publication and allied rights for the rest of the world. International Copyright Secured. All Rights Reserved.

One Dime Blues, Words and Music by Blind Lemon Jefferson. Edited with New Material by Alan Lomax. TRO - © Copyright 1959 (Renewed) Folkways Music Publishers, Inc., New York, NY. International Copyright Secured. All Rights Reserved Including Public Performance For Profit. Used by Permission.

One of Those Songs, English Lyric by Will Holt. Music by Gerald Calvi. Copyright © 1958, 1965 by EDITIONS MUSICALES DU CARROUSEL. Copyright Renewed. All Rights for the USA and Canada Controlled and Administered by UNIVERSAL MUSIC CORP. International Copyright Secured. All Rights Reserved.

Orange Blossom Special, Words and Music by Ervin T. Rouse. Copyright © 1938, 1947 UNIVERSAL MUSIC CORP. Copyright Renewed. All Rights Reserved. Used by Permission.

Perfect Winter Day, A, Words and Music by Teresa and Paul Jennings. Copyright © by Plank Road Publishing. International Copyright Secured. All Rights Reserved.

Acknowledgments, continued

Rage and Roar, Words and Music by Elizabeth Gilpatrick. Copyright © by Elizabeth Gilpatrick. International Copyright Secured. All Rights Reserved.

Ride on the Wind, Words and Music by Mark Patterson. Copyright © Shawnee Press, Inc. International Copyright Secured. All Rights Reserved. Reprinted by Permission.

River of My People, Words and Music by Pete Seeger. Copyright © by Stormking Music, Inc. International Copyright Secured. All Rights Reserved.

Rock Around the Clock, Words and Music by Max C. Freedman and Jimmy DeKnight. Copyright © 1953 Myers Music Inc. and Capano Music. Copyright Renewed 1981. All Rights on behalf of Myers Music Inc. Administered by Sony/ATV Music Publishing, 8 Music Square West, Nashville, TN 37203. International Copyright Secured. All Rights Reserved.

Samba de Orfeu (Dance of Orpheus), Words by Antonio Maria. Music by Luiz Bonfa. Copyright © 1959 by Nouvelles Editions Meridian. Copyrights for the United States of America and Canada Renewed and Assigned to Chappell & Co. and United Artists Music Co., Inc. All Rights Administered by Chappell & Co. International Copyright Secured. All Rights Reserved.

San Antonio Rose by Bob Wills. Copyright © 1940 by Bourne Co. Copyright Renewed. International Copyright Secured. All Rights Reserved.

Sing Hosanna, Words and Music by Michael Jothen. Copyright © 1977 by Beckenhorst Press, Inc. International Copyright Secured. All Rights Reserved.

Slap That Bass, Music and Lyrics by George Gershwin and Ira Gershwin. Copyright © 1937 (Renewed 1964) GEORGE GERSHWIN MUSIC and IRA GERSHWIN MUSIC. All rights administered by WB MUSIC CORP. All Rights Reserved.

Step into the Spotlight, Words and Music by Emily Crocker, John Higgins and John Jacobson. Copyright © 2004 by HAL LEONARD CORPORATION. International Copyright Secured. All Rights Reserved.

'Taint What You Do (It's the Way that Cha Do It), Words and Music by Sy Oliver and James Young. Copyright © 1939. (Renewed) by Embassy Music Corporation (BMI) in the United States. All Rights outside the United States Controlled and Administered by Universal MUSIC CORP. International Copyright Secured. All Rights Reserved. Reprinted by Permission.

Texas, Our Texas, Words by Gladys Yoakum Wright and William J. Marsh. Music by William J. Marsh. Copyright © 1925 by William J. Marsh. Copyright renewed 1953 by William J. Marsh. Used by Permission of Owen E. Thomas and Mary C. Hearne, Copyright owners. Published by Southern Music Company.

That Great Come and Get It Day, from FINIAN'S RAINBOW. Words and Music by E.Y. Harburg and Burton Lane. Copyright © 1946 by Chappell & Co. Copyright Renewed. International Copyright Secured. All Rights Reserved.

There Was a Blue Flower, Words and Music by Libby Larsen. Copyright © 2001 by Libby Larsen Publishing. International Copyright Secured. All Rights Reserved.

They Call the Wind Maria, from PAINT YOUR WAGON. Words by Alan Jay Lerner. Music by Frederick Loewe. Copyright © 1951 by Alan Jay Lerner and Frederick Loewe. Copyright Renewed. Chappell & Co. owner of publication and allied rights throughout the world. International Copyright Secured. All Rights Reserved.

This Pretty Planet, Words and Music by John Forster and Tom Chapin. Copyright © 1988. The Last Music Company (ASCAP) and Limousine Music Co. (ASCAP). International Copyright Secured. All Rights Reserved.

Troika, Based on a Traditional Russian Folk Song. Additional Words and Music by Dave and Jean Perry. Copyright © 1986. Shawnee Press, Inc. International Copyright Secured. All Rights Reserved.

Waiting for Life, From MTI's Broadway Junior Broadway for Kids ONCE ON THIS ISLAND Junior. Lyrics by Lynn Ahrens. Music by Stephen Flaherty. Lyrics Copyright © 1991 Hillsdale Music. Music Copyright © 1991 by Stephen Flaherty. All Rights Reserved. Used by Permission.

Walk by the River, Words and Music by Holly Jo Turnquist Fischer. Copyright © 1986. RHODA Publishing, 413 E. 7th St., Northfield, MN 55057, (507) 645-8338. International Copyright Secured. All Rights Reserved.

Water Is Wide, The, English Folk Song. Arranged by Luigi Zaninelli. Copyright © Shawnee Press, Inc. International Copyright Secured. All Rights Reserved. Reprinted by Permission.

When I Sing, Words and Music by Bill Henderson. Copyright © by Boosey & Hawkes, Inc. International Copyright Secured. All Rights Reserved. Used by Permission.

Why We Tell the Story, From MTI's Broadway Junior Broadway for Kids ONCE ON THIS ISLAND Junior. Lyrics by Lynn Ahrens. Music by Stephen Flaherty. Lyrics Copyright © 1991 Hillsdale Music. Music Copyright © 1991 by Stephen Flaherty. All Rights Reserved. Used by Permission.

Yellow Bird, Words and Music by Irving Burgie. Copyright © 1957; Renewed 1985 Cherry Lane Music Publishing Company, Inc. (ASCAP), Lord Burgess Music Publishing (ASCAP) and DreamWorks Songs (ASCAP) Worldwide Rights for Lord Burgess Music Publishing and DreamWorks Songs Administered by Cherry Lane Music Publishing Company, Inc. International Copyright Secured. All Rights Reserved.

You Sing for Me, Words and Music by Raymond K. McLain. Copyright © 1975 by McLain Family Music. International Copyright Secured. All Rights Reserved.

Literature

I Asked a Little Child, edited by Sara and Stephen Corrin, from *Once Upon A Rhyme.* Copyright © 1982 by Faber and Faber Limited. All Rights Reserved.

Kwanzaa is . . . by Cedric McClester, Copyright © 1990. Reprinted by permission of the author in *Make a Joyful Noise,* edited by Deborah Slier. Checkerboard Press, Inc. Copyright © 1991. All Rights Reserved. Used by Permission.

A Minor Bird by Robert Frost, from *Collected Poems, Prose, & Plays.* Copyright © 1949. Reprinted from *Complete Poems of Robert Frost,* by arrangement with Henry Holt and Company. All Rights Reserved. Used by Permission.

Songs for the People by Frances E.W. Harper. Copyright © 2000. Reprinted in *The Vintage Book of African-American Poetry,* edited by Michael S. Harper and Anthony Walton. A Vintage Original, a division of Random House, Inc. All Rights Reserved.

Unfolding Bud by Naoshi Koriyama, from The Christian Science Monitor. Copyright © 1957 by The Christian Science Monitor. All Rights Reserved.

CREDITS

Illustration Credits: Kathryn Adams: 126. Esther Baran: 103, 104-105. Kristin Barr: 172-173. Rose Mary Berlin: 91. Elizabeth Britton: 346-347, 348-349. Jannine Cabossel: 154-155. C.B. Canga: 334-335, 372-373, 374. Mike Carina: 14, 15. Pamela Carroll: 342-343, 344. Peter Church: 310-311. George Clark: 231. Giovannina Colalillo: 6-7. Bob Dombrowski: 58-59. Bill Farnsworth: 326-327, 328. Stan Fellows: 134-135, 136-137. Tina Fong: 241. Parker Fulton: 340-341, 381, 382. Steve Gardner: 166-167, 168-169. Patrick Jones: 210-211, 212-213. Patrick Kelley: vi, Spotlight on Performance (2). Alan King: 22, 25, 376-377. Doug Knutson: 184-185. Lori Lohstoeter: vii, Spotlight on Celebrations (2). Stephen Marchesi: 329, 330-331, 332. Robin Moore: 114-115, 116-117. Craig Orback: 323, 324-325. Walter L. Porter: 362-363, 364. Cindy Revell: 365, 366-367, 368-369. Adam Rogers: 378-379, 380. Charlie Shaw: 312-313. Stephen Snider: 4, 5, 318-319, 320-321, 322. Frank Sofo: 204. Craig Spearing: 74-75. Greg Stevenson: 221. Nicole Tadgell: 359. Brad Teare: 128-129. Mary Teichman: 219, 220. Jeff Thompson: 336-337, 338. Meryl Treatner: 350, 352-353, 354-355. Jeremy Tugeau: iv, Spotlight on Concepts (2). Kristen Varner: 46-47. Sally Jo Vitsky: v, Spotlight on Music Reading (2). Jane C. Wright: 98, 99.

Photography Credits: All photographs are copyright of Macmillan/McGraw-Hill (MMH) except as noted below.

Allan Landau for MMH: iv-vii: trombone, A-H: t.r., 2-3: bkgd., 4: t.l., 5: b.l., t.r., 19: b.r., 82-83: c., 90: l., r., 93: c., 97: b., 101: t.l., t.c.r., t.c.l., t.r., 108: t.r., 118: b.r., 122-123: r., 140: c.r., 163: b., 202-203, 218: r., 436: c.r., 437: t.l., c.r. . Jade Albert for MMH: cover, i: b.r. Shane Morgan for MMH: 71: t.l., t.r., 86: t.l., t.c.l., t.c.r., t.r.

iv-vii: side drum, cowbell, frame drum, soprano saxophone, congas, keyboard, tuba, wood blocks, Chinese wood blocks, PhotoDisc, Inc.; trumpet, silver drum, decorated drum, French horn, Corbis. A: c. Fred Prouser/Reuters NewMedia, Inc./Corbis; b.r. Richard Carson/Reuters NewMedia, Inc.; b.l. Redferns Music Picture Library; border, flag, Richard Cummins/Corbis; border, map, Cartesia/PhotoDisc, Inc./Getty Images; border, rabbit, Darrell Gulin/ Corbis; border, mission, Andre Jenny/Alamy Images, Ltd. A-B: t.l., border, bkgd. PhotoDisc, Inc.; border, hat and boots, Jules Frazier/ PhotoDisc, Inc./Getty Images. B: t.r., border, derricks, cactus, PhotoDisc, Inc.; b.l. Reuters NewMedia, Inc./Corbis; b.r. AP/ Central City Productions/Randy Piland; t.c. Buddy Mays/Corbis; border, bird, Jeremy Woodhouse/PhotoDisc, Inc./Getty Images; border, bridge, Corbis. C: t.r. Jim West/The Image Works; border, flag, The Granger Collection, New York. C-D: border, cactus, PhotoDisc, Inc.; border, hat and boots, Jules Frazier/PhotoDisc, Inc./Getty Images. D: border, flag, The Granger Collection, New York. E: b.l., border, flag, Richard Cummins/Corbis; b.r. Texas Secretary of State; t.r. Tim Mosenfelder/Getty Images; c. Bettmann/ Corbis; border, map, Cartesia/PhotoDisc, Inc./Getty Images; border, rabbit, Darrell Gulin/Corbis; border, mission, Andre Jenny/Alamy Images, Ltd. E-F: border, hat and boots, Jules Frazier/PhotoDisc, Inc./Getty Images; border, bkgd. PhotoDisc, Inc. F: t.l. Bettmann/ Corbis; t.r. Cartesia/PhotoDisc, Inc.; b.l. B. G. Thomson/Photo Researchers, Inc.; c. John Svoboda/FoodPix/Getty Images; b.c. Animals Animals/Earth Scenes; b.r., border, derricks, cactus, PhotoDisc, Inc.; border, bird, Jeremy Woodhouse/PhotoDisc, Inc./ Getty Images; border, bridge, Corbis. G: border, riverwalk, PhotoDisc, Inc.; border, children, Bettmann/Corbis; border, mission, Andre Jenny/Alamy Images, Ltd.; border, flag, The Granger Collection, New York. G-H: border, storm, Hulton Archive/Getty Images. H: t. Rob Atkins/The Image Bank/Getty Images; border, derricks, PhotoDisc, Inc.; border, engraving, MPI/Hulton Archive/ Getty Images; border, rocks, David Muench/Corbis. I: t.r. The Granger Collection, New York; c.l. Hulton Archive/Getty Images; b.r. PhotoDisc, Inc.; b.l. MetaCreations/Kai Power Photos; border, dome, G. E. Kidder Smith/Corbis; border, Alamo, Kean Collection/ Hulton Archive/Getty Images. I-J: border, dam, Underwood & Underwood/Corbis; border, oil field, H. P. Meissner/Hulton Archive/ Getty Images. J: t.c. Lindsay Hebberd/Corbis; b.c. The Granger Collection, New York; c.l. Corbis; t.r. Henry Griffin/AP/Wide World Photos; t.c.r. AP Photos; b.c.r. Susan Walsh/AP Photo; b.r. LM Otero/AP Photo; border, gusher, factory, Hulton Archive/Getty Images. K: border, dome, G. E. Kidder Smith/Corbis; border, Alamo, Kean Collection/Hulton Archive/Getty Images. K-L: bkgd. PhotoDisc, Inc.; border, dam, Underwood & Underwood/Corbis; border, oil field, H. P. Meissner/Hulton Archive/Getty Images. L: border, gusher, factory, Hulton Archive/Getty Images. M: c.l. Corbis; c.r. Rita Maas/The Image Bank/Getty Images; b.l. Museum of South Texas History. M-N: c. Museum of South Texas History; border, peppers, maracas, flag, PhotoDisc, Inc.; border, piñata, Image Club; border, taco, Comstock. N: t.r. Eric Gay/AP/Wide World Photos; t.l. AP Photo/Las Cruces Sun-News, Vladimir Chaloupka. O-P: bkgd. George H. Huey/Corbis; border, peppers, flag, maracas, PhotoDisc, Inc.; border, piñata, Image Club; border, taco, Comstock. Q: t.r. Danny Lehman/Corbis; c.l., b.r., border, riverwalk, PhotoDisc, Inc.; border, children, Bettmann/Corbis; border, mission, Andre Jenny/Alamy Images, Ltd.; border, flag, The Granger Collection, new York. Q-R: bkgd. PhotoDisc, Inc.; border, storm, Hulton Archive/Getty Images. R: border, derricks, PhotoDisc, Inc.; border, engraving, MPI/Hulton Archive/Getty Images; border, rocks, David Muench/Corbis. S: border, flag, The Granger Collection, New York. S-T: bkgd. George H. Huey/Corbis; border, cactus, PhotoDisc, Inc.; border, hat and boots, Jules Frazier/ PhotoDisc, Inc./Getty Images. T: t.r. Smithsonian American Art Museum, Washington, D.C./Art Resource, NY; border, flag, The Granger Collection, New York. U: t. David Muench/Corbis; border, flag, The Granger Collection, New York. U-V: border, cactus, PhotoDisc, Inc.; border, hat and boots, Jules Frazier/PhotoDisc, Inc./Getty Images. V: bkgd. David Muench/Corbis; r. Kevin Winter/ ImageDirect/Fox/Getty Images; border, flag, The Granger Collection, New York. W: t.r. Lindsay Hebberd/Corbis; b.r., c.l. Bob Daemmrich/PhotoEdit, Inc.; border, flag, Richard Cummins/Corbis; border, map, Cartesia/PhotoDisc, Inc./Getty Images; border, rabbit, Darrell Gulin/Corbis; border, mission, Andre Jenny/Alamy Images, Ltd. W-X: bkgd. The Image Works; border, hat and boots, Jules Frazier/PhotoDisc, Inc./Getty Images; border, bkgd. PhotoDisc, Inc. X: t.r. Robert Landau/Corbis; c.l. Bob Daemmrich/Bob Daemmrich Photography; b. Wally McNamee/Corbis; border, derricks, cactus, PhotoDisc, Inc.; border, bird, Jeremy Woodhouse/PhotoDisc, Inc./Getty Images; border, bridge, Corbis. 6-7: t. Dover Publications, Inc. 8: b.l. Comstock. 8-9: t. Dover Publications, Inc. 9: b. Pablo Corral V/Corbis; c.r. PhotoDisc, Inc. 10: t.r. Lebrecht Music & Arts Photo Library. 10-11: bkgd. Dover Publications, Inc. 11: b. 20th Century Fox Film Corporation, all rights reserved, courtesy Everett Collection. 12-13: bkgd. Dover Publications, Inc. 13: t.r., b. Bettmann/Corbis. 14-15: bkgd. Jon Burbank/The Image Works, Inc.; t. Jack Fields/Corbis. 15: t.r., c. Kenneth Hamm/Photo Japan; b.r. Kate Mount/Lebrecht Music & Arts Photo Library. 16: t.r. Toshiro Morita/HAGA/The Image Works, Inc.; b.l. S. Grant/Art Directors & Trip Photo Library; b.r. Kenneth Hamm/Photo Japan. 16-17: t. Jack Fields/Corbis; bkgd. Jon Burbank/The Image Works, Inc. 17: b.r. Robert Brenner/PhotoEdit, Inc.; t.l. Camera Press Digital/Retna, Ltd.; t.r. Camera Press/Paolo Negri/Retna, Ltd.; t.c. Kenneth Hamm/Photo Japan. 18: t.r. Bettmann/Corbis. 19: b.l. AP Photo/Mike Albans. 20: t.r. Chris Delmas/Zuma Press. 21: b. AP/Wide World Photos. 26: c. Dover Publications, Inc.; t.r. Victoria & Albert Museum, London, UK/Bridgeman Art Library. 26-27: bkgd., t. Dover Publications, Inc.; bkgd. Corbis. 27: t. Ancient Art & Architecture Collection, Ltd.; b. Private Collection/Bridgeman Art Library. 27-28: bkgd. Dover Publications, Inc. 28: t. Columbia/ Sony/Chan Kam Chuen/Kobal Collection; b.l., b.r., b.c. Keren Su/China Span. 28-29: t., bkgd. Dover Publications, Inc. 29: t.r. Columbia/Sony/Chan Kam Chuen/Kobal Collection; b.c. Lebrecht Music & Arts Photo Library; b.r. Keren Su/China Span; b.l. tk/China Span. 30: t.l. PhotoDisc, Inc. 30-31: bkgd. Dover Publications, Inc. 31: b. Alan Band/fox Photos/Hulton Archive/Getty Images. 32: c. courtesy of the John Cage Trust; t. Ebet Roberts/Ebet Roberts Photography; b. Bettmann/Corbis. 32-33: bkgd. Dover Publications, Inc. 34: t.r. David Bergman/Corbis. 34-35: bkgd. MetaCreations/Kai Power Photos; t. Corel. 35: c.r. www.hossamramzy.com; b.r. Chris Stock/Lebrecht Music & Arts Photo Library; c.r. J. Highet/Lebrecht Music & Arts Photo Library; t.l. Shirley Borchardt/Inner Visions Photographic Services. 36-37: bkgd. MetaCreations/Kai Power Photos; t. Corel. 39: t. PhotoDisc, Inc. 42: l. Dennis MacDonald/ PhotoEdit, Inc. 42-43: t. PhotoEdit, Inc. 43: t.l. Aneal Vohra/Unicorn Stock Photos. 44: t.r. David Young-Wolff/PhotoEdit, Inc. 45: b. Indianapolis Children's Choir; b.r. San Diego Children's Choir; t.r. The Image Works; t.l. Syracuse Newspapers/The Image Works,Inc. 47: b.r. National Gallery of Art, Washington, D.C./SuperStock. 48: t.r. Jeff Greenberg/Visuals Unlimited. 48-49: b. Vicky Alhadeff/ Lebrecht Music & Arts Photo Library. 50: bkgd. Vicky Alhadeff/ Lebrecht Music & Arts Photo Library. 51: t.r., bkgd. Vicky Alhadeff/ Lebrecht Music & Arts Photo Library. 52: t.r. Associated Press, AP/AP/Wide World Photos. 54-55: bkgd. Corbis; bkgd. The Gilbert and Sullivan Collection/The Pierpont Morgan Library, New York, NY/Art Resource, NY; bkgd. AP/Wide World Photos. 55: t.r. Corbis. 56: t.r., b.r. Photofest. 56-57: bkgd. The Gilbert and Sullivan Collection/The Pierpont Morgan Library, New York, NY/Art Resource, NY; bkgd. AP/Wide World Photos; bkgd. PhotoDisc, Inc. 60: t.r. Corbis; c. PhotoDisc, Inc. 60: t.r. Corbis; c. PhotoDisc, Inc. 60-61: bkgd. Erich Lessing/Art Resource, NY. 61: b.l. Corbis; b.r. Kit Houghton/Corbis; c.r., t.r. PhotoDisc, Inc. 62: t.l., b.r., t.r. PhotoDisc, Inc. 62-63: bkgd. MetaCreations/Kai Power Photos. 64: b.l., b.r. PhotoDisc, Inc. 64-65: bkgd. MetaCreations/Kai Power Photos. 65: c.r. Eric L. Wheater/Lonely Planet Images; c.r. Czech Boy's Choir Boni Pueri. 66: b., c.r. courtesy of Korg USA/Korg USA. 66-67: bkgd. Barry Lewis/Corbis; t. reproduced by permission of The State Hermitage Museum, St. Petersburg, Russia/Corbis. 67: b. reproduced by permission of The State Hermitage Museum, St. Petersburg, Russia/Corbis; b.l. Paul Almasy/Corbis; b.r. Adam Woolfitt/Corbis. 68: r. Adam Tanner/The Image Works, Inc.; l. Dave G. Houser/Corbis. 68-69: t. reproduced by permission of The State Hermitage Museum, St. Petersburg, Russia/Corbis; bkgd. Barry Lewis/Corbis. 70-71: bkgd. Dover Publications, Inc. 72: t., b. Charles O'Rear/Corbis; c. Olivier Cirendini/Lonely Planet Images; bkgd. Dover Publications, Inc. 73: b. Olivier Cirendini/Lonely Planet Images. 76: b.r. Tim Mosenfelder/Corbis. 76-77: bkgd. R. R. Jones/courtesy of the Cabrillo Festival of Contemporary Music. 77: t.r. R. R. Jones/courtesy of the Cabrillo Festival of Contemporary Music. 84: b. Alan Schein Photography/Corbis; b.r. Kevin O. Mooney/Odyssey Productions; t.r. Will & Deni McIntyre/The Image Bank/Getty Images; l. PhotoDisc, Inc. 85: b. Bob Krit/Stone/Getty Images; t. Phil Leo/Stone Getty Images; r. PhotoDisc, Inc. 86: b. Hulton-Deutsch Collection/Corbis. 87: b. Pete/Marlene Woronowski/ Raylene Design Studio. 90-91: bkgd. Robert Y. Ono/Corbis; t. Craig Aurness/Corbis. 91: b.c. Heather Titus/Photo Resource Hawaii; b.r. Ann Cecil/Photo Resource Hawaii. 92: b.r. David Schrichte/Photo Resource Hawaii; l. PhotoDisc Green/Getty Images; r. Photo Resource Hawaii; b.c. Heather Titus/Photo Resource Hawaii. 92-93: bkgd. Robert Y. Ono/Corbis; t. Craig Aurness/Corbis. 94-95: bkgd. Corel; bkgd. PhotoDisc, Inc. 96: c.r. Bettmann/Corbis; t.r. Kevin Fleming/Corbis. 97: c. Steve Rubin/The Image Works, Inc.; t. A. Ramey/PhotoEdit, Inc. 98: b.c. Archivo Iconografico, S.A./Corbis. 98-99: t. Gerard Blot/Réunion des Musées Nationaux, Ecouen/Art Resource, NY. 100: b. Daniel Arnaudet/Réunion des Musées Nationaux, Ecouen/Art Resource, NY. 100-101: t. Gerard Blot/Réunion des Musées Nationaux, Ecouen/Art Resource, NY. 101: b.l. R. G. Ojeda/Réunion des Musées Nationaux, Ecouen/Art Resource, NY; b.r. Erich Lessing/Art Resource, NY; c.r. Chuzeville/ Réunion des Musées Nationaux, Ecouen/Art Resource, NY. 102: texture Dover Publications, Inc. 104: b.r. Richard Nowitz. 105: b. Tim Graham/Corbis. 106-107: t. PhotoDisc, Inc. 107: t. Kevin Fleming/Corbis. 108-109: t. PhotoDisc, Inc. 110: c.l. John Springer/ Corbis; c.r. MPI/Hulton Archive/Getty Images. 110-111: bkgd. John Stark, c1899/New York Public Library. 111: b.l. J. S. Zamecnik/ West/Duke University Digital Scriptorium/Historic American Sheet Music. 112: t.r. Hulton-Deutsch/Corbis. 112-113: bkgd. E. O. Hoppe/Corbis. 113: t.r. MGM/Kobal Collection. 114: c.r. Bettmann/ Corbis. 114-115: t. Corel. 116-117: t. Corel. 121: c. Redferns Music Picture Library. 126-127: bkgd. PhotoDisc, Inc. 127: b.l. Corbis; t.l., c.l. PhotoDisc, Inc.; c.r. Ludwig Musser/Steinway Musical Instruments, Inc., a subsidiary of Steinway Musical Instruments, Inc. 128: t.r. Bettmann/Corbis; b. Lebrecht Music & Arts Photo Library. 130: t.c.r. Michael Boys/Corbis; t.r. PhotoDisc, Inc.; t.c.l. R. Booth/Lebrecht Music & Arts Photo Library. 131: t.c. Associated Press/Keystone, Franco Greco; t.r. Christopher Cormack/Corbis; t.l. Adalberto Roque/AFP/Getty Images. 133: t.r. Erich Lessing/Art Resource, NY. 135: t.r. PhotoDisc, Inc. 138: t.r. David Arky/Corbis; l., t.c.r. Henry Diltz/Corbis. 138-139: bkgd. gkphotography/Alamy Images, Ltd. 140: t.r. Neal Preston/Corbis; b.c. Corbis; b.r. Kevin R. Morris/Corbis. 140-141: bkgd. Dorling Kindersley Picture Library. 141: t.l. Hulton-Deutsch/Corbis. 142: t.r. Michael S. Yamashita/ Corbis. 142-143: t. Kenneth Hamm/Photo Japan; bkgd. Michael S. Yamashita/Corbis. 144-145: t., bkgd. Kenneth Hamm/Photo Japan. 145: c.r., b.r., t.r. Michael Yamashita/Corbis; b.r. Kenneth Hamm/ Photo Japan. 146: t.l. Mosaic Images/Corbis. 146-147: c. PhotoDisc, Inc./Getty Images. 147: b. Private Collection/Lebrecht Music & Arts Photo Library; b.c.l., b.c.r. Bettmann/Corbis; b.r. PhotoDisc, Inc./Getty Images. 148: l. G. Salter/Lebrecht Music & Arts Photo Library; r. Chris Stock/Lebrecht Music & Arts Photo Library. 149: inset, r. Associated Press/AP. 150: bkgd. Lebrecht Music & Arts Photo Library. 150-151: bkgd. Lebrecht Music & Arts Photo Library. 151: bkgd. Lebrecht Music & Arts Photo Library. 152: t.r. Antoine Gyori/Corbis; c.r. The Granger Collection, New York; b.c. Richard H. Smith/Lebrecht Music & Arts Photo Library; t. Lebrecht Music & Arts Photo Library. 152-153: b. Laurie Lewis/ Lebrecht Music & Arts Photo Library; bkgd. Lebrecht Music & Arts Photo Library. 153: c.r. David Redfern/Redferns Music Picture Library; t.r. Lebrecht Music & Arts Photo Library. 156: c.r. Robert Holmes/Corbis; t. Philip Gould/Corbis. 157: b. Gai Terrell/Redferns Music Picture Library; t. Bettmann/Corbis. 162: t. Underwood & Underwood/Corbis; b. AP/Wide World Photos/Deutsche Grammophon/Grossman. 163: t. Bettmann/Corbis. 164: b. Frank Driggs Collection. 165: c., t. William Gottlieb/Redferns Music Picture Library; t.r. Lebecht Music & Arts Photo Library. 166: t.c.r. Peter Stackpole/Time Life Pictures/Getty Images. 166-167: t. MetaCreations/Kai Power Photos. 168: b. Peter Stackpole/Time Life Pictures/Getty Images. 168-169: t. MetaCreations/Kai Power Photos. 169: t. Jack Vartoogian/FrontRowPhotos. 170: l. F. J. Mortimer/Hulton Archive/Getty Images. 171: t.r. Bettmann/Corbis; b. Corporation of London/Topham-HIP/The Image Works. 173: t. Mike Powell/The Image Bank/Getty Images. 174: l. Bettmann/Corbis. 174-175: t. Corbis; bkgd. PhotoDisc, Inc. 175: b. Hulton Archive/ Getty Images. 176: inset, Neal Preston, Corbis; t. Kathy McLaughlin/The Image Works. 176-177: t. Corbis; bkgd. PhotoDisc, Inc. 177: r. Corbis. 179: t. Rob Day. 180: t. Frank Driggs Collection/Hulton Archive/Getty Images. 181: t.r. Frank Driggs Collection/Hulton Archive/Getty Images. 182: bkgd. David Karp/ AP/Wide World Photos. 182-183: t. Bob Krist/Corbis. 183: bkgd. Jeff Greenberg/Index Stock Imagery; t.r. Michael Kim/Corbis. 184-185: t. Bob Krist/Corbis. 186-187: bkgd. Musee des Arts Decoratifs/ Bridgeman Art Library. 187: b.r. Archivo Iconografico, S.A./Corbis. 188: b. Kit Breen; t.r. Philip James Corwin/Corbis. 188-189: bkgd. PhotoDisc, Inc. 190: l. Oliver Benn/Alamy Images, Ltd. 190-191: bkgd. C. VonTuempling/Robert Stock Photography. 191: t.r. Bob Thomas/Stone/Getty Images; t.l. Jeff Greenberg/PhotoEdit, Inc. 192-193: bkgd. Ricardo Azoury/Corbis. 193: t.r. I. Evangelista/ Lebrecht Music & Arts Photo Library. 194: l. NASA. 194-195: bkgd. Corbis. 195: c.l., b.l., b.r. NASA. 196: b.r. John and Lisa Merrill/Corbis; c. Bettmann/Corbis; bkgd. Stapleton Collection/ Corbis. 197: t.r. Stapleton Collection/Corbis. 201: b.r. courtesy of Austin Symphonic Band. 204: t. Bebeto Matthews/AP/Wide World Photos. 205: t. Mitchell Gerber/Corbis. 206-207: t. Richard Day/ Panoramic Images. 208: t.r. Mary Evans Picture Library. 208-209: bkgd. Macduff Everton/Corbis. 209: c.r. Corbis. 210-211: t. Corbis 212-213: t. Corbis. 214: t.c.l., b.c.l. Gail Mooney/Corbis. 214-215: bkgd. Dave G. Houser/Corbis. 215: t.r. Gail Mooney/Corbis. 216: t.r. Gail Mooney/Corbis. 217: bkgd. Dave G. Houser/Corbis; r. Gail Mooney/Corbis. 218: b.l. Roberto Borea/AP/Wide World Photos; t. Francisco Kjolseth/The Salt Lake Tribune. 221: c. Ann Marsden/ Libby Larsen. 223: Joe Maierhauser. 224: Art Archive/Biblioteca Nazionale Marciana Venice/Dagli Orti (A). 225: c. Arvind Garg/ Corbis; b.r. Bennett Dean, Eye Ubiquitous/Corbis. 226-227: bkgd. Corbis. 228-229: bkgd. Corbis. 230-231: bkgd. Corbis. 233: b. Hideo Haga/HAGA/The Image Works, Inc.; t.r. Wolfgang Kaehler/ Corbis. 234: l. PhotoDisc, Inc. 234-235: bkgd. Culver Pictures. 235: t.r. Photofest. 236: t.r. Mark Humphrey/AP/Wide World Photos. 236-237: bkgd. Culver Pictures/AP. 242: t. Mary Evans Picture Library. 244: b.l. PhotoDisc, Inc. 246: b. Comstock. 247: b.l. Museum of Music, Bologna, Italy/ET Archive, London/SuperStock, Inc. 248: b. Corel. 251: b. PhotoDisc, Inc. 252: b.l., b.r. PhotoDisc, Inc. 253: b.l. Artville, LLC. 257: b. Mary Evans Picture Library. 263: b.r. Christopher Felver/Corbis. 267: t. PhotoDisc, Inc. 270: b. Comstock. 276: b.l. PhotoDisc, Inc. 276-277: c., t. PhotoDisc, Inc. 277: t.r., t.c., b.c. PhotoDisc, Inc. 278: t., b. MetaTools. 280: bkgd. PhotoDisc, Inc. 281: b.c. Image Club; b.l. PhotoDisc, Inc. 287: b.r. PhotoDisc, Inc. 290: c. PhotoDisc, Inc.; l. Corel; b.l. MetaCreations/ Kai Power Photos; r. Musical Theatre International. 291: b.l., b.r. PhotoDisc, Inc. 293: c.r. PhotoDisc, Inc. 294: b. Music Theatre International. 295: t. Music Theatre International. 300: b. PhotoDisc, Inc. 301: t. Music Theatre International. 302: b. Music Theatre International. 304: b. PhotoDisc, Inc. 305: t.r., b.l., b.r. Music Theatre International. 306: t.r. Corbis/Sygma. 307: t. PhotoDisc, Inc. 308: l. PhotoDisc, Inc. 309: t.l., b.l., t. PhotoDisc, Inc. 311: t. PhotoDisc, Inc. 313: t. PhotoDisc, Inc. 314: t. Joan Marcus, Ahmanson Theatre/AP/Wide World Photos. 315: t. PhotoDisc, Inc. 317: t. PhotoDisc, Inc. 318: b.r. Bettmann/Corbis. 319: t.r. Artville. 321: t.r. Artville. 323: t.r. Artville. 325: t.r. Artville. 327: t.r. Artville. 329: t.r. Artville. 331: t.r. Artville. 333: t.r. Artville. 335: t. PhotoDisc, Inc. 337: t. PhotoDisc, Inc. 339: t. PhotoDisc, Inc. 341: t. PhotoDisc, Inc. 342: t.r. Archivo Iconografico, S.A./Corbis. 343: t. PhotoDisc, Inc. 345: t. PhotoDisc, Inc. 347: t. PhotoDisc, Inc. 349: t. PhotoDisc, Inc. 351: b. Francesc Muntada/Corbis; t.r. MetaCreations/Kai Power Photos. 353: t.r. MetaCreations/Kai Power Photos. 355: t.r. MetaCreations/Kai Power Photos. 357: b. Paul A. Souders/Corbis; t.r. MetaCreations/Kai Power Photos. 358-359: b. Yann Arthus-Bertrand/Corbis. 359: t.r. MetaCreations/Kai Power Photos. 361: t.r. MetaCreations/Kai Power Photos. 363: t.r. MetaCreations/Kai Power Photos. 365: c.r. Nathan Benn/Corbis; t.r. MetaCreations/Kai Power Photos. 367: t.r. MetaCreations/Kai Power Photos. 369: t.r. MetaCreations/Kai Power Photos. 370: l. PhotoDisc, Inc.; t.r. Ariel Skelley/corbis; b.r. David Young-Wolff/PhotoEdit, Inc. 371: t.r. Corbis. 373: t.r. Corbis. 375: t.c.r. Bettmann/Corbis; t.r. Corbis. 377: t.r. Corbis. 379: t.r. Corbis. 381: t.r. Corbis. 383: t.r. Corbis. 386: c.r. PhotoDisc, Inc. 386-387: bkgd. PhotoDisc, Inc. 388-389: bkgd. Image Club Graphics; bkgd. PhotoDisc, Inc. 390-391: bkgd. PhotoDisc, Inc. 391: b.r. SuperStock; b.c.l. United States Marine Corps; t. Underwood Photo Archives/SuperStock. 392: t. PhotoDisc, Inc. 393: b.c.r. Corbis; b.r., b. PhotoDisc, Inc. 394: r. Atmotu Images/Alamy Images, Ltd.; l. PhotoDisc, Inc. 395: b.r. Sakchai Lalit/AP/Wide World Photos. 397: t.r. Omni Photo Communications, Inc./Index Stock Imagery; b.r. Robert Holmes /Corbis; c.l. Devendra M. Singh/AFP/Getty Images Editorial. 398: t.r., b.r. Hideo Haga/HAGA/The Image Works, Inc.; c.l. Reuters/ Corbis; t.l., b.l. PhotoDisc, Inc. 398-399: bkgd. PhotoDisc, Inc. 400-401: bkgd. Corbis. 401: t.l., t.c., t.r. PhotoDisc, Inc. 402-403: bkgd. Corbis. 403: b.r. Bettmann/Corbis; c.l. PhotoDisc, Inc.; c.r. Corbis. 404: t. MetaCreations/Kai Power Photos. 406: l. Image Club; r. MetaCreations/Kai Power Photos. 406-407: bkgd. PhotoDisc, Inc. 407: b. PhotoDisc, Inc. 408-409: bkgd. PhotoDisc, Inc. 410: c. Thinkstock; l., r. PhotoDisc, Inc. 410-411: bkgd. PhotoDisc, Inc. 411: b.r. Lovely Hula Hands, Inc.; c.l. Douglas Peebles/Corbis; c.r. Lucy Pemoni/Reuters NewMedia, Inc./Corbis. 412-413: bkgd. PhotoDisc, Inc. 414: b.r. Ariel Skelley/Corbis. 415: t. Lawrence Midgale/Photo Researchers, Inc.; b. Leon Morris/Redferns Music Picture Library. 416: t.r. Hulton Archive/Getty Images. 417: l. Central Press/Hulton Archive/Getty Images; r. SuperStock. 418: t. Reuters/Corbis; b.PhotoDisc, Inc. 419: r., l. PhotoDisc, Inc. 420: t. Hasan Sarbakhshian/AP/Wide World Photos; b. Paul Almasy/ Corbis. 425: c. Vladimir Mnev. 427: l. Corbis; t.r. MetaCreations/Kai Power Photos; b.r. Diamar Portfolios. 428: t.r. Cheryl R. Richter/Cheryl R. Richter Photography; b. Deborah Davis/ PhotoEdit, Inc.; t.l. PhotoDisc, Inc. 429: t. Jon Chase/Harvard University News Office/Harvard University Gazette; b.r. PhotoDisc, Inc. 430: l., b.l. The Bettman Archive. 432: t.l., b.r. PhotoDisc, Inc.; b.l. Getty Images. 433: c.l., c.r. PhotoDisc, Inc.; b.r. Jules Frazier/ PhotoDisc Green/Getty Images. 434: t.l. PhotoDisc, Inc. 435: b.l., t.r. PhotoDisc, Inc. 436: t.r. PhotoDisc, Inc. 437: c.l., b.r. PhotoDisc, Inc. 438: t.r. PhotoDisc, Inc.

All attempts have been made to provide complete and correct credits by the time of publication.

Classified Index

**YOUR BROADWAY
MUSICAL**

Alphabetical Index

Global Voices

Interviews

 INDEX OF SONGS AND SPEECH PIECES

Pronunciation Key

Simplified International Phonetic Alphabet
VOWELS

ɑ	f<u>a</u>ther	o	<u>o</u>bey	æ	c<u>a</u>t	ɔ	p<u>a</u>w
e	<u>a</u>pe	u	m<u>oo</u>n	ɛ	p<u>e</u>t	ʊ	p<u>u</u>t
i	b<u>ee</u>	ʌ	<u>u</u>p	ɪ	<u>i</u>t	ə	<u>a</u>go

SPECIAL SOUNDS

β say *b* without touching lips together; *Spanish* nue<u>v</u>e, ha<u>b</u>a

ç <u>h</u>ue; *German* i<u>ch</u>

ð <u>th</u>e; *Spanish* to<u>d</u>o

ɬ put tongue in position for *l* and say *sh*

ṇ sound *n* as individual syllable

ö form [o] with lips and say [e]; *French* ad<u>ieu</u>, *German* sch<u>ö</u>n

œ form [ɔ] with lips and say [ɛ]; *French* c<u>oeu</u>r, *German* pl<u>ö</u>tzlich

ɾ flipped r; bu<u>tt</u>er or r native to language

r̄ rolled r; *Spanish* pe<u>rr</u>o

ǂ click tongue on the ridge behind teeth; *Zulu* n<u>gc</u>wele

ü form [u] with lips and say [i]; *French* t<u>u</u>, *German* gr<u>ü</u>n

ü̆ form [ʊ] with lips and say [ɪ]

x blow strong current of air with back of tongue up; *German* Ba<u>ch</u>, *Hebrew* <u>H</u>anukkah, *Spanish* ba<u>j</u>o

ʒ plea<u>s</u>ure

ˈ glottal stop, as in the exclamation "uh oh!" [ˈʌ ˈo]

~ nasalized vowel, such as *French* b<u>on</u> [bõ]

˥ end consonants *k, p,* and *t* without puff of air, such as s<u>k</u>y (no puff of air after *k*), as opposed to *kite* (puff of air after *k*)

OTHER CONSONANTS PRONOUNCED SIMILAR TO ENGLISH

ch	<u>ch</u>eese	ny	o<u>ni</u>on; *Spanish* ni<u>ñ</u>o
dy	a<u>di</u>eu	sh	<u>sh</u>ine
g	<u>g</u>o	sk	<u>sk</u>y
ng	si<u>ng</u>	th	<u>th</u>ink
nk	thi<u>nk</u>	ts	boa<u>ts</u>

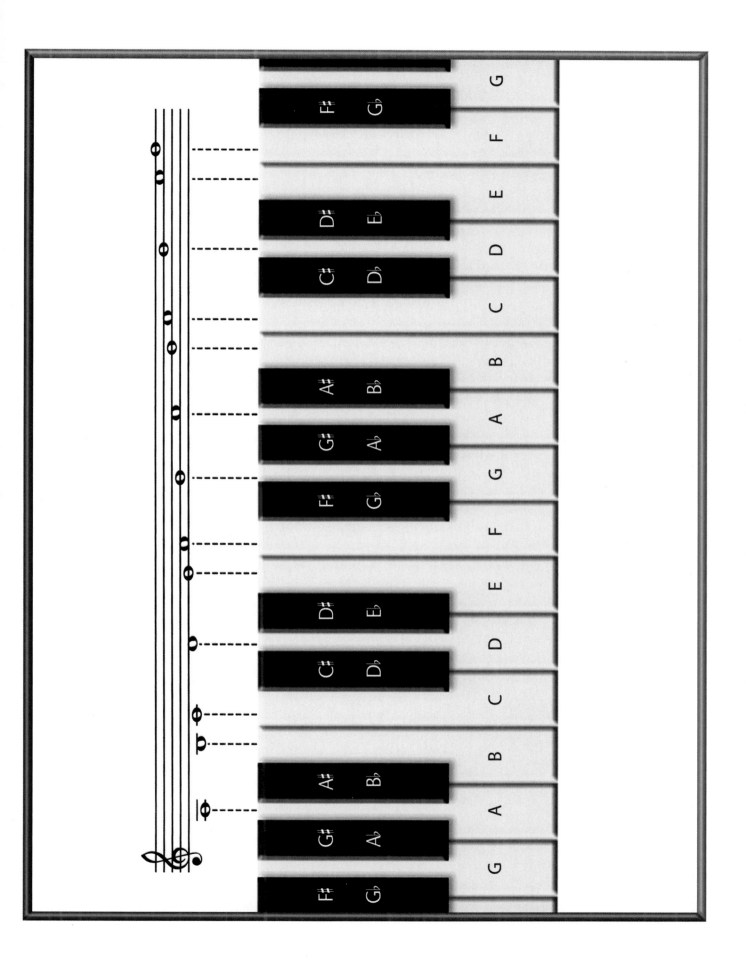